THOMAS L

THE FIRST SPIN DOCTOR
(c. 1363–1437)

A POLITICAL BIOGRAPHY OF THE FIFTEENTH CENTURY'S
GREATEST STATESMAN

IAN C. SHARMAN

with an introduction by Professor Colin Richmond

1999

DOVECOTE–RENAISSANCE

Cover design and print   by HILLSIDE PRINT and DESIGN, Dyehouse Lane, Rochdale

Dovecote–Renaissance

To contact the author write to
268 Manchester New Road
Middleton
Manchester
M24 1JR
England

CONTENTS

FOREWORD

PROFESSOR COLIN RICHMOND

Books about civil servants are not often written. Civil servants are notoriously shy of publicity: they have always been the classic backroom boys. Yet no one has ever denied their influence on political life. Indeed, the definitive portrayal of a civil servant by Nigel Hawthorne in "Yes Minister" is of a man who wields such power behind the scenes that politicians positively jump to follow his advice. Ian Sharman gives us such a figure from what we might be tempted to think of as a distant and therefore different past. Lancastrian England was neither. I write as chauvinistic sentiments are being cranked up by one of England's political leaders, and specifically anti-French attitudes are being adopted by journalists and others, many of whom ought to know better. The major difference between then and now is that the government of Henry V, while being even more pro-European than that of Mr Blair, was decidedly anti-French. Thomas Langley was one of the promoters of that policy which led to Agincourt, the conquest of Normandy, and an English empire in France. Not only did he promote policy, he helped plan it. Whatever the morality of Henry V's anti-French policy, it is a resounding success, so that if qualities of management were to be detached from morality we would unreservedly applaud it. And, therefore, to applaud Thomas Langley amongst the rest.

France was not only his achievement. As Ian Sharman shows, an even bigger and better feather in Langley's cap was the formative part he played in the establishment and defence of the Lancastrian regime. Here too morality, or lack of it, is an issue. Civil servants as we know from the case of Adolf Eichmann, his being only the most extreme example of countless instances of amoral careerists implementing the Holocaust, servants of the state will stoop to anything either to serve the state, or to advance their careers, or, if they are compatible (as they usually seem to be), both. Thomas Langley was involved in nothing so vile, nor can we ever imagine him being so, medieval churchman as he was and medieval culture being as it was. He was, however, implicated in the murder of the deposed Richard II and in the execution of archbishop Richard Scrope, a state "crime" which troubled Henry IV's conscience for the remainder of his uneasy reign. Without Langley the reign would have been far more disturbed than it was; without Langley it conceivably might never have happened at all. That is a large claim, yet not an improbable one.

By 1400 civil servants, most, although not quite all of them, clergy, were more important than they had been in 1300. It was not only that bureaucracy had blossomed, principally as a result of a major was effort against France beginning in the 1330's, but also that the arts of political management were in 1400 of far greater importance. Taxes, for example, had to be argued for in what we have to come to call the "House of Commons"; England was to all intents and purposes a constitutional monarchy by 1400, and kings could take taxes without the assent of the Commons, let alone the Lords, in parliament. Smooth talkers, effective organisers, able accountants, good propagandizers, were in demand. Those who showed the least sign of such skills in their earlier years were patronised and promoted, whatever their origins and wherever they came from, the sons of those we might call peasants, whether illegitimate or not, included.

Lancastrian England was a meritocracy; there were probably more opportunities for boys like Langley in Middleton and beyond Middleton then than there are now. Langley, after all, became a lord of the church, the bishop of Durham being third or fourth in the hierarchy of the church in England. That bishopric did not come late in life as a reward for years of sterling service. Thomas was appointed bishop of Durham in 1406; he did not die until 1437: he had thirty years as a wealthy prelate. He was not, of course, a bishop the pursuits would have us wish him to be, but his long absence from the diocese did not mean that the men and women in the north east went without religion. The church in 1400 was as bureaucratic as the state: Langley's Durham diocese functioned just as well without him. It was expected to: its head was busy elsewhere, chiefly at the hub of government in Wesminister.

Thomas Langley was not just "at the hub"; for seven years he *was* the hub, being Chancellor of England from 1417 to 1424, so "knew the ropes". He would have known them anyway having served successively as the king's secretary and as keeper of the Privy Seal before becoming Chancellor in 1405. For the talented and ambitious these were stepping stones to the highest office, Chancellorship being reserved for the king's "prime minister". But ambition without talent counted for nothing in Lancastrian England: its most glittering prizes were reserved only for the very best of men. We can be assured that Langley, from the point of view of his devoted masters, Henry IV and Henry V, two of the most intelligent of English kings, was the best of men. He served them ably; they, we can have no doubt, treasured him. It was a great achievement for a Middleton boy to have ended up in the Episcopal palace at Bishop Auckland, to have ended up there via the highest office at Westminster was a triumph. Thomas Langley made not simply good, he made the best there was. And Ian Sharman has done him proud.

Colin Richmond
Keele
28 October 1999

INTRODUCTION

DON PICKIS, FORMER HEADMASTER,
QUEEN ELIZABETH SCHOOL

Until I read this book and talked with the author I knew very little about Thomas Langley. I now know that he became the foremost political figure of his time. His name came to my attention in Middleton and in particular through an association with Middleton Grammar School known more recently as Queen Elizabeth's. In 1412 Langley had founded a chantry school or more probably regularised one already existing in Middleton; one at which he may himself have been a pupil. The Elizabethan Foundation of 1592 succeeded the earlier endowment when Alexander Nowell made the school the responsibility of the fellows of Brazenose College, Oxford.

Langley's position of political eminence appears to have been achieved not only swiftly but to have been sustained. To be near, or at, the centre of affairs for some thirty–eight years during four successive reigns indicates a sure grasp of the affairs of state few others have equalled. He must have been trusted, respected, and when ruthlessness was called for, feared as well.

In following Langley's career one is impressed by its intensity and the rapid, even dramatic way it unfolds. Influential at least, pivotally important on occasion, Langley is surely to be seen as worthy to take his place with Becket, Wolsey, More, Cecil, – chancellors, ministers, administrators, right hand men whose policies shaped dynasties and altered our history.

To be successful at this level of influence, and to survive, requires a plentiful supply of reliable information, but while intelligence may be the basis of power its effective deployment depends on judgement, decisiveness and discretion. Comprehensively skilled as a manager Langley would have become indispensable to those fortunate enough to obtain his services; a prince of statecraft, a true prototype of the Machiavellian ideal.

Before coming to Middleton I had encountered the name Langley in the place names Abbots Langley and Kings Langley and once only as a persona surname. The coincidence is interesting and one that has not gone unre- marked by the author. Langley, Virginia is the location of the headquarters of the Central Intelligence Agency and was once where the Research Center for the National Air and Space Administration had its home. Acquiring, processing, and presenting data is of course the larger part of the raison d'être of both organisations.

Lightowlers, Littleborough
October 1999

KEY DATES IN LANGLEY'S LIFE

In compiling this list events and occurrences that had a bearing on Langley's life have been included as well as the major events in his career

1361–2		Second visitation of the plague
c.1363		Born in Middleton, Lancashire
		Establishment of the Wool Staple at Calais
1368	12th September	Death of Blanche, Duchess of Lancaster, aged 26/7
1369		Gaunt appointed Captain of Calais
1372	January	Gaunt created King of Castile and Leon
1374		Gaunt tours his Lancashire estates
		Peace conference at Bruges
1375		Attends St. Mary's, Thetford and Corpus Christi, Cambridge
1376	8th June	Death of Edward, The Black Prince
1377	21st June	Death of Edward III at Sheen
	16th July	Ascension of Richard II
		Palatinate powers granted to the Duchy of Lancaster
1378		Beginning of the Great Schism
1381	Saturday, 15th June	Outbreak of the Cambridge Poll Tax riots
June		Corpus Christi sacked
1385	4th August	Appointed Rector of Radcliffe
1386		Begins employment in Gaunt's household as a clerk in the treasury
		Death of William Llangley.
		Impeachment of the Chancellor, Michael de la Pole.
		Birth of Henry of Monmouth
1388		The Merciless Parliament
1394		Death of Anne of Bohemia, Queen to Richard II
	24th March	Death of Constance, Gaunt's 2nd wife
		Marriage of Richard II and Isabella

1394	September	Langley attends Richard II in Wales on Gaunt's behalf
1395	23rd July	Awarded the prebend of St. Martin-le-Grand
1396	12th February	Rector of St. Alphange
	13th February	Gaunt marries Catherine Swynford
1397	15th February	Given canonry of St. Asaph Cathedral and prebend of Meiford
	17th March	Ordained as a priest in Coventry Cathedral Beauforts legitimised. Thomas Arundal, Archbishop of Canterbury exiled
1398	26th September	Presented to Castleford church Bolingbroke exiled for 10 years Richard II granted the wool subsidies for life
1399	3rd February	Death of Gaunt at Leicester Langley appointed as an executor Bolingbroke exiled for life
	June	Langley joins Bolingbroke at Pontefract Appointed Bolingbroke's secretary and keeper of the Ducal Signet
	30th September	Richard II deposed
	13th October	Bolingbroke crowned Henry IV
	23rd October	Henry of Monmouth invested as Prince of Wales
	29th October	Langley appointed archdeacon of Norfolk
1400	January	Richard II murdered Appointed Keeper of the Kings Signet
	18th September	Beginning of Glyn Dwr's rebellion
1401		Granted prebends in York minster and Bridgnorth
	1st July	Appointed Dean of York
	3rd November	Hertford Castle, appointed Keeper of the Privy Seal
1402		Boniface IX refuses the York provision
1403	10th May	Death of Catherine Swynford in Lincoln
	12th July	Percy rebellion
	21st July	Battle of Shrewsbury
	8th August	Installed as Dean of York
1404	10th October	Elected Bishop of London Innocent VII refuses his candidature

1405	2nd March	Appointed Chancellor
	23rd March	Rebellion of the Archbishop of York Scrope
		Scrope executed in York
		Langley elected Archbishop of York
		Innocent VII refuses to accept Langley
		Henry IV, Langley and others excommunicated
	August	Visitation to Norfolk
1406	1st March	The Long Parliament begins
		Commons demands the naming of the King's Councillors.
		Henry announces his support for Innocent against the Avignonese Papacy
	12th May	Excommunication lifted, receives Papal Bull to the see of Durham
	8th August	Consecrated in St. Paul's
1407	30th January	Resigns as Chancellor
		Appointed *de facto* 1st Foreign Secretary on same day
	4th September	Enthroned in Durham
	23rd November	Louis of Orleans assassinated
		Rebellion of Northumberland Bardolf
	December	Meets French embassy at Gloucester
	7th December	Agrees terms of a truce in Gascony
1408	19th February	Rebels defeated at Brabham Moor
		Offers to support the French clergy in dispute with Avigonese Pope. Truce extended
		Cardinal Uguccione visits England.
		Northern Convocation at York chooses Langley to represent them at the Convocation of Pisa.
	December	Meets a delegation from France in London
1409	7th March	Arrives in Pisa
	13th June	Celebrates mass before the council
	26th June	Alexander V elected
1410		Prince Henry assumes control of government, Langley named as a member of the council
1411	6th June	Created a Cardinal. Henry IV declines on his behalf

1411	1st September	Appoints vicars-general for his diocese
		Expeditionary force under the command of the Earl of Arundel dispatched to France
	22nd October	Force enters Paris
1412	February	Langley meets an Armagnace delegation in his London House. Restoration of Aquitaine offered
	June	Prince Henry lodges with Langley whilst a reconciliation with his father is brokered
	22nd July	Burgundians and Armagnacs renounce agreements with England. English force despatched to France
		Henry IV seriously ill
	22nd August	Langley consecrates St. Leonard's, Middleton
1413	20th March	Death of Henry IV at Westminster
	9th April	Langley in attendance and named as an executor
	9th April	Henry V crowned
	August	John, Duke of Burgundy expelled from Paris
		The Armagnacs take control of the French government
	23rd September	Treaty of Leulinghem
1414	January	Langley meets envoys from Charles VI at Durham house
		Agreement made for the marriage of Henry V and Catherine
	May	Langley meets envoys from the Duke of Burgundy in Leicester. Marriage of Henry and Burgundy's daughter discussed
	31st May	Langley named as head of embassy to France
	8th August	Arrives in Paris
1415	24th January	Further embassy to France
		Langley interviews the Celestines on behalf of Henry V
	12th March	Negotiations open, talks break down after ten days
	June	Bedford appointed Lieutenant of the realm
	2nd–6th July	Meets French embassy at Winchester

1415	24th July	Named as an executor in Henry V's will
		Southampton plot
	25th October	Battle of Agincourt
	18th December	Death of Dauphin
1416	March	Meets French embassy
	May	Meets the Emperor Sigismund in London
	June	Bedford defeats French/Genoese naval force
	October	Meets Burgundians in Calais
	8th December	Begins negotiations with the Scots
1417	18th January	Opens secret talks with the French prisoners at Pontefract
	23rd July	Appointed Chancellor for the 2nd time
		Henry V embarks for France
	August	Fall of Caen
	November	Opens Parliament
	December	Oldcastle captured
	14th December	Oldcastle executed
1418		Assumes complete control of the government
	14th July	Burgundy occupies Paris
1419	Rouen falls	10th Septembe
		Burgundy murdered at Montereau
1420	23rd March	Treaty of Troyes
	2nd June	Catherine and Henry V married
1421	February	Henry returns to England
	23rd February	Catherine crowned Queen
	March	Meets Scottish embassy at Howden
		Duke of Clarence killed at Bauge
	10th June	Henry embarks for France
1422	31st August	Death of Henry V at Vincennes
	28th September	Resigns as Chancellor
	7th November	Henry V interred in Westminster Abbey
		Langley informs the Great Council of the terms of the will
		Gloucester named as Protector
	16th November	Appointed Chancellor for the third time
1423	August	Meets Scots at York
	10th September	Agreement with the Scots ratified by Parliament
	20th October	Last address to Parliament

1424	28th March	James of Scotland and Joan Beaufort in Durham where treaty is sealed
	16th July	Resigns as Chancellor at Hertford Castle
	October	Mediates between Gloucester, Bedford and Henry Beaufort
1429	6th November	Henry VI crowned
1430		Virtually retires from public life at the age of 67
1437	20th November	Dies in his Palace at Bishop Auckland after an illness of a year

PREFACE

When a country becomes embroiled in turmoil
and violence, injustice gives birth to genius.

For those who are glancing at this book wondering who Thomas Langley was and why a biography is merited, may I ask you too consider the following. During the course of his life England witnessed the rise of John of Gaunt the founding father of the Lancastrian dynasty, the Poll Tax riots, the usurpation by Bolingbroke, the glory of Kingship that was the reign of Henry V, and the chaos of the reign of Henry VI. The Beauforts were legitimised, the repercussions of which so profoundly affected England's history in that the seeds of the Wars of the Roses were sown, the power of Parliament substantially increased, Chaucer wrote his masterpiece, The Canterbury Tales and the mythology of the Lancastrian Dynasty was established.

One common thread runs throughout: Thomas Langley, who was intimately involved in all these events. From humble beginnings he rose through the patronage of Gaunt to become Bishop of Durham, Chancellor to three English kings, and England's first Foreign Secretary, as well as being the fulcrum upon which the Lancastrian myth was based.

In today's language he would have been known as a spin-doctor and fixer, a practitioner of the devious arts so well described 150 years after his death by Machieveli. I have endeavoured to present a book that will appeal to both the academic and to those who read history because they enjoy the subject. His loyalty to the House of Lancaster and the lengths he was prepared to go to preserve its status and persona are a classic example of medieval power brokering. His time as Bishop of Durham has been the subject of two studies, one in 1961 the other in 1963, and given the advance in scholarship since their publication I feel that his church career would benefit from a re-evaluation where the political events have a bearing on his religious career.

The advantage for me is that no detailed study of this unique man has ever been compiled. Whilst the book by Dr. R. L. Storey provides an exhaustive study of his period as Bishop of Durham it only gives an overview of Langley's political career, no full analysis is undertaken into the background behind his actions. Nor has any consideration been given to his personal involvement in the politics of the time. I hope that this book redresses this historical oversight. For those of you who are familiar with the area adjacent

1

to Middleton near Manchester that is known as Langley, you will be surprised that such a famous man once lived on the land now covered by a mundane council estate. I hope that by reading this book the residents of Langley will gain a sense of pride and identity. It is in part thanks to the support and encouragement of certain residents of Middleton that this book has come about.

Further thanks are due to Professor Colin Richmond, the first person who encouraged me to study medieval history seriously, this book is my way of thanking him for the kindness he has shown me. Thanks are also due to Mike White, he has painstakingly poured over this book, correcting my many errors of grammar and punctuation. This he has done with enthusiasm, and with a ready smile, the world would be better place if more people were of the same demeanour. Lastly, but to me most importantly, please allow me the indulgence of thanking my partner Marie, who has for many years endured my passion for history, and it is thanks to her that this book has come into being.

Middleton
November 1999

PART ONE

THE DECADES OF CHANGE

The age that Thomas Langley was born into was a time that saw the beginnings of the Lancastrian dynasty and with it the rise of the clerics who were attached to the Duchy household. Through a fortunate set of circumstances combining together, a number of members of the lower middle classes were given the opportunity to build careers on the wider stage that access to the ruling house always gave to its trusted and loyal servants. Since the period of the Norman Clergy transplanting itself into the English Bishoprics through to the promoting of their own followers to the offices of state by the Plantagenets, a pattern of consolidating the chief Clerical and Lay positions under the control of the Crown had been at times controversially undertaken to underpin the position of the ruling family and its closest allies and supporters. Whilst the middle echelons of the Civil Service were not altered, the hierarchy that was linked to the ruling classes, their families and tenants shifted with the alliances that the diktats of policy and events in Europe brought to bear on Royal policy. From the signing of Magna Carta, the Royal House's reliance on a compliant Parliament had shifted the endowment of patronage towards the more powerful of the titled classes. Those Earldoms which enjoyed Palatinate status built up powerful courts of their own together with all the trappings of semi-regality that embraced both lay and clerical control and these Earldoms exercised power as a counterweight to the worst excesses of Royal repression. Conversely there are cases of overpowerful Earls acting with overmuch self- interest which frequently split the Royal Courts and often polarised Parliament.

Palatinate powers were granted to Henry of Lancaster in 1351 when Edward III formally conferred a Dukedom on his nephew. Henry was granted the *"liberties and jura regalia pertaining to a Count Palatine as fully and freely as the Earl of Chester is known to have them in the County of Chester"*. He established a new chancery and appointed his own judges for the Shire, money and the law first. Even in the medieval period the government's priorities were the same as today.

A new tier of government required a new tier of civil servants, based on Lancaster and Preston. Nevertheless Edward III still reserved the right to demand Parliamentary taxation from the Shire. 15 years later Gaunt had this rescinded and in 1390 gained permission from Richard II, who needed Gaunt's political support, the right to entail both the Duchy, which covered the lands outside Lancashire, and the Palatine, on his heirs male. The Duchy Council was established under Gaunt's son Bolingbroke, it had its own seal, Chancellor, courts and officers. Henry Haydock was the first Chancellor, he was given the seals of both the Duchy and the Palatine, Bolingbroke later joined the two seals together.

The Crown's increasing reliance on the powers of Parliament to assist the funding of home and foreign policy aims brought with it a new breed of civil servant.

This new breed were more than mere clerics, they acted also as brokers, advancing the relative positions of their masters both in terms of influence and profit, and were diplomats both at home and abroad. This new caste of civil servants also held the reigns of patronage which they used with varying degrees of success dependent on the outcome of the overall policies which they pursued on behalf of this new breed of Earl, whose fortunes and horizons widened with the advent of the Crusading movement and the questioning of the fundamental tenets of religion begun in England by Wyclif, who was to some extent protected by John of Gaunt, Langley's first great patron. Wyclif's heresy shook the very foundations of the church, the fact that the Lollard movement continued long after his death, exemplifies the cord his teaching struck in the thinking of medieval man. His attack on the wealth of the church in particular alarmed the clergy more than his questioning of the basic teachings of the church. The transansubstiation argument inevitably became lost in the welter of propaganda produced by both sides.

The ebb and flow of successful royal policy abroad and its effects on England became inextricably linked with the expansion of the greater Lords, as, through marriage the network of kinship expanded across Europe. Through these alliances of marriage, a web of co-operation between the principal Lords of various countries came to rival the powers of the Royal houses of Europe. This shifting of power was not confined just to continental alliances; the strategic betrothals between the higher echelons of society created power blocks which unified large areas of land and reversed the policy of divided landholding instigated by William the Conqueror which had done much to maintain the reins of power in royal hands.

This influence permeated down through to a network of courtiers and court officials whose pursuit of policies transcended European boundaries through treaties of commerce to facilitate the import and export of a variety of commodities. These policies, at various times, became detached or were in direct contravention to the aims and ambitions of the ruling cliques.

To bolster this burgeoning form of regional government an increasingly larger number of posts with positions attached to the Ducal households were created, to be filled by the junior members of those families which held influence at the Ducal courts. These civil servants in turn exercised the powers of patronage and advancement practised by those above them. The movement that expanded and increased during the 14th, 15th and 16th Centuries, could be termed as the *Stratification of Society* being the reinforcement of a new layer of society which burgeoned as the environment became more complex and interwoven.

This did much to redistribute the wealth of the country as this new category of professional civil servants increased its status in society until such time as the entire governance of society would have ceased to operate without these functionaries. The formation of the Guilds and the Inns of Court created bodies that at times rivalled the power of the ruling houses. Many of these guilds, particularly the merchant guilds banded together to create banks.

Those Lords who recognised this new grouping that was spreading became the Lords with more influence as each sought to perfect their secretariat. This shift in the structure of society should be compared with the large continental mergers we see today between various conglomerates who seek through merger and financial take-over to extend their economic and corporate powers so that they transcend territorial boundaries. This extension of commercial and territorial power produced a profound effect on national policies when they directly affected the ability of the inter-continental grouping of lordships to continue their commercial trading. These increasingly influential factors competed at times with the strategies of the ruling houses who wished to enter into policies of expansion for reasons that were entirely contrary to the commercial interests of the country.

In turn the King's growing dependence on Parliament to provide the finance to pursue royal interests meant that the pendulum of power swung towards a wider number of people who judiciously exploited their positions to weaken Royal power to the extent that a more pluralistic form of governance came into being. This greater pluralism led to a new class of civil servant; a body of men sprang up who were able to manipulate the dialogue between the parties so that they effectively became the real power brokers of the middle ages. Those Lords who laid the foundations of these new structures were the ones who recognised the need to sponsor education and by the power of patronage to control who was admitted to this closed world. They can be likened to the press barons we have today.

The foundations of firstly monastic orders and later the universities, enabled the upper classes to promote their tenant's relations into positions of service based on their ability to, through education, perform with varying degrees of adroitness, the duties of civil servants. This widening of influence was mainly filled by second and third sons whose access to promotion was decreased by the sub-infeudation of the family's landholdings, the only prerequisite to entry to this new sphere of influence being the family's connection with, and having enough influence to gain for the younger branches, the patronage of these greater lords.

This power of patronage instilled a deep sense of gratitude in those who owed their increased standing in society to their patrons. This bred a loyalty that was rarely retracted but was at times ruthlessly pursued through the legal process which had, as a result of the increase in the diversity of the creation of wealth, produced a burgeoning legal process which in turn had its own exponents who exploited the power this gave them. Those Lordships who retained the control of the chancery and criminal courts, coupled with the control of the right to appeal, became the most autonomously powerful group and came to rival the power of the Crown.

The Palatine of Lancashire rivalled all the major Lordships in England. Its landholdings were vast and varied, its connection through blood with the royal house placed it in a unique position of influence both nationally and, increasingly, over a European scale. A fortunate set of circumstances brought John of Gaunt, the 3rd son of Edward III and Phillippa of Hainault and brother of Edward (the Black Prince), the Palatine of Lancaster and with it an influence that culminated in Gaunt's son, Bolingbroke replacing his cousin as monarch. This rise to the pinnacle of power coincided with the rising career of one Thomas Langley whose influence increased as the house of Lancaster moved from a base centred on its Palatinate lands, to a base that encompassed England and extensive holdings across Europe.

Those servants who were able to obtain positions in both the lay and clerical bodies were the best placed to take advantage of the changing circumstances which culminated in the shift of power that occurred with the deposition of Richard II by Henry of Bolingbroke. The treatment that the house of Lancaster had endured under the regime surrounding and controlled by Richard II gradually brought about the replacement of the higher civil servants and officers of state by Lancastrian appointees whose loyalty was beyond question.

Bolingbroke's usurpation was not universally welcomed. The feelings of a significant number of people that Bolingbroke had no legitimate right to the throne led to the need to create a religious blessing to his reign. To bring this about the new Lancastrian ruling house had to rely on those in the clergy who were loyal to, or owed their appointments to, Lancastrian patronage.

This was the beginning of the Lancastrian Myth which occupied Langley throughout his political career. The perpetuation of this myth, the creation of a religious climate of acquiescence for Bolingbroke's actions through very public proclamations of support from the clergy, were fundamental to the stabilising of the country, particularly the neutralising and coercion of the baronial movement that stood to lose from a change in the ruling house.

The creation of this myth of Kingship laid the foundations for Bolingbroke's son, Henry of Monmouth, to depict himself as God's divinely ordained representative on earth. This perceived position of religious authenticity was used to influence the parliaments of Henry V's reign into financing the resumption of the war with France. The victory of Agincourt was widely seen, and indeed promoted as, a sign that God had clearly shown his support for the Kingship and ideals of the new King. Langley ruthlessly exploited this sense of public opinion to strengthen the power of the royal house in Parliament and the country at large. Langley's acute perceptiveness served him throughout his career and is the hallmark of a life spent in the unwavering service of the House of Lancaster. The Lancastrians benefited from a pool of servants whose training was grounded in the structure that John of Gaunt had instigated.

Gaunt has received a mixed press over the years, the chroniclers being, at the outset, very critical of the reign of Henry IV. Indeed Gaunt had suffered from an increasingly anti-movement that culminated in his being the principal target of the Poll Tax rioters. The shock to Gaunt's court led to the Lancastrians adopting a policy of rigid centralisation of the mechanism of government when power was seized. Those servants already in the junior ranks of service who in later years rose to the positions of power and who had experienced the shock of Gaunt's fall from public grace, carried throughout their careers deep suspicions of anyone who did not overtly support through deed and parliamentary action the policies of the Lancastrian dynasty.

The epitome of patronage was reached in the legitimisation of the children of Gaunt and Catherine Swynford, creating the Beaufort clan, who through a clause later inserted in the legitimisation document were unable to grasp the reins of the ultimate power that was the throne of England. This creation of a web of Lordships and Ecclesiastical appointments that were awarded to the three sons and one daughter, (John became Earl of Somerset and Marquis of Dorset, Henry Bishop of Lincoln and later of Winchester, Thomas Duke of Somerset and Joan through her second marriage to Ralph Neville founded the Warwick dynasty as well as the house of Tudor), provided the Lancastrian dynasty with supporters that were related in blood and owed their entire wealth to the ruling family. The principal figure in the bringing about of the legitimisation was Thomas Langley who through his brokering of the legitimisation with the supporters of Richard II, assured the unstinting support and gratitude of a family clique whose power was second only to that exercised by the crown.

The upheavals of the church that began with Wyclif and spread across Europe, culminating in the great schism allowed England to regain some of its influence within the Papacy, and this in turn led to a strengthening of the position of the English Clerics at the Royal Court. The reliance which the Lancastrian Dynasty was forced to place on the Church produced a new religious fervour and an expansion, through royal patronage, of the influence and security of the Bishops and the Ecclesiastical lands. The new climate of religion brought about the increase in the reporting of miracles which in turn created a renewal in the belief of the virtues of pilgrimage.

This greater tolerance helped to expand the areas of writing and poetry as expressions of the greater piety that had returned to the fabric of society. The increase in commerce that accompanied this expansion in the literal arts was not an accident. The greater freedom that interchange and the increase in the interaction of different cultures brought about a whole new set of chroniclers who benefited from the insights they gained from other societies. This new-found wealth of literature that sprung up created about itself an aura of respectability through the patronage of culture towards those who produced these arts. The ideals of Chivalry and Virtue were at the centre of the literature, verse and song, that spread across the European peoples. The astuter civil servants learnt about the power of imagery through the Church's use of such symbolism so that they too utilised the creative arts to expound the virtues of their office in the hierarchical structure of society.

The successes of Crécy (1346) and Poitiers (1356) enabled Edward III to capture Calais which was extensively fortified. This led to the Treaty of Brétigny (1359) which traded Edward's claim to the French throne for the sovereignty of Aquitaine. The French renounced the terms of the treaty when Charles V succeeded his father John II, the ensuing war proving catastrophic for the English. The English land holdings were reduced by over 80%. The pursuit of war was affected by the spread of the ideals that permeated

European Society. Chivalry and the virtues attached to the practice of the Arthurian ethos created the climate of the "just war", sanctioned and blessed by God. Man fought for the benefit of God, not himself, a country's triumph in a war being depicted as a sign that God had judged his cause to be just (1). Propaganda to justify conflict to the populace is not a new trend. The Lancastrians became experts in this use of religion and symbolism to expand their war effort through a taxation which carried the stigma of assisting with a war that was God's will.

The success of a mans career can be measured in many ways. The expansion of his wealth and landholding marked the expansion of the Baronial movement, how they used their new found influence depended to a large extent on the quality of advice that they received. This led to the creation of "new men" whose forte was in the understanding of and the practice of the intricacies of governance. This new breed of professional clerics exhaustively sought to perfect their offices by continually seeking to control all aspects of governance. This drawing together of the reins of power enabled the best exponents of this new discipline to rise to positions of great prominence. The change of emphasis in the reasons for war, from the greed for enlarged territorial holdings to an emphasis aimed at increasing the wealth of a nation through enlarged opportunities for trade, created a powerful role for these new men.

The responsibilities these new men undertook and the policies they pursued can be followed by the actions they took to bring these policies about. The ability to exercise Lay and Clerical power was given to very few, history having taught the ruling classes the dangers that accompanied the giving of power, both Lay and Clerical, to men who endeavoured to use this power against the Crown. Becket is the classical example of a man who rose through the civil service to the highest post in the Church of England. His understanding of political and Ecclesiastical power shook the foundations of the Monarchy to such an extent that the lessons learnt were still considered centuries later when Bishoprics were being filled. This led to the creation of the Political Bishops who were able to balance the needs of the monarchy with the policies of the Papacy, and they became the greatest exponents of the art of compromise politics as they performed a balancing act between their two masters.

One can chart the influence of a person by the promotions that he received through the gift of titles and land that he accumulated throughout his career. The value of their service to the crown can be assessed in this way. For others, the virtue of service as an ideal carried its own rewards. This ethos applied to Langley as it did to others whose raison d'être was the preservation of royal authority and the continuance of the stability which an ordered, structured society, gave to the country. Their reward was the maintenance of their rank and position, many saw their life's vocation to be the furtherance and extension of their master's powers through the structures that they themselves had instituted. They followed prescribed paths that were designed to control the system of government, both regional and national, so that a steady course was steered that avoided the unrest that led to fratricide. Their sole purpose was to progress the policies that benefited the upper echelons of society with a percolation downwards of the benefits of these expansionist policies, they regarded service as a virtue. They in effect became the non-executive directors of England P.L.C., the main shareholders being the chief landowners and later the Commons representing the minor shareholders, their Parliamentary seats being the proxies of the minor classes.

The ability to control the decisions of Parliament became an art form of its own. The practitioners of this art were aided by the fact that there was no collective unity in party groupings, and that those summoned to Parliament were always going to vote along the lines that were dictated to them by their overlords. The highest art of all was the ability to be able to placate both Crown and Parliament so that both felt that they had achieved their aims; this added the virtue of policy advice to the functions of the civil servants. Langley on numerous occasions managed to weave together many different strands of policy for the crown and the Duchy of Lancaster whilst at the same time assuring that the power of the Bishops was not adversely affected. The diplomatic function of the civil servants had been finely honed over the years by the negotiations with the Flemish towns over wool and later cloth exports. Increasingly the clauses of treaties that dealt with trade and commerce took on an importance that equalled the territorial settlements that were the usual principal aims of such agreements.

England's increasing dependence on the revenues from the territories that Eleanor of Aquitaine had brought to the Angevin throne gave these civil servants influence in an area that stretched from Ireland in the west to the borders with the Ile de France down to the Pyrenees and Northwards to the Flemish towns that were, in part, satellite states dependent upon the whims of the English Wool market. The English art of diplomacy was practised on behalf of the country's national interest, not in the role as broker between opposite parties. Prior to this England's position with its continental neighbours was as an aggressor not a trading partner.

It was in the area of Ecclesiastical diplomacy that Langley played a prominent part that he has to date not received credit for. England acted as a major power broker between the conflicting parties during the period of the great schism. Prior to this the English Church was at various times isolated from and at odds with the Papacy. This was in part due to England's continuance of the territorial wars in France, the papacy drawing more of its support from France than it did from the English clergy who were more rigidly controlled by the crown than their continental neighbours.

The encouragement given to Wyclif provides a good indication of the policies and tactics of the crown. Wyclif was actively encouraged to voice his doctrines on a wider stage than the University of Oxford provided. Royal policy was clearly intended to embroil the church in debates that questioned its riches and structures. The clergy were more concerned with the heretical aspects of Wyclif's teachings, and the Crown, not unsurprisingly showed more interest in Wyclif's views on the accumulation of the wealth that the church enjoyed. If one wishes to trace the beginnings of the Protestant religion they began in Oxford during Wyclif's period. The great schism which lasted from 1378 to 1419 allowed England to regain some of its prominence within the hierarchy of the church. However by the beginning of the reign of Richard II a number of tensions were tearing at the fabric of the old order.

The culmination of this was the Peasants Revolt, the old order tried to reassert its ancient rights against an increasingly more powerful agrarian society who united around a common cause, the applying of a statutory relief across the board. The Chancellor, Michael de la Pole, earl of Suffolk, was impeached in October 1386, which led to Parliament being given the rights to supervise certain aspects of government. This preceded the crisis of 1387 when Richard persuaded some judges to secretly rule that some of Parliament's measures were treasonable in intent and action, the wording of the judgement was leaked. The consequence of this was the raising of an army by Woodstock and the Earls of Arundel and Warwick. An appeal of treason was lodged against the five main councillors of Richard, and significantly when Robert de Vere, Duke of Ireland brought an army to the King's defence, Henry Bolingbroke joined the appellant Earls. De Vere was defeated and Richard was forced to admit the appellant Earls into the Tower of London to begin negotiations.

The following Parliament of 1388 came to be known as the Merciless Parliament, a number of Richard's advisors and councillors being found guilty and executed. The English defeat at Otterburn was viewed as a consequence of the Lords Appellant having left the North of England undefended, this allowed Richard to reassert his control over Parliament. Gaunt was out of the country during these events but Langley was working diligently in the Duchy on Gaunt's behalf. His possible knowledge of

Bolingbroke's planned rebellion will be discussed as part of the debate concerning how much Gaunt did know of his son's plans.

The tensions that beset the social fabric were exacerbated by the main outbreaks of plague that visited England in 1348/49 and 1361/2. Those people who lost their spouses in the first visitation remarried as soon as possible, the visitation of 1348/9 striking the older members of society. One estimate of the mortality rate by J. R. Russell put the lethality rate at 20%; combined with the later outbreaks it is further estimated that by the end of the century, 50% of the population had been wiped out by the various visitations (2). The population of England, based on the poll tax returns of 1377, has been calculated at 2,250,000, prior to the visitations, i. e. in 1348 the population had been estimated at circa 5/6 millions (3). Lancashire's population by the time of the lay-poll tax returns of 1377 was 23,880. The main consequence of this drop in the available labour market was that prices for goods fell and this led to the increase in the leasing of estates, creating a new grouping of the peasantry who benefited from this shortage of labour. A further effect of the plague was that wages rose, 33% during 1340-8 and by a further 60% over the next decade.

The response was the Statute of Labourers which sought by statute to bind the working class to a single lord for life, thereby halting the peasant's ability to transfer his labour to the highest bidder, the precursor of the wage freeze (4). Remember the strikes of the 60's and 70's, the medieval equivalent was to riot and the statute became unworkable. Legislation was enacted to constrain the bondsmen, the various acts of parliament that followed began to unite the peasants to the extent that the seeds of the poll tax riots can be traced back to the years after the plague visitations (5). This was hardly the beginnings of the trade union movement, however, the unity that the peasantry's of certain shires showed were the seeds of the formation of collectives which, through their banding together, enabled them to negotiate with the landholders from greater positions of strength than had been possible, in effect strength through unity. The Poll Tax riots, in part, presented the peasants with a piece of legislation that they could unite behind; the grievances that led to the rioting had their roots in the consequences of the plague.

This was the world that Langley came into, the changes and trends that had their beginnings in the mid 1350's coming to a head at the precise time that Langley entered the national civil service. His coming could not have been better timed, the conditions and changes to the fundamental structures of society presented a unique opportunity for someone who was fully conversant with the mechanics of governance, someone who was seen as "our man", someone who could traverse the minefield of politics in the late 1300's. There had been a number of famous Bishops who through Royal service became politicians. It now became the time of the Political Bishops, men who chose the civil service first and then added the mantle of Bishop to further their political aims and ambitions.

These men framed policies which controlled the direction of the country for the next 160 years. A number of the issues which so convulsed Tudor England had their origins in the policies that these new men adopted or encouraged. The policy of commerce and trade coupled with the increase in the powers of Parliament came into being as a result of the creation by society of the need for a new group of men, the political civil servants. Today we know them as the permanent secretaries of the departments of government, their chief being the Cabinet Secretary, who is the modern-day equivalent of the position that Thomas Langley held with such distinction throughout the reigns of the three middle Henry's. The fact that he made no enemies throughout his career is testimony to his adroitness, and everyone of power and influence, both lay and Clerical, owed something to Langley, he in turn always repaying his favours, often before the favour was called. Such was the propensity of the man, the fact that he was mostly unobtrusive in his dealings partly explaining why his place in history has never been given the recognition that it deserves. As a model of service his career could not be bettered, his is the classic story of the local boy made good.

Notes and References

(1) Robbins, R. H. "Historical Poems of the 14th and 15th Centuries", New York, Columbia University Press, (1959).
(2) Russell, J. C. "British Medieval Population", (1948), Albuquerque.
(3) Myers, A. R. ed, "English Historical Documents", vol. iv, 1327–1485, doc no. 562, pgs 993/4, (1969), London, Eyre and Spottiswoode.
(4) Bean, J. M. W., "Plague, population and economic decline in England in the later Middle Ages". Economic History Review. 2nd series, 15, (1962–3), London.
(5) Douglas. D. C. (ed), "English Historical Documents", vol. iv, 1327–1485, doc no. 362, pp 993/4, (1969), London, Eyre and Spottiswoode.

For a General Overview:

Ziegler, P. "The Black Death", (1969), London.
Mc Kisack. M. "The Fourteenth Century", The Oxford History of England, (1959), Oxford. *chaps xi & xii.*

Keen. M. H. "England in the Later Middle Ages", (1973), London, Routledge. *section iii, chap. 8.*
Scot. T. "The Peasantries of Europe", (1998), London, Longman.
Wilkinson. B. "The Later Middle Ages in England, 1216–1485". (1969), London, Longman, *chap. 6.*

There is also a great deal of material available on the effects of the plague on different counties. This type of material is usually published by Local History Societies.

BIRTH and BACKGROUND

The clue to the date of Thomas Langley's birth lies in remarks he made in 1433 when he complained of feeling his age and that he was suffering from infirmity, which for a septuagenarian was not surprising (1). This would place his birth in Middleton, a small parish that is approximately six miles north of Manchester, around the mid-1360's. Middleton lay on the Manchester to York road; the River Irk is joined by a number of small brooks in the centre of the town before joining the River Irwell some five miles downstream near Manchester's medieval boundaries. The area was typical of the land that occupied the lower parts of the foothills that bordered the Pennines, open uncultivated moorland that led to the outskirts of Tottington Forest which in turn ran to what is now known as Rossendale Forest. The farms and houses were built on the small hillocks that dotted the area. Until the upsurge in the need for wool, there was little pastoral farming and virtually no arable farming in the area. The area was sparsely populated, with, until the advent of the wool trade, not many opportunities to earn a living. The damp inhospitable climate was ideally suited to sheep farming and unless a landholder could obtain employment in the forests that bordered the area life was a continual struggle. The lessons of thrift and austerity were quickly learnt and, as a fourth son, Langley's only hope of improvement lay as a cleric. His position was replicated across the country. Had it not been for the rise to power of the Lancastrians through John of Gaunt and his family together with the factors that placed the production of wool at the economic heart of English policy, the area would have lain dormant until the advent of the industrial revolution some four hundred years later.

Wool and Economy

Since Domesday the chief tenants in the area had subsidised the running costs of these outlying manors from the revenues of their more prosperous holdings. With the increased demand for wool, this demand was both in terms of its export value and its value as a tool of taxation and the raising of loans by the crown, so the outlying manors moved into a self-sufficiency which since their creation they had lacked.

This new found importance in wool also afforded the main producers a greater influence than they had previously enjoyed. Many of the small landholders and their tenants underwent an upturn in their fortunes as a result in the increase in the value of wool. Consequently the effects of national commerce and politics directly affected a wider section of the population during the 14th. This linkage between national events and the local economy meant that families such as Langley's took a greater interest in national politics than they previously had done. In 1309, Edward II had been forced by economic necessity to grant all the wool customs from Scotland and Ireland to the Italian bankers the Frescobaldi, his debt to them having since been estimated at £21,635 (2). The dependence that the Flemish towns of Ghent, Bruges and Ypres placed on receiving regular supplies of English wool, enabled England to exercise a great influence on Flemish policy.

The Flemish ports were strategically placed and attracted a number of mercenary captains and their followers, wool proving an important tool as the Hundred Years War progressed. Louis de Nevers, Count of Flanders, tended to lean towards Philip VI, the Valois king of France, in matters of allegiance, France having come to his assistance in helping to quell the rebellion of his subjects at Cassel in 1328. Consequently, any English attempt in controlling the wool staple was, at this time, counter-productive. Edward III countered by bribing Duke John of Brabant with the sum of £60,000 as well as establishing a wool staple at Antwerp. A further wool staple was established at Calais in 1363 in part to endeavour to make Calais more financially independent. The great Council held at Nottingham in 1336 granted a subsidy of 20 shillings and a loan of 20 shillings per sack, equivalent to approximately £70,000 a year. In the following year, William de la Pole and Reginald Conduit negotiated an exclusivity contract with the king whereby the main group of wool contractors would buy 30,000 sacks of wool for the King's use. The King had cleverly restricted the export of wool to the Flemish merchants in the preceding year thereby creating a shortage from which this group could profit, providing an inducement to pay such a high price. This tactic is used today by OPEC to manipulate the forward spot market in crude oil.

Tensions soon began to appear between the wool exporters and the King. Smuggling became commonplace as did sharp practice by the port workers, again nothing new. After much underhand manoeuvring by Edward III the King eventually repurchased the bonds of the merchants at a discount through intermediaries (3). The resultant collapse in confidence between all parties led to the bankruptcy of the Crown, the exporters understandably holding back a significant number of sacks, over 85%, in the following year (4). By 1338 a crisis point had been reached, despite the English sea victory at Sluys, Edward III was being pressed by the Italian bankers and his Flemish creditors. The wool count had been ignored by at least 12 counties. Exasperated, the King used the age-old tactic, still used to this day, of blaming his ministers, and removed Stratford his Chancellor. It is salient to remark that during the crisis the differences between the French *parlement* and its English counterpart come sharply into focus. The French version was staffed by professional lawyers, the English version relying upon amateur politicians backed up by the group of professionals who staffed the chancery created a climate of "us and them" in terms of parliament and the King's full-time staff, with the king retaining the ultimate power of dismissal should his ministers not carry out the policies that he wished to pursue.

The wool trade was not as affected by the plagues as the agrarian industry was. Consequently the customs profits rose, putting them on a par with the religious orders who did not include the profits from wool in their assessment returns.

This part of the financial preferment became a prime target for Wyclif. A further consequence of the increase in the value of wool was that the value of the rental charges for meadows and pasture land rose sharply. This eased some of the pressures but the respite was brief in these tensions between crown and parliament; coming to a head during the reign of Richard II. From 1328 to 1399, the number of wool sacks that were exported rose from 31,000 to 37,000 (5). The threat to Calais posed by a resurgent French Monarchy meant that the Calais Staple became too unstable to maintain the confidence of the wool producers of England. The staple was relocated to Bruges, for diplomatic reasons, on condition that an Anglo-Flemish alliance was agreed, but the capture of Bruges by the French halted this plan. The location of the Staple became a political football as those with interests in different cities competed with each other. It was at this time that the "wool interest" in parliament began to exploit, on a collective basis, the economic muscle that they had acquired.

Richard II's disastrous handling of affairs in France precipitated the collapse of the Calais Staple with the consequent knock-on effect upon the

English Wool Merchants and producers. This unrest, created by the utter failure in France in 1381 of Richard's army, fuelled the seeds of dissension across the country amongst the agricultural labourers. During this time there was a significant rise in the formation of craft and trade guilds. The reasons for the Poll Tax Riots were more diverse than is normally stated, England's commercial trade having had deep effects on the economy both nationally and regionally. Today, we see this each time Britain has a dispute with one or more of its fellow E. E. C. members. Britain's withdrawal from the E. R. M. produced the same crisis as relocation of the wool staple amongst the merchants – for "the city" read the "companies of merchants". Nevertheless, by the end of the century England's wool exports had risen to 8,000,000 fleeces a year (6). In 1398 Richard II obtained a grant of the wool subsidy for life, and the financial freedom this gave to the crown was exploited by Langley throughout the next three reigns.

John of Gaunt was the instigator of Langley's rise, the debt that Langley owed to Gaunt being quite simply his whole career. It is because of this that a brief biography of Gaunt's life and career up to the time when Langley entered his service follows. Langley became one of the ablest talents that Gaunt spotted; today we call it head-hunting, in the middle ages it was called patronage, the forerunner to indentureship. Every age has its examples of advancement from humble beginnings.

Gaunt noticed the traits in Langley that later became apparent to a wider public and, this speaks as much about Gaunt's judgement as it does about Langley's qualities. A number of Historians have questioned Gaunt's judgement in matters of politics, and in their partially justified analysis many of them have overlooked the career of Langley having been instigated by Gaunt.

JOHN of GAUNT

Many people who came into contact with John of Gaunt benefited from this contact; still more owed their entire careers to Gaunt's wealth and patronage. During his lifetime and immediately afterwards, Gaunt received a significant amount of critical comment from the main chroniclers of the period. The criticism was mainly aimed at Gaunt's wealth, and given the audience that the chroniclers were writing for, a good deal of bias clouded their observations. Much like the newspapers of today the chroniclers relied to some extent on the patronage of the wealthy, and this in varying degrees affected their judgements on the character of the people they were writing about, Thomas Walsingham, the St. Albans monk, being the most critical. There is a rhyme from Daniels book of 1595 **(7)** that perfectly composites the ill-will felt towards Gaunt by the chroniclers:-

Too great a subiecte growne, for such a state
The title of a king and what h'had done
In great exploits his mind did eleuate
Above proportion kingdomes stand vpon,
Which made him push at what his issue (i.e. Henry IV) gate ...

John was born in March 1340 at the Abbey of St. Bravo in the town of Ghent, known as Gaunt in English. He was the third son of Edward III and Phillipa of Hainault, and had two older sisters as well as two younger brothers and two younger sisters. When he was barely a year old he was granted the earldom of Richmond **(8)**, the guardianship of which was entrusted to his mother. On 20th May 1359 at Reading, Gaunt married Blanche, co-heiress with her elder sister Maud, of Henry Grosmont, Duke of Lancaster. Her elder sister was married to William of Hainault, Count of Holland and Zealand; consequently the running of her share of the Dukedom was left in the hands of her younger sister. Blanche was eulogised by Geoffrey Chaucer in "The Boke of the Duchess" and he described her as "bothe fair and bright". In the same year, a chronicler records that blood flowed from Thomas of Lancaster's tomb, attracting many pilgrims to Pontefract Priory, this was seen as a portent months later when Gaunt accompanied his two elder brothers, Edward (the Black Prince), Lionel and his father Edward III when they sailed to France. Gaunt led one of the battles which made an unsuccessful attempt to storm the city of Rhiems. He accompanied his father-in-law on a number of raids around the region before moving with the army towards Paris. The campaign ground to a standstill and was concluded by the Treaty of Brétigny, and Gaunt arrived back in England on 20th May 1360, shortly after his first child Philippa was born. Within a year Henry Grosmont died at Leicester of the plague, and two days later Edward III granted custody of Grosmont's estates to the twenty-one-year-old Gaunt.

Directions for the division of the estate were given in July 1361, the lands north of the Trent which included the Lancaster and Derby Earldoms being added to the estates he held as Earl of Richmond, and Gaunt was now the largest single landowner in northern England. His full title was now, John son of the king of England, Earl of Lancaster, Richmond, Derby and Lincoln, and High Steward of England **(9)**. In September of that year Gaunt's sister Mary Duchess of Brittany died, possibly of the same plague that claimed another sister Margaret Countess of Pembroke two months later. Gaunt's sister-in-law, Maud Countess of Leicester, died childless, her portion of Grosmont's estate being passed to Gaunt who was named Duke of Lancaster by his father on 13th November at Westminster. Maud was in England in 1361, and although it seems probable that she contracted the same plague as the sisters, nevertheless, rumours started in Leicester that Maud had been poisoned to unite the inheritance. This story first came to light when Gaunt visited Leicester with Blanche in the June of 1362. Just like certain of the stories that appear in the Sunday Redtops, this story was more appealing than what was the more likely truth, scandal and innuendo having always proved more popular than fact. In November 1366 three year's after Langley's birth Gaunt's involvement with Castile began when he sailed to join his brother the Black Prince in Dax. Gaunt was using his new found power by pledging some of his lands to the Crown against a loan of 5,000 marks. He also called on the service owed to him by a number of his tenants, including Langley's grandfather John.

By an alliance signed in 1362 between Edward III and Pedro I (the Cruel) of Castile Edward had embroiled England in the struggles between Pedro, Pere III of Aragon and Enrique of Trastamara, who was the illegitimate half-brother of Pedro. Naturally Charles V of France supported Pere. This brought about the invasion of Castile by Betrand de Guesclin at the head of an army of mercenaries financed by the French crown. To counter this incursion Pedro sought help from the Black Prince who was in Gascony when he was deposed in favour of Enrique. The campaign came to a head with the battle of Najera, where Gaunt commanded the vanguard together with Sir John Chandos who commanded the Castilian contingent.

The usually reliable Froissart commented that *"... there was done many a noble feat of arms. And on the English part specially there was Sir John Chandos, who on that day did like a noble knight and governed and counselled that day the Duke of Lancaster in like manner"* (10). Knighton and a number of the English chroniclers followed Froissart's lead in praising Gaunt. The price of victory was high as the Black Prince began to show signs of deterioration in his health, and he was to die 10 years later in 1376, one year before his father. Gaunt left for England before the winter weather set in, Blanche having borne their first son Henry of Bolingbroke. She died on 12th September 1368 aged either 26 or 27, her death being attributed to childbirth (11). She and Gaunt had five children in nine years, two of which, both boys, died in infancy. She was buried in St. Paul's Cathedral. Froissart and Chaucer wrote movingly of her, Gaunt's grief was genuine, and the fact that he chose to be buried next to her is a testimony to his feelings for her.

By July of the following year Gaunt was again in France, he had contracted with his father to serve for six months. He was duly appointed captain and lieutenant of Merck, Guines and Calais, arriving on 14th July, again many of his retinue being drawn from the duchy. His mother's death on 15th August prevented his father from joining him, the Black Prince being still in Aquitaine when Gaunt landed. Charles V of France had been gathering an army with the intention of invading England, Gaunt's landing changing the French strategic aims. The French under the command of the French king's brother, Philip duke of Burgundy, moved towards Normandy. Gaunt meanwhile, relieved the town of Ardres and harried the besiegers south-eastwards taking the towns of Therouanna and St Pol. After taking the town of Pernes, Gaunt withdrew towards Guines, and on 23rd August they sighted Burgundy's army. Both armies took up defensive positions, and a stand-off lasting two weeks ensued during which time skirmishes took place.

All armies dislike inactivity while both commanders waited for the other to advance. The impasse was broken at the beginning of September when a force from England under the command of the earls of Warwick, Oxford, Salisbury and March, joined Gaunt, and on the night of 12–13th September, the French withdrew. Gaunt's army marched back to Calais, and after three days they set out on a chavaunche towards Harfleur, the base established by Charles V for the invasion of England.

After twelve days of Harfleur being besieged, Gaunt withdrew to Calais not having achieved any significant victory. He has received a good deal of criticism for his handling of his first sole command. Whilst Gaunt failed to push home the advantage reinforcements had given him, it should be borne in mind that the French had learnt the futility of confronting English armies in pitched battles, the battles of Crécy (1346) and Poitiers (1356), bearing testimony to the slaughter English armies could inflict in a pitched battle. The French had adopted a policy of allowing the English armies to carry out their chevaunches whilst staying behind well-fortified cities, this tactic greatly frustrating the English. In hindsight the French tactics were eminently sensible.

The only time that the French abandoned this ploy the result was more damaging than Crécy and Poitiers, and it became known as Agincourt. I believe that Gaunt acted prudently in that he did not risk his army in attacking the French positions, and it is the fact that he had as his eldest brother the darling of the chroniclers, Edward the Black Prince, which made comparisons unfavourable.

In April of 1370 Gaunt sent letters from London to his Lancashire retainers summoning them to join him at Plymouth, the king having ordered him to reinforce his brother in Aquitaine. The brothers met at Cognac. By this time the Prince's health had deteriorated to the extent that he could not even sit on a horse, he was carried by litter to the siege of Limoges (**12**). Gaunt took over the lieutenancy from his brother who was so ailing that he did not stay for the funeral of his youngest son. The campaign again petered out but not before Gaunt married Constance of Castile who had fled to Bayonne after the assassination of her brother Pedro (the cruel) by her half-brother Enrique of Trastamara at Montiel in 1369. They married at Roquefort near Mont-de-Marsan and landed in England on 4th November at Fowey, arriving at the Savoy before the end of November.

By January of 1372 Gaunt was given permission by the English council to style himself King of Castile and Leon, and this began a whispering campaign that haunted Gaunt for the rest of his life. He had offended English Nationalism, which after the successes of Poitiers and Crécy, was arrogantly high, Gaunt's desire to act like a king of a foreign country offending the xenophobes. Compare this with the nationalism that was rampant during the Falklands war, our worst traits are deeply ingrained.

Langley was approximately 9 at this time. Given Gaunt's use of his Lancashire retainers on his last expedition, news of the events of the last year in France would have filtered down to places like Middleton as the army dispersed. How much of the news Langley remembered would be hard to gauge; however, in the decades to come Langley acted on a number of very important diplomatic missions to the French court, in his own way following in the steps of his forbears in thwarting the French. His key roles in the campaigns of Henry V, both diplomatically and financially, inflicted more damage on the French than any of Gaunt's campaigns, for once the pen proved mightier than the sword.

Constance was well treated and she was showered with gifts, and publicly she won over the English public who eventually became to feel sorry for her trapped in a country she could not call her own. Gaunt further incurred the wrath of the chroniclers with his continued affair with the widow of a Lancastrian knight, the daughter of one of Queen Philippa's household knights, Catherine Swynford. One called her ''a she-devil and enchantress'' (**13**), another remarked that Gaunt was frequently upbraided by members of his household for his adultery (**14**). Her sister Philippa was married to Geoffrey Chaucer who alluded to her in *The Monkes Tale*. She bore Gaunt three sons and a daughter before she died four years after Gaunt in 1403. These children became inextricably linked to Langley later in their lives.

For diplomatic reasons Edward III agreed to Duke John of Brittany's request to have returned his ancestral earldom of Richmond, and, Gaunt was given Tickhill and Knaresborough to compensate him. Diplomacy rather than war came to control English foreign policy, given the debts owed to Gaunt by the crown, in excess of £30,000, this must have suited the bankrupt Gaunt. He set out on a tour of his estates during the second half of 1374 before travelling abroad the following year to lead the English delegation at the Bruges peace conference. Gaunt completely mis-handled the negotiations, his failure to properly consult England's allies being deeply criticised at home.

He continued with further negotiations whilst in London, Edward III ' s grip on court and parliament was slipping. Criticism of the Crown's chief ministers had been growing for some time, and the movement began to replace the clerics with laymen. The lessons that Gaunt learnt at this time in regard to the politics of court must have left an impression. Coupled with his semi-regal council in his Duchy he began to gather around him men who were skilled in the intricacies of governance.

An excellent point has been made by Anthony Goodman **(15)** regarding the effect of the policies that England had used towards France and the effects these policies had on Gaunt. He has argued, correctly I believe, that Gaunt had witnessed at first hand the folly of England's policies and the heavy financial costs incurred, and that Gaunts attempts to make peace show him to be a man who could admit a mistake. An interesting reference to exemplify Gaunt's personality. Gaunt found himself at odds with the Commons when, through their insistence, new councillors were appointed. Relationships worsened when, after the death of the Black Prince on 8th June 1376, the Commons, as a counter to Gaunt, insisted that the nine-year-old heir to the Black Prince, Richard, be granted the principality of Wales. A number of rumours had been circulating that Gaunt was plotting to succeed to the throne **(16)**. If these rumours were true, and given parliament's actions they certainly had concerns, I believe that Gaunt's part in his son's usurpation would benefit from fresh analysis.

The king's health continued to deteriorate and Gaunt became *de facto* ruler. The ordinances of parliament were defeated in the lords and the Commons blamed Gaunt, not without justification. One by one during the course of the next year, Gaunt brought down his main opponents, Wykeham was deprived of his temporalities and Sir Peter de la Mare was imprisoned.

At the beginning of the next year, Gaunt took a prominent part in the celebrations held in London for Richard Prince of Wales. Two days later parliament sat, Gaunt's new tactic of the populist politician paid dividends, one of his retainers, Sir Thomas Hungerford, was appointed speaker and through Gaunt's influence pardons were granted to all those who were impeached during the last parliament, there being but two exceptions,

Wykeham and De la Mare. This was the parliament that brought in the first poll tax which, by including the clergy, put Gaunt on a collision course with the church. Wyclif was summoned to answer charges of unorthodoxy at St. Pauls and Gaunt very publicly escorted him there where he harangued the church officials and asked for their arrest. Rumour spread across the city that the bishops had been beheaded, causing crowds to form who were intent on attacking the Savoy, only the appearance of Courtney stopping them. Gaunt next promoted a bill to curtail some of the liberties of the Londoners. On the 20th February rioters attacked Gaunt and Percy whilst they were dining in the city and they escaped by being rowed across the Thames.

Gaunt was proclaimed a traitor to knighthood and taunted that his real father was a butcher in Ghent. It was only when the ring leaders were summoned before the king at Sheen that they backed down. They were made to apologise and to pay for and erect a marble pillar at Cheapside to which they would affix Gaunt's coat of arms. Edward III died in the following year, at Sheen on 21st June 1377.

There is no doubt that Gaunt's preoccupation with foreign affairs weakened his political power in England. During the years 1367–72 he spent more time abroad than he did at home, and between 1372 and 1376 he veered towards a settlement of England's foreign policy through diplomacy. Whilst the Black Prince was alive Gaunt could be reasonably assured that when his brother ascended the throne he would occupy a position of prominence in the political structure, but his brother's premature death changed this. Many in the Commons perceived Gaunt as a danger to their positions; the propaganda war was bitter with those opposed to Gaunt using innuendo and smear tactics to undermine Gaunt's position. The real issue was who would control the council advising Richard Prince of Wales?

Those lords who prior to the Black Prince's death were in the second or third tier of government seized their chance to achieve a greater influence than they ever could have expected prior to 1376, the chief beneficiaries of the minority being Robert de Vere, earl of Oxford and Thomas Mowbray, earl of Nottingham. Both had not previously distinguished themselves at home or abroad in the service of their country and also crucially neither were Lancastrian supporters. A modern-day parallel would be between Edward III and Margaret Thatcher, both having become tired and losing touch with the mood of the country and the Commons. The succession issue became one of not who was best for the country but who could stop Michael Heseltine who was the Conservative Party's best hope of retaining office. The fudge that gave power to John Major was the beginning of the Conservative's fall. For Heseltine read Gaunt, the comparisons are justified, both had wealth and power, both polarised parliament, and the self-interest of others eventually contributed to their removal from power. For Labour's landslide victory read Henry of Bolingbroke's usurpation. Langley was now approximately 14 years of age and through Gaunt's patronage, was taking his first steps along the path of advancement.

Langley's Family and the Duchy

The Lancashire V. C. H. carries a reference to a document dated 1270 which states that the homage and service of Robert son of Ellis de Holt and heirs for tenements held of Sir Geoffrey de Chetham in land called Langley to Roger de Middleton. This is the earliest record of the Langley land that I have so far discovered. It implies that the land was previously owned by Sir Geoffrey de Chetham who transferred the land and the rights attached to it to the Middleton family. A pedigree appears in C. S. Macdonald's book **(17)** that dates the family from circa 1220. I am far from convinced of the accuracy of this pedigree, especially in the light of the V. C. H. reference. It is more likely that soon after this the de Middleton's transferred the ownership to the Langley's as the dowry for one of the six daughters of Agnes and the last de Middleton, who died in 1313.

William Langley was the second son of John whose elder brother was also called Richard. The elder brother married Joan de Tetlow whose dowry included lands at Agecroft which is situated some three miles from Langley on the banks of the River Irwell. This left the second son, William, as heir to the Middleton lands. This was the second time that the Middleton lands had passed to a second son, William's father, Thomas's Grandfather John, was the younger brother of William who was the Rector of St. Leonard's the parish church. William and Alice Langley had five children, Henry, John, William, Thomas and Margaret. At the time of Thomas Langley's birth the household consisted of his parents, Grandfather, Great Uncle and his three elder brothers, eight people in all. There is an understandable tendency in local histories to overstate the importance of personages who are the subject of local histories. Whilst it cannot be disputed that the Langley family were land owners their estate was not substantial, there is no record of any under-tenants or of their holding lands in any other part of the Duchy of Lancaster. In the subsidy of 1332, William de Longley was assessed at 8 shillings. Their neighbours the Hopwoods and the Radcliffes held more substantial parcels of land.

The coats of arms of the three main families in the area, the de Middleton's, the Langley's and the Hopwood's were very similar indicating that all three families were descended from the original land holders the de Middletons. The de Middleton coat of arms are a paly of six argent and vert, the Langley family's displays a mullet in the second pale, the Hopwood's display an escallope in the second pale. When Thomas Langley became a bishop he used the device of a mullet on his signet ring, and this could have been a reference to his being a fisher of men's souls, the symbol of a fish being an old Christian symbol first seen in the catacombs that ran besides the Appian Way leading to Rome.

The last male de Middleton died in 1313 leaving a widow, Agnes, and six daughters. The landholdings of the de Middleton's then became sub-infuedated as settlements were made on the various marriages of the daughters, hence the similarity in the coats of arms. The area of land held by the Langley family is today fairly flat, arable farming as well as sheep farming may have been possible and indeed, given the number of people living in the house, would have been necessary. Excavations by the Greater Manchester Archaeological unit were carried out on the site of Langley Hall in March 1990. This was as a result of an enquiry by a Mr. S. White of the Middleton Civic Society who had found what turned out to be the base of a cheese press dating from the sixteenth century. The hall was demolished in 1886. A local man is reported as having found a roof timber with an inscription dated 1358. Mr. White produced an excellent plan which is reproduced in the appendices showing the original hall and the later additions. It appears that the hall was 15 metres by 14. I am grateful to the Middleton Civic Society and its members for their assistance in providing this information. There is evidence of a pond, marked as "dried up" on the tithe map of 1840, fish being an important part of the medieval diet and it is probable that this was a medieval pond. Three fields adjacent to the site of the house are marked as Little Eddish Meadow, Carre Hay Meadow and Dove House Meadow. Three meadows fits the pattern of sheep farming that was prevalent in the fourteenth century. A further field is named Mill Field indicating the obvious. If indeed a mill was situated on the Langley lands this would prove a valuable source of income. A brook dissects the land which again indicates that fresh water fish would have been available. The site is marked as moated although I feel that the moat was an addition of a later generation and was purely ostentatious.

Education and Religion

John of Gaunt held the advowson of St. Leonard's Church Middleton and presented William Langley, Thomas's great uncle, as rector in 1351. The only career open to a fourth son of a family with a small land holding was in the church, access to which was limited. Fortunately for Thomas Langley, his great-uncle was able to provide this access. Seven was the normal age for the start of one's education "litel clergeon, seven year of age" **(19a)**. He would have been taught the basis of Latin grammar and logic by his great-uncle,

"Swich manere doctrine as men used there, This is to seyn, to syngen and to rede, As smale children doon in hire childhede." **(19b)**

In the mid 1370's he was sent to St. Mary's Thetford, Norfolk, which was a Clunic Priory under the patronage of John of Gaunt. The order had originated in Capetian France being founded in 909 **(20)**. It was highly centralised and looked to Rome instead of Episcopal authority. There were thirty eight Clunic priories in England comprising a powerful body which, because of its prime allegiance to its Norman houses, became known as the alien priories. The abbey of Cluny, founded by the family of Eleanor of Aquitaine, originally followed the rule of St. Benedict although the original abbots insisted that the abbey followed a regime of strict observance of the Benedictine rule. Due to the centralism that was practised, the abbey at Cluny became known as the "mother house".

Gaunt was orthodox in his religious beliefs and much has been made of his initial support for Wyclif. The commentaries on this aspect of Gaunt's life have swung between those who condemned his support for Lollardy to those who see him as a liberal. It is important to remember that the doctrines espoused by Wyclif meant different things to different people. To the church, Wyclif represented an attack on the fundamentals of religious beliefs. To Edward III and the lords, Lollardy in the beginning was used as a tool to restrain the church, and, through the Commons, a device to assist with the passing of legislation to tax the clergy. There is no evidence to show that Gaunt attacked the church. It should also be remembered that his support for Wyclif cooled as Wyclif carried his attacks too far. Gaunt was more of a liberal in that he sought to patronise all the main religious orders.

Given the vast tracts of lands under his control, each area and country tended to favour different religious orders based on the historical institution of these orders. Gaunt's patronage of so many different doctrines merely reflected his wider geographical land holding. This could appear as an over-simplification but I would offer the thought that some of the theses that have been put forward have tried to "over-humanise" Gaunt and his benefactions and personal piety. Dukes such as Gaunt were constantly on the move as they perambulated around their lands. In 1359, Gaunt was given Papal permission to use a portable altar as well as being able to choose his own confessor and in 1363 this was extended to allow the administration of the sacraments to Gaunt, Blanche and the household **(21)**.

His son, Bolingbroke, generally followed his father's liberalism, although, because of the usurpation, relations were strained at times with the Papacy, particularly after the beheading of Archbishop Scrope. Henry V's piety bordered on the piety of the zealot, and this will be discussed later in this book. Gaunt's orthodoxy is exemplified by his devotion to the cult of the Virgin Mary which had prominence from 1389 onwards, when, in an attempt to end the schism, Pope Boniface IX instituted the Feast of the Visitation (2 nd July) **(22)**. Gaunt's orthodoxy was rewarded with the legitimisation of the children he had with Catherine Swynford, this and Langley's role in the negotiations having profound effects not only for the country but also for Langley. Much has been made of Gaunt's having made a number of bequests to Lincoln Cathedral including furnishings for the St. Mary chapel, as he was earl of Lincoln. Whilst not wishing to in any way demean his bequests, it should be remembered that Catherine Swynford was married to a Lincoln-shire knight. Was this was a case of contrition? The Cathedral also received bequests of a gold chalice made in Bordeaux that bore an engraving of a crucifix, a large candelabra and an altarpiece which cost over £387.

A contemporary description exists:

"One great sapphire within a circle on the foot of a Majesty, worth £40; within the circle are twelve clusters, each of four pearls, with a diamond in the middle, each cluster worth 100s, and the whole £60; above the circle, the figure of a pope, having a small ruby and sapphire on his feet, worth 20s." **(23)**

The access to benefices that service in Gaunt's household could provide meant that his patronage was highly valued and positions in his service were the subject of much competition. Gaunt did not overtly abuse his powers in this regard, indeed the benefices that were given during Gaunt's stewardship of the Duchy were considerably fewer in number than his predecessor Henry Grosmont. Despite this competition Langley received considerable patronage almost continually from the time that he formally entered the Duke's service. Gaunt's preoccupation with, and support of, Lincoln, reached its zenith when he obtained the see for his eldest son by Catherine Swynford, Henry Beaufort. Catherine was entombed in the cathedral in 1403.

Why Gaunt should choose a priory so far from Middleton to further Langley's education is unclear. It is likely that the priory acted as a "feeder" for Christ Church University, Cambridge as they were only thirty miles apart. Another possible alternative is that the great-uncle William studied at Thetford. In sending Langley to Thetford Gaunt was following the trend started by William Wykeham of preparing scholars for university, Cambridge in Gaunt's case. These scholars were groomed to replace the high numbers of educated clerics who had died as a result of the black death, the policy being to create a society of monks and seculars. St. Albans had lost its abbot, prior, subprior and forty-six monks in 1349, Westminster lost its abbot and twenty-six monks being just two examples.

There is an old adage that one does not forget a good teacher, and, given Langley's later church career, it is interesting to contrast the centralism of the Clunics with the policies that Langley followed when dealing with his church duties. The Clunics, as has already been stated, looked to the mother house first and Rome second more than to the Bishopric in matters of supremacy, Langley not overtly favouring the Papacy in his later political and clerical dealings. Nor is there any real evidence that he gave preferential treatment to the Clunics. Contrast this with his contemporaries, who at times favoured the orders who ordained them into the priesthood. The broad sympathy and support for the doctrines of Wyclif's and the Lollards had a distinct bearing on Langley's policies, and this is but one example of Langley's correct understanding of public opinion, an understanding that he carried throughout his career. The promotion of favoured candidates who were clearly not deserving of promotion was one of the features of Papal policy that did so much to weaken the respect and standing of the Church of Rome in the mid to late thirteenth century. The statutes of Provisors and Praemunire (1344 and 1353) were the culmination of the anti-Papal mood that marked the later years of Edward III's reign. The counter-argument to this runs that Papal influence was "the only effective check on the dominance of strictly material class interests within the church" **(24)**.

The schism, which will be discussed later in this book, did much to assist the supremacy of Royal over Papal policy during its duration. Benefices became a tool of the political arena used by both Pope and King equally, with the filling of the various benefices being governed by the wider European political situation. Today, this is seen in the appointments to quangos, Health Care Trusts and European Commissioners. The prime example of this is the appointment of William of Wykeham to the see of Winchester. Wykeham was the nominee of Edward III and was duly elected by a compliant chapter, the King having to write to twenty four cardinals as well as three letters to the Pope before the appointment was ratified **(25)**. This form of horse trading between Crown and Papacy percolated down to the second tier of church offices, and Maitland described the trade in canonries, prebends and arch-deaconaries as "the staple commodity of the papal provisors" **(26)**. A check by the Papacy in the imposition to high church office affected Langley early in his church career and showed precisely where Langley's true loyalties lay (see the chapter on Henry IV).

The third Statute of Praemunire issued by the Commons in the parliament of 1393 contained provisions prohibiting the Pope from issuing sentences of excommunication, citations or bulls of provision in England **(27)**.

Thomas Radcliffe, the younger brother of James, both of whom were neighbours of Langley's family, was an esquire in Gaunt's household and it is probable that he drew the Duke's attention to Langley's abilities, and through James Radcliffe Langley received Gaunt's patronage. As will be seen later, Langley repaid the Radcliffes when he rose to high office.

In 1385, Langley was described as a clerk **(28)** showing that he was by that time in minor orders. It therefore follows that he joined the Clunics whilst he was at Thetford. The Clunic's centralisation and their close connections with the Papacy will have given Langley an invaluable insight into the views of Rome on the English Church. The knowledge he gathered would have added to his later career as clerk to Gaunt and later as Chancellor of England. Such understanding of both lay and clerical policy and the machinery behind it greatly assisted Langley in his rise and proved invaluable to both Henry IV and his son Henry V. The Council of Constance and Langley's pivotal role in its proceedings can be attributed in part to the grounding in church politics that he received from the Clunics.

Cambridge

How long Langley was at St. Mary's is not known, but from here he went to Corpus Christi College, Cambridge. Gaunt had received the patronage of the college through his wife Blanche, and Gaunt is recorded in 1382 as maintaining a scholar at Cambridge in the previous year **(29)** which would make Langley 18 years of age. It was customary for scholars to enter Cambridge when they were around the age of 14; this would place Langley at Cambridge in 1377. Langley did not take any formal degree; there is no record of Langely ever bearing the title "master".

He would have studied canon and civil law which was customary for those who were to become secular clerks. The fact that Langley had a patron indicates that his education at Cambridge was aimed at his following a career outside the church. Together with the grounding in church politics that he received from the Clunic Order, he was in effect doing a double degree course similar to that which is taught at certain English Universities today, Keele for example. Corpus Christi was the youngest of the seven universities founded at Cambridge in the fourteenth century being founded in 1352, against the three foundations in the same period at Oxford. The Cambridge foundations were: King's Hall (c. 1316), Michaelhouse (1324), (both became absorbed into Trinity), Clare (1326), Pembroke (1347), Gonville Hall (1349) and Trinity Hall (1350).

Control of Cambridge lay with the Archdeacon, the *magister glomerie* was subject to the archdeacon's whim. The early history of Cambridge is slightly obscure due to the destruction of the university archives by the rebels. Episcopal control held Cambridge in its grip for a longer period than it did at Oxford, and confirmation of the Chancellor and the canonical oath he had to swear was still controlled by the Bishop of Ely in 1400. Criminal jurisdiction which the chancellor of Oxford had exercised for a 100 years was only given to the Cambridge Chancellor in 1383 **(30)**. Corpus Christi was founded by one of the Cambridge gilds giving the university access to commercial wealth as well as clerical endowments. The university day started at 6. 00. a. m. with the first lecture of the day, and finished at 6. 00. p. m. . The halls were small with only twenty to thirty students, and for a boy of fourteen it was a very austere adolescence.

Notes and References

(1)   *Reg. no. 1041.*
(2)   Fryde, E. B. "Studies in Medieval Trade and Finance", (London 1983). Also in "The Cambridge Economic History", vol iii, (Cambridge 1961).
(3)   Sayles, G. O. "The English Company of 1343", *Speculum,* vol vi (1931).
(4)   Unwin, G. ed. "Finance and Trade under Edward III", (Manchester, 1918).
(5)   Gray, H. L. "The Production and Export of English Woollens in the Fourteenth Century", *E. H. R. xxxix*, (1924).
(6)   Wilkinson, B. "The Later Middle Ages in England, 1216–1485". Longman, London, (1969).
(7)   Daniel, S. "The first fowre Bookes of the ciuile wars between the two houses of Lancaster and Yorke", (London, 1595).
(8)   C. P. R. 1343–5, pp. 4–5, 42–3.
(9)   C. P. R. 1361–4 pp. 171, 202–3 and in Somervile, R. "History of the Duchy of Lancaster", (London, 1953).
(10)   Froissart, J. "Chronicles", ed Macaulay, (1895, London).
(11)   Armitage-Smith, S. "John of Gaunt", (Constable, London, 1904). pp 21, 94.
(12)   Froissart. J, p 200.
(13)   Knighton. "Chronicon Henrici"
(14)   Thompson, E. M. ed. Chronicon Angliae, Rolls Series, (London 1874).

(15) Goodman, A. "John of Gaunt, The Exercise of Princely Power In The Fourteenth-Century Europe". Longman, (London 1992). Invaluable both for its new appraisal of Gaunt and also a mine of information for sources. I could not have written the first part of this book without this work.
(16) Macdonald, C. S. "A History of Hopwood and the life of Cardinal Langley of Langley. (Waldegrave, London, 1963).
(17) Holmes, G. "The Good Parliament", Oxford University Press, (1975).
(18) "Exchequer Lay Subsidies", (Rec. Soc. of Lancs and Cheshire, 31), 36.
(19a & b)
    Chaucer, G. "The Complete Works", ed. W. W. Skeat, (O. U. P. 1951).
(20) Jumieges, William of, (and Orderic Vitalis and Robert of Torigni), *Gesta Normannoram Ducam*, ed. E. M. C. van Houts, 2 vols, (Oxford, 1992–5).
(21) Bliss, W. H. et. al. eds, "Calendar of Entries in the Papal Registers relating to Great Britain and Ireland", H. M. S. O. , (London 1896). Also "Petitions to the Pope, vol 1, 1342–1419, (1897), Papal Letters, vol. 3, 1342–1362. vol. 4, 1362–1404.
(22) Pfaff, R. W. "New Liturgical Feasts in Later Medieval England", (O. U. P. 1970).
(23) Goodman.
(24) Barraclough, G. "Papal Provisions", (O. U. P. 1935).
(25) Highfield, J. R. L. "The Promotion of William of Wykeham to the see of Winchester", Journal of Ecclesiastical History, IV, (1953), 44.
(26) Maitland, F. W. "Roman and Canon Law in the Church of England", (Cambridge 1898).
(27) Myers, A. R. ed, English Historical Documents IV, 1327–1485, (Eyre and Spottiswoode, London 1969). p 881 doc no. 383.
(28) Lambeth, "Register of Archbishop Courtney, p 350 and 353 v.
(29) John of Gaunts Register, 1379–83, no. 856.
(30) McKisack, M, "The Fourteenth Century 1307–1399, (Oxford, 1959) p 506

PART TWO

Falstaff: *"To die is to be a counterfeit, for he is but the counterfeit of a man who hath not the life of a man; but to counterfeit dying, when a man thereby liveth, is to be no counterfeit, but the true and perfect image of life indeed. The better part of valour is discretion, in which better part I have sav'd my life"* **(1).**

THE FIRST STEPS OF HIS CAREER

The Poll Tax Riots

The Poll Tax riots were the apogee of a tide of discontent that had started at the beginning of the 1350's when the effects of the first visitation of the black death which occurred in 1348/9 began to affect the labour market. The shortage of workers that resulted and the opportunity it gave to the peasantry to improve their status in society created tensions between the royal administration, parliament, the major landholders and their tenants. Gaunt's position as one of the largest landowners in England and his wealth, the gross income from his estates has been calculated to be as high as £11,750 at its peak **(2)**. made him one of the prime targets of the rioters.

The rioting in Cambridgeshire began on Saturday 15th June, 1381, when John Greystone, who had taken part in the rioting in London, led the people of the north of the shire in an orgy of looting and robbery whilst John Hanachach led an assault on the Hospitallers manor at Duxford. On the following Monday, a group headed by Richard of Leicester seized and beheaded Sir Edmund Walsingham who was a justice of the peace. On the same Saturday the Great Bell of St. Mary's gave the signal for the rioters to begin the sacking of the universities, their principal target being Corpus Christi which was so badly sacked that the college was gutted. Gaunt's patronage of the College had ensured that it became the focal point of the rioter's discontent. The rioting continued over the weekend, St. Mary's was sacked whilst mass was in progress; its plate, jewels and archives were seized and much of its records were publicly burned in Market Square. A document was drawn up which required the University to surrender its privileges to the town, and it also had to agree to be governed by the municipal authorities.

The mayor had led the rioters, clearly a case of self interest in the attack on the university's rights. How often have we seen a person using a populist movement to extend their personal position? Langley was 18 years old and would be regarded as a senior student. The effect the rioting must have had on a young mind must have been profound. His life up to this time had been one of order and logic controlled by the daily offices of the Clunic order. Society was viewed as a series of hierarchical structures, a place for everyone and everyone in their place. The riots and the upheaval to the calm orderliness of the cloistered world that Langely knew must have terrified such a young impressionable mind. Proof of this came 36 years later, when, as Bishop of Durham, Langely threatened to excommunicate some disorderly tenants; clearly the scars of the poll tax riots had left their mark. Excommunication was the direst penalty a person could suffer, no Christian charity here, more a case of once bitten. The threat of God used as a tool of oppression, makes it appear that Langley had forgotten his roots.

There is a gap in the chronology of Langleys life from 1381 to 1385 Storey throws no light on Langleys education or for how long he was at Thetford. Indeed Storey, the only available source for Langley's life, is fairly dismissive of his early career. I hope that the comments that have preceded this paragraph have filled in the gaps. One has to analyse the early upbringing and influences that shaped Langley in order to arrive at conclusions in respect of his later actions. It is also relevant to remark that Langley's rise from 1385 was rapid, and that this could not have been achieved if he had not received the type of education previously described. In the absence of documentary records, destroyed by the poll tax rioters, one has to follow by deduction the path that personages like Langley would take. The first official line of his career traces his rise from the 4th of August 1385 when he was instituted as the Rector of the church of Radcliffe. Radcliffe is situated on the red cliff banks of the River Irwell on the outskirts of Bury, he was presented to the church by James Radcliffe.

In the four years between his leaving Cambridge and his presentation it is likely that he assisted his great-uncle William in the parish church. Langley stated in 1407 that he had served the Duke of Lancaster since his youth; "*ab annis teneris*" (3). It is conceivable that because of the damage at Corpus Christi suffered Langley would have returned North. He would have been about 18 at this time which would fit in with his later remarks. Gaunt later (1390) granted the Cambridgeshire manor of Landbeach to the college. He was never recorded as "Master", indicating that he did not take any formal degree. Gaunt's need for clerics, particularly in the aftermath of the riots, would have meant that Langley, as a sponsored scholar of Gaunt's, would have entered into Duchy service at this time.

The Duchy Household and Chancery

I am again indebted to Anthony Goodman (4) for the itinerary of Gaunt's perambulations around his estates during 1382, the first year of Langley's service. From January to May he was at Hertford Castle, his principal residence near London. The Savoy was never rebuilt after its destruction the year before. In the 1390's he leased the Bishop of Ely's house in Holborn midway between St. Paul's and Westminster. This will have been Langley's place of residence when he was in London. Gaunt and Catherine Swynford entertained the new Queen Isabella at Holborn; Langley was in London at this time and would have attended the banquet. In July he was at Higham Ferrers on route to Leicester Castle, the *caput* of his Lands south of the Trent. August saw him in Yorkshire visiting York, Pontefract and Pickering before returning to London in October. Langley accompanied him on these per-ambulations which were necessary as much for hygienic reasons as any other.

The Palatinate powers that had been attached to the Duchy enabled its civil servants to exercise their authority safe in the knowledge that the judiciary was under their control. Considering the vast size and diversity of the Duchy estates, there are very few complaints regarding the maintenance of the Ducal estates. The violence of the Poll Tax riots, particularly in London where Gaunt's residence the Savoy Palace was sacked, was widespread. Many commentators have written that Gaunt was the principal target of the rioters due to the events in London, and whilst this is partially true, it should be remembered that Gaunt was the largest landowner in the country. Therefore he had more to lose than most, and on a pro-rata basis he did not suffer more than anyone else, but it was Gaunt's political standing specifically in the council where the most damage was done.

Tensions between Gaunt and both the citizens of London and the Bishops had been fomenting for some time, the Poll Tax riots providing a pretext to settle old scores. It must also be remembered that Edward III had been in poor health for some time, and politically those factions who were against the Lancastrians, and Gaunt in particular, were jockeying for positions of control of the minor Richard, Prince of Wales. Gaunt and Percy had been forced to flee from the Savoy Palace to Kennington where Princess Joan offered to act as a mediator. These events were taking place whilst Langley was beginning his studies at Cambridge, and Gaunt's favouring of Wyclif would have been the main topic of debate within both the university and the abbey at Thetford. At the first Parliament of the new reign Gaunt had faced down his opponents. The gist of his speech was that he had too much to loose by being disloyal, a good point. The rioting had not touched the Duchy heartland, the land of which was principally held on a leasehold basis. The expenditure of the Duke was high, but leaseholds gave a greater degree of forward financial planning than did reliance on fluctuating incomes that depended in turn on climatic conditions and their effects on the agricultural yield. In the years 1394 and 1395 the gross income of the Duchy was circa £11,750, nearly 25% of which was spent on annuities for his retainers (5).

Langley's institution into the church of Radcliffe in August 1385, albeit for a brief five months, shows that Gaunt was able where possible, to augment his retainer's income from advowsons. Langley's early service at the Duchy court will have brought him into contact with Henry of Bolingbroke and the rest of the Duke's offspring. Bolingbroke was three years younger than Langley and whilst Constance was the de facto Duchess, it was Katherine Swynford who supervised the ducal household.

As a clerk in Gaunt's chancery, Langley would have had to learn more than accountancy. Gaunt rigidly controlled the shire knights who were elected to parliament, and Langley would be well aware of Gaunt's political aims and objectives. All assignments of estates, grants and benefices would have passed through the chancery office. Again, Langley will have seen these documents and in a number of cases would have drafted them himself. Langley's later success in raising money for Henry V shows how well he learnt his trade.

There is an old saying about government chancellors; "they have more pockets than Fagin"; in Langley's case this was to become an apt adage. Gaunt was absent from the Duchy for three years from 1386–9, during this time the administration of the Duchy fell on the Sheriffs and chancery. Various instances can be found in the Duchy records of riotous behaviour that continued after the poll tax riots. Langley will have accompanied Gaunt when he attended parliament so that he could go through the various petitions that the Duke brought to the Commons. His understanding of the mechanics of parliament were of the greatest assistance to him during his chancellorships. His was a long apprenticeship earned through hard work not gained by titled position, the professional and the amateur, it is little wonder that Langley was so adroit.

There is an incident that occurred in 1385 that would have given Langley his first experience of court politics. The tensions between the lords advising Richard II and Gaunt were frequently strained. The Earldom of Chester bordered the Lancastrian lands, and Sir John Stanley, probably encouraged by the royal lieutenant, had entered the manor of Lathom pleading the excuse that he entered as ward due to the minority of the previous heir. Gaunt, who held the estate of Halton in the shire, appealed to the Commons on the basis that Stanley before entering, should have, sought leave to do so from the Palatine court. The Commons found in Gaunt's favour, ordering that he could only proceed through the Palatine's Chancery. Langley at this time was serving in chancery and would at the very least have been aware of, if not involved in the preparation of the case.

The next year Robert de Vere who, as well as being justiciar of Chester and lieutenant of Ireland was bitterly opposed to Gaunt, rewarded Stanley by appointing him as his deputy. Langley's appointment to the church of Radcliffe could have been a reward for his part in the Stanley case. A further indication that Langley had been involved is that, within five months of his receiving Radcliffe, he was appointed treasury clerk to Gaunt and returned to Lancaster. Clearly, after only four years service in the household his talent was being recognised and rewarded. As treasury clerk, Langley will, mostly, have travelled with Gaunt and his court. The ducal court mirrored the royal court in its composition and workings. This gave Langley the most intermit insight into the workings of the Duchy and, just as importantly, will have brought him into contact with a wide selection of people both in the royal and baronial circles, as well as giving him contact with the other chancery clerks and civil servants.

It is whilst he was serving as a chancery clerk that Langley came into contact with parliament both professionally and politically. In today's jargon this is known as networking. All and any comment regarding Langley in books on the period gave as the reason for his rise, especially under Henry IV, his "Lancastrian roots". Whilst this was obviously a factor in his promotion I feel that it is too trite a view. By the time he was 23 in 1386, he had been receiving various forms of education for 11 years or so, and by the time of Gaunt's death he had been in service for 17 years. Anyone who had spent 28 years of their life learning principally the workings of the ducal chancery would be extremely well qualified to deserve a promotion. Being Lancastrian was only part of the picture, and it is this sort of reasoning that has meant that Langley's role in history has been considerably overlooked.

The delicate position that Bolingbroke found himself in on his assumption of the throne meant that he could ill afford to antagonise parliament by appointing incompetent ministers. The same was true for his father after the poll tax riots. An inefficient chancery would have given more ammunition to Gaunt's opponents. Langley would always have to have an eye to the wider picture. His diplomatic training had also started, his duties would also will have brought him into contact with parliamentarians. A person who was in a position to learn all these facets of governance coupled with his church background was uniquely placed on the slippery slope of promotion and patronage. The work that passed through the ducal chancery was varied, from the fixing of the value of leases & assessing farming yields through to the expenditure of the ducal court. As one example in March 1381, the tenants of Rochdale complained that they were being summoned and constrained to answer outside their franchise by the bailiffs of Staffordshire. A report by the auditors in 1388 states that the falling profits can be blamed on the local administrative officials for laxity, Langley would have had a hand in framing this report.

The Duchy had followed a policy of leasehold tenure amongst its farms, and this bound a family by land and economic ties, something the Victorians did in owning the houses the mill workers lived in. This was a big inducement to keep the peace, which partially explains why the poll tax riot did not affect Gaunt's estates . The success of the chancery officials in increasing the ducal income can be seen in the increase in revenue from £8,380 in 1331 to £11,750 gross in 1395 **(6)**, an increase of 40%. Of this Lancashire contributed £1,763 net, 17% of the net figure for 1395. This net income was split nearly 50/50 between the northern and southern lands. The Ducal income received a windfall in 1388 when Gaunt received £100,000 in settlement from Juan I of Castile. The chancery will also have had to deal with foreign income and expenditure further expanding Langley's knowledge and experience.

It has been necessary to dwell on the diversity of the ducal income to exemplify the work that Langley was undertaking which is why Gaunt appointed him as one of his executors. This will have been because of his intimate knowledge of the ducal estates, and as a junior executor Langley will have dealt with the majority of the paperwork. His work will have also brought him into contact with the beneficiaries of Gaunt's will. His closeness to the heart of the court will also have brought him into close personal contact with Gaunt's immediate family. Given that Bolingbroke was still in exile when his father died, and the fact that Bolingbroke immediately appointed Langley to his inner household shows that he was well known to the Duke's family. Coupled with the political events that Langley had to partially deal with from 1381 to 1399, his rise was achieved on the foundations of a long intimate education in the mechanics and minutiae of the office of chancery. For someone to serve so diligently and with so little reward in terms of landed estates exemplifies Langley's unswerving loyalty to the House of Lancaster. Such deep-seated service was the only service the son and grandson of Gaunt really trusted. Of all the civil servants appointed to the higher offices by Henry's IV, V and VI, only Langley had the length of service that warranted his promotion through virtue of endeavour. His personal reward was the opportunity to serve, service as a virtue and virtue in service, a roundness to one's life.

Politics

A good deal of the main political issues that affected Langley have been discussed in the preceding sub-section. To complete the political picture it is necessary to look at the two significant events that were to place Langley at the centre of the political stage. One was Bolingbroke's involvement on the national scene and the effects on Langley. The other was the legitimisation of the Beauforts with, as a significant side issue, the exiling of Thomas Arundal Arch-bishop of Canterbury.

    Following the poll tax, Gaunt trod a delicate path between the lords of his nephew's court and those who were increasingly at odds with the Ricardian regime. Gaunt was well aware of the nasty streak in Richard II; he was also well aware of the discontent with his councillors. Whilst Gaunt had to appear friendly and co-operative with his nephew, he was careful to keep as much distance as he could from the unpopular decisions of the ministers. The fact that both he and Bolingbroke were abroad for a significant period, Gaunt's exile by choice but Bolingbroke's being forced on him, had the effect that the publics perception was that Gaunt was not blamed for a lot of the tyranny of the later years of the reign. A number of the trips abroad that Bolingbroke undertook were funded by the Duchy chancery which would have brought Langley into close personal contact with the heir to the Duchy. The detail that the chancery would have had to go to in organising the expenditure and letters of credit was complex. The son of one of Europe's premier lords had to travel in style and had to distribute gifts that befitted a son of such importance. The friendships and alliances that one made on such journeys were designed to assist spread of one's spheres of influence, personal contact bought. Today's equivalent would be a trade mission.

    This closeness to the very heart of the ducal household helped Langley to cope with the crisis that Bolingbroke's exile brought. Only someone who was conversant with the political climate in the country could have decided to stay in England and prepare the platform for Bolingbroke's return. Langley's position as executor was key to preserving the Lancastrian finances against the king's rapaciousness.

By the early 1390's Gaunt was the eldest surviving child of Edward III, the death of the childless Queen Anne of Bohemia in the summer of 1394 having brought yet more tensions to the royal court. Richard had no children; his cousin Henry Bolingbroke had, herein lay the problem. In the same year Gaunt's second wife Constance died on 24th March. This left Gaunt free to marry Catherine Swynford by whom he already had four children all born in the 1370's. Richard's choice of bride was the seven-year-old Isabella, daughter of Charles VI of France. She brought with her a 800,000 franc dowry together with a 28–year peace treaty which removed the heavy costs of financing an increasingly desperate defensive position in France. Richard had asked for a clause stating that the French monarchy would'' (support him) against all manner of folks and to sustain him with all their power against any of his subjects'' **(7)**. The clause was not inserted in the marriage agreement but the point had been made, and the king felt sufficiently secure to again turn his attention to his particular style of governance. Gaunt had taken part in the negotiations, and given the age of the bride, it would be at least seven years before an heir was in place, the clause having been requested at the behest of those who recognised Gaunt's increasingly powerful position.

The Beauforts

The Duke's prime concern at this time was to obtain the legitimisation of his children known as the Beauforts, in this he needed a Papal dispensation as well as the support of the king. Gaunt had wanted to legitimise the children for some time, and this would require some delicate negotiation, not least to assuage any concerns his eldest son might have. The methodology needed to bring this about required tact, it needed someone who was well versed in the politics of the court, and someone who was also able to gain the Pope's ear, one Thomas Langley. He is noted as being in Wales in 1394 to attend on the king concerning certain matters of the Duke's affairs **(8)**.

The appointments that followed the next year, whilst in Gaunt's gift, will have had to receive ratification by the king, and this indicates that affairs that Langley conducted were considered important matters by both parties. Richard II embarked for Ireland from Haverfordwest at the end of September 1394. On 24th August of that year whilst he was at Pontefract, the Earl of Rutland, and Gaunt's two brothers, Edmund of Langley, Earl of Cambridge and Thomas of Woodstock, Earl of Buckingham had stopped there Edmund was due to depart for Gascony, and Rutland and Woodstock were to join the king on his expedition to Ireland.

Gaunt wrote an effusive letter to the king in which he thanked him for warranting a grant and stressed his goodwill towards the king's person. He went on to state that certain persons of "low standing, I know not whom", had uttered remarks in the royal household touching the king's honour. The letter continued, "I believe and truly hope, my lord, that you always had such proof of my loyalty by experience of all my dealings with you, that you would not be inclined to believe such utterances tending to contradict my said dealings" **(9)**. The tone of the letter shows the concerns that Gaunt still had regarding those at court who were opposed to him.

He intended to be in Aquitaine as indentures had already been issued **(10)**. Talbot, who was still at court, had accused Gaunt of treason. Within five weeks of the letter being written, Talbot was in the Tower of London. Richard had previously struck Talbot in Westminster Abbey when he was late for the funeral of the Queen. Given that Richard II was only in Wales in 1394 at the end of August and for the first three weeks of September and this is the only record of any correspondence during this period between Gaunt and the king, this has to be the "duke's affair" that Langley dealt with. He will have accompanied Woodstock and Rutland to Wales Langely at the age of thirty-one Langley was dealing with matters other than what one would expect for a mere chancery clerk. and such a delicate matter would not have been entrusted to anyone other than a trusted servant, the rewards that Langley received from both Gaunt and the crown show that he had made an impression, hence his being entrusted with the task of legitimising the Beauforts.

On 23 July in the following year he was ratified as a prebendary of the royal free chapel of St. Martin-le-Grand **(11)**. Seven months later (12th February), he was given the rectory of St. Alphege, London. On 15th February 1397, he exchanged his London posts for the canonry of St. Asaph together with the prebend of Meifod **(12)**. On 17th March 1397, he was ordained a priest in Coventry Cathedral taking his prebend as his title **(13)**. On 26th September 1398, Gaunt presented him to the church of Castleford. These various awards of offices attached to a church did not place the recipient under any obligation to personally attend on the church. It was customary to employ a vicar who would receive either a fixed stipend or a third of the revenue of the church **(14)**. Dispensations were given for spiritual and political work, in Langley's case Gaunt would have obtained the relevant dispensations. The benefices were given to supplement Langley's income; as he rose through promotion so his own personal expenditure would increase, he would need servants and clothing appropriate to his station. Whilst the Duchy met much of this expenditure Langley would still have had to pay for a number of items, and he would have been entertaining more as he flexed his political muscles and began to meet with a wider circle both at court, exchequer and Commons.

His entertaining was done at the Bishop of Ely's house in Holborn, midway between church (St. Paul's) and the political centre of the realm (Westminster). This was one of the busiest thoroughfares in the city, and all important visitors from abroad and the country would pass by. The town houses of the bishops, officers of state and the major lords, were in and around Holborn, a far cry from Langley's boyhood days in rural Lancashire.

The bells of St. Paul's would awaken him, with the gossip of politics following him to bed, secular and clerical life co-existing side-by-side inextricably linked in the service of the realm. An apt analogy for Langleys life and career is that all his career was spent between one or the other, his time spent serving two masters, one in this world and one in the other, religion and politics, the habit and the robes of state, the power of patronage the only constant. The rewards for success were great, the price of failure disgrace and sometimes worse, and it required a delicate touch on the tiller of life to steer a steady course between the two, which Langley did to perfection. His long years of uncriticised service are a testimony to this.

He and Thomas Radcliffe were also amongst the tenants of Gaunt's manor at Barnoldswick (**15**). Langley was now bound by clerical and landowning ties. Clearly his promotion through the ranks of the church was planned by Gaunt, the Duke had obviously decided that Langley was to rise higher than a mere chancery clerk. The positions in the church helped to strengthen his religious status, and this would be needed so that Gaunt could petition Pope Boniface IX for the legitimacy of his four children by Catherine Swynford. As a purcusor to this, Gaunt married his long time mistress on 13th February, 1396, in Lincoln. The marriage was confirmed in the same Papal bull as the legitimisation. In the parliamentary sitting in Hilary 1397, the Beauforts were granted a charter of legitimacy (**16**).

Archbishop Arundal, the chancellor, recited the charter after which Sir John was created Earl of Somerset. Whilst Langley had been preparing the ecclesiastical ground, Gaunt had been assuaging his son's concerns. Given Langley's rapid promotion when Henry took the crown it would appear that the new king bore no malice towards those who, in fact, had reduced the size of his inheritance. As important as this act was for the contemporary period, the consequences for the future of England can, in hindsight, been seen as one of the most important acts of legitimacy in the history of this country. John the eldest Beaufort was the great-grandfather of Henry VII, the first Tudor king. Henry became bishop of Lincoln then Winchester and as well as wearing a cardinal's hat he occupied for a time the post of chancellor. Joan was the youngest and her second marriage was to Ralph Neville from which came the Warwick dynasty and through marriage Richard III. Her grand-daughter was the mother of Edward IV. The Somerset Lords came from a branch of the Beauforts and Jane, John's daughter, married James I king of Scotland.

Within a hundred years all the major titled families could claim a connection with the original Beaufort family. The four children were aged between 19 and 25, and given the great schism that was in progress and the current Anglo-French alliance Boniface would hardly have wanted to alienate one of the most powerful lords in the country. Richard II needed his uncle's support and so in some ways the legitimisation was not to difficult to obtain. Nevertheless, by being so associated with the procurement of the document Langley benefited. He now had as friends, and in some ways debtors, an adjunct of the most powerful house in England, who, due to a clause inserted later by Bolingbroke 1406 were excluded from inheriting the crown, thereby making their existence dependant on the continuance in power of the Lancastrian dynasty. The lordships, marriages and positions the Beauforts obtained ensured that Langley's influence and support spread across the baronage and brought more families into his sphere.

Langley must have been aware of the ennoblement's that Gaunt wished to bestow on these children. Langley was politically astute enough to realise how the addition of more Lancastrian nobles would benefit Gaunt and his sons. Langley's role in this issue added immeasurably to his reputation in Lancastrian circles, and, as will be seen in his later career, the Beauforts proved good allies to Langley particularly in the later parliaments, as did their spouse's families.

By this one single act, Langley assured himself of the future political support of what was to become the majority power at court, in the Commons, and across the country. It is hard to believe that Langley had not calculated at least some of the plus factors to be had from assisting in the legitimacy. He had by this time been involved at the hub of political life for 16 years, the last 3 years of which had been spent in and around the court of Richard II. The factionalism that had developed around the throne will have been noted by Langley who would have viewed the legitimisation as contributing as a counterweight against those ranged against Gaunt and his eldest son. The support the Beauforts were to give Gaunt's grandson was the plank upon which Henry V's throne rested; the debt the king owed to Langley was not lost on the most famous of the Lancastrian kings. They were 15 years older than Henry V and as such were regarded as the elder branch of the family.

Langley's dealings with the Beauforts will be dealt with later in this book when Henry V ascended the throne.

Bolingbroke's reaction to the legitimisation of his half brothers and sister is difficult to assess. Clearly Gaunt had discussed the matter with his eldest son. The fact that Bolingbroke did not dissent publicly either during or after his father's death indicates that he had received sufficient assurances regarding his inheritance. The insertion of the clause excluding the inheritance of the crown should be viewed as a prudent father endeavouring to secure his son's inheritance to the throne. Relations between the half brothers remained cordial and co-operative after the clause had been ratified by the Commons, the Beauforts having too much to loose by open dissension, theirs being initially a tenuous position.

Also, Henry of Bolingbroke had only been two years old when his mother Blanche died at the age of twenty-six. His governess was Catherine Swynford whose son by her first marriage, Sir Thomas Swynford, accompanied Henry on his later travels in Prussia. He was also to act as the jailer of Richard II and it was he that was most likely to have been the King's murderer. The intimate childhood contact between the half brothers and sister would have been a reassurance. Froissart claimed that Gaunt's legitimisation of the children was due to his fondness for his children (17). I do not doubt that this altruistic act was in part brought about for the reasons Froissart states, but Gaunt was too politically astute not to see the wider picture. Also Froissart was the type of writer who followed popular opinion, Gaunt's stock at this time being high in the country. Just as the tabloids today endeavour to editorially cater for their readership, so too did the medieval chroniclers.

Bolingbroke, crisis and exile

Richard II's actions of 1398 were preceded in 1397 by the exiling of the Arch-Bishop of Canterbury, Thomas Arundal. Warwick, Arundel and Gloucester were all impeached for their parts in the events of 1387/8. Gloucester was murdered in Calais (18), Warwick was exiled to the Isle of Man, and Arundel was executed. Gaunt, in his capacity as Steward of England, pronounced the sentences although at the time that he did so he was unaware that his brother, Gloucester was already dead; Langley was in attendance in London. The exiling of the arch-bishop was to prove the king's biggest mistake. Gaunt at least outwardly obeyed the king's orders, but privately he must have viewed with alarm the vindictiveness that was so publicly displayed by his nephew.

The crisis provoked by Richard II in 1398 set the Lancastrians on a course the outcome of which was inevitable. Langley as Gaunt's executor occupied a position that was of fundamental importance as events unfolded. The king's actions would have been viewed by someone with Langley's education and background as spiteful and unjust. The disinheritance would have been an affront to Langley's religious and legal training. Civil servants with his long service had a deep appreciation of the need to correctly administer the law in a legal, fair way. Despotic use of the judicial powers of the monarchy would have deeply offended the clique that Langley was a member of, Richard could hardly afford to alienate the core of the civil service, many of whom were leading prelates. His treatment not only of Bolingbroke but also of the Arch-Bishop of Canterbury polarised the clergy, council, Commons, judiciary and civil servants.

Langley's decision to remain in England when Bolingbroke's exile was extended to life was made taking cognisance of the political undercurrents that he did so much to encourage. His decision was based on political "nous", not blind loyalty, for blind loyalty would have seen him joining the disinherited duke in exile. Many commentators have opined that Langley remained in the country to carry out his duties as executor to Gaunt, but I would offer the further point that by remaining he was able to protect the Lancastrian inheritance. Richard's actions meant that the only option open to Bolingbroke was to rebel against his cousin, and the only outcome of that would be that one of them would occupy the throne, with Bolingbroke never being able to trust his cousin again even if Richard had rescinded his confiscation. Langley was too shrewd not to have read the situation correctly as his actions and rapid promotion by Bolingbroke showed.

The crisis of 1399 was the accumulation of two events that had taken place earlier, one of which took place between 1387/8. The humiliations the king had suffered at the hands of the lords appellant had left deep scars, and it was ten years later that Richard exacted his revenge. The harbouring of a grudge for so long is a telling insight into the kings true self, even neutrals being compelled to take sides. The king informed Gaunt and his brother Edmund of Langley that their brother Woodstock, together with the earl of Arundel was plotting to seize him. To show that they had no part in these allegations they withdrew from court, leaving their brother with few allies. Gaunt faced the dilemma of supporting his brother, and by inference Bolingbroke, who had joined the earls in 1387/8. Gaunt was now nearly sixty years of age, and Richard was still childless.

The king, understandably, had to consider how his cousin would act once he had inherited the wealth of Lancaster. Arundel was tried and executed on

21st September, Gaunt pronouncing the sentence. Woodstock had been taken to Calais under Mowbray's custody and he was murdered sometime before 24th September. Langley was present with the ducal household during these proceedings. It is a possibility that Gaunt knew of his brother's murder, his silence being brought with the award of the earldom of Hereford for his son Henry **(19)**. Previous historians have offered varying views as to whether Gaunt had a hand in the crisis of 1398 partly to avenge his brother's murder. There is no doubt that Gaunt and his brother were close, both had made good marriages and were wealthy, and the effect of the policies pursued by Richard II and his advisers served to bind together his uncles and their extended families. Their unity increased as the reign progressed, and it would be perfectly natural for Gaunt to consider the possibility that should Richard die childless, his eldest son would be in line to ascend the throne. The murder of his brother polarised the two groups, Gaunt had over the years learnt the benefit of patience and diplomacy. It is inconceivable that father and son did not discuss the situation, and in doing this they would have turned to their inner circle of senior ministers for advice, Langley being part of this clique. Of prime concern would have been their financial position, and Langley, with his knowledge of the workings of the ducal chancery, would have been in constant attendance at this time.

In December 1397 Bolingbroke accidentally met Mowbray on the road from Brentford to London. On January 30th when parliament was sitting at Shrewsbury, a transcript of the conversation, Bolingbroke's version, was read out. His account slandered Mowbray, the account being implausible in some of its detail. Mowbray was plotting, and Adam of Usk commented that Mowbray:-

> *laid snares of death against the duke of Lancaster as he came thither; which thing raised heavy storms of trouble. But the duke, forewarned by others, escaped the snare.* **(20)**

The allegations brought out into the open the undercurrents of dissatisfaction with the king and his ruling clique that had been simmering for some time; polarisation had begun. A number of the nobles made public statements pledging loyalty to both sides, hedging their bets. A commission was convened to look into the allegations. It's membership would certainly have alarmed Mowbray, as it contained all the senior Lancastrian lords, Edmund Langley, his son Aumale, Exeter, Dorset (John Beaufort), William Scrope and Thomas Percy, and it was headed by Gaunt. Gaunt was to absent himself from the commission. The previous year he had made arrangements to negotiate a truce with the earl of Carrick, son of Robert III of Scotland **(21)**.

They met on 11th March 1398 at Howden Stank, Roxburghshire. Three weeks before this, on 23rd April Bolingbroke and Mowbray appeared before the king at Oswestry where Mowbray formally denied the accusations. The proceedings were adjourned to Bristol where it was decided that the issue should be decided by battle (22). Gaunt met with his son at Windsor on 25th March (23), and from here they moved to Windsor to attend the great council held on 28–9 April. Here one of Bolingbroke's retainers also accused Mowbray of the murder of Woodstock, and trial by combat was set for 16th September at Coventry (24). Gaunt and his son returned north. From the king's point of view this quarrel suited him. By occupying the polarised factions in this dispute he was able to rule unchecked and one party or the other had to lose, this succeeding in removing an obstacle to his reign. His later actions were to show that he had reviewed the issue and had come to recognise the danger to his throne that a victory for Bolingbroke would bring (25). Not only could it be inferred that if Bolingbroke won then by implication Richard was indeed guilty of Woodstock's murder.

Furthermore Richard was still childless, and a victory for the Lancastrians would make a coup d'etat a distinct possibility. These thoughts would also have exercised the Lancastrian's minds, particularly Gaunt's who was shrewd enough to have weighed all the options. The parties met at Coventry on 16th September, the king shocking all those present by halting the proceedings. The drama of this, so well depicted by Shakespeare, caused great disappointment amongst those present. Trial by combat was rare, a modern day equivalent would be the Cup Final. Very few members of the populace ever witnessed a fight to the death by two knights. The elaborate chivalry involved in such an event emphasised the belief that God, through victory to one of the protagonists, would signify his judgement.

The crowds had been flocking to Coventry for many days, peddlers, mummers and the like were all drawn to the gathering. Many visitors from abroad attended, trail by combat being such a rare event. The expectations were high, the disappointment mirrored this expectation. He altered his judgement to a penalty of a ten-year exile for Bolingbroke and exile for life for Mowbray.

Bolingbroke was made to swear that he would refrain from contacting the exiled archbishop, an oath that he was later to break. The warning signs were there for the king to see. Froissart wrote that *"there were in the stretes, no less thanne forty thousde men, wepying and crying after hym, that it pytie to here, and soe said: O gentyl erle of Derby, shall we thus leave? This realme shall never be in joye tyll ye retourn again"* (26). Allowing for poetic licence, there is no doubt that the people were genuinely upset at the treatment meted out to Derby. From a Lancastrian point of view, this display of public support, particularly after the treatment Gaunt had suffered at the hands of the Londoners twenty-seven years before, would serve to encourage them should they decide to challenge the King. Langley was at Eltham with Gaunt when Derby took formal leave of his father.

Gaunt presented Langley to the church of Castleford in the honour of Pontefract and this was formalised on 26th September when he was also granted a licence for non-residence for three years (**27**). The licence was necessary for two reasons. Firstly, Langley had by now become fundamental to the administration of the Duchy, and secondly, he was now held in considerable esteem by his counterparts at court.

Gaunt's failing health meant that Langley was constantly at his master's side, particularly as the banishment meant that someone of Langley's abilities would be needed principally to co-ordinate and manage the Lancastrian retainers in the Commons. Bolingbroke's sentence was reduced to six years after Gaunt had interceded. Many have opined that Gaunt was pleased to see his son exiled as it removed him from immediate danger. If the king had sought to harm Bolingbroke then the Lancastrians, with the greater pool of support and finances, would have won. The timescale of even six years would work against the Lancastrians in that the king could by that time have produced an heir. I believe that it was at Coventry that Gaunt and his sons realised that they would never be safe whilst Richard occupied the throne. This upheaval to the running of the Duchy as well Bolingbroke's estates will have involved Langley in long hours of work. Bolingbroke, under his father's sage advice, went to the Valois court of Charles VI and his sons in Paris. Gaunt's health began to deteriorate and his physicians wrote to Bolingbroke advising him to remain in Paris. As a named executor, Langley was now with Gaunt permanently.

During the later part of the year, Gaunt retired to Lilleshall Abbey from where he moved to Leicester Castle. As one of the inner circle Langley would have been corresponding with Bolingbroke, particularly as the position of an exiled heir would have to be resolved. The possibility of the heir returning to the country, including all the options if he was refused entry by the king, would have to be considered. Langley, as both an executor and from his position in the chancery, would have had to ensure that should Bolingbroke return, his inheritance would be intact. Gaunt died on 3rd February 1399 at Leicester Castle (**28**), having the previous day made the final version of his will; Langley was present when Gaunt died. He was buried on Passion Sunday (16th March) in St. Paul's and the cortege had stopped at the abbeys of St. Albans and Barnet where Langley joined the monks in their all-night vigils **(29)**. The executors had been instructed to summon the duke's family and friends, and the chroniclers mention that Richard II attended **(30)**.

The York Minster Window

His first great patron's death had a profound effect on Langley, and towards the end of his life he dedicated a window in the south choir aisle of York Minster. The figure of St. Cuthbert is surrounded by people styled in attitudes of devotion. The window bears the inscription, *"Johannes dux acquitannie et lancastrie"*. Gaunt is depicted kneeling, wearing a crown, pink robe, white mantle and ermine-bordered girdle, his hands together in supplication. A book is open on the desk by which Gaunt is kneeling with the 38th psalm inscribed on its pages,

1. "O Lord, rebuke me not in thy wrath: neither chasten me in thy hot displeasure.
2. For thine arrows stick fast in me, and thy hand presseth me sore.
3. There is no soundness in my flesh because of thine anger; neither is thre any rest in my bones because of my sin.
5. My wounds stink and are corrupt because of my foolishness.
7. For my loins are filled with a loathsome disease: and there is no soundness in my flesh.
8. I am feeble and sore broken: I have roared by reason of the disquietness of my heart.
10. My heart panteth, my strength faileth me: as for the light of mine eyes, it also is gone from me.
11. My lovers and my friends stand aloof from my sore: and my kinsmen stand afar off.
12. They also seek after my life lay snares for me: and they that seek my hurt speak mischievous things, and imagine deceits all day long.
18. For I will declare mine iniquity; I will be sorry for my sin.
19. But mine enemies are lively, and they are strong: and they that hate me wrongfully are multiplied".

All biblical quotations can be interpreted in various ways. Shortly after Gaunt's death rumours began to circulate that he had died of a venereal disease. Langley's choice of psalm 38 could be his answer to these rumours. St. Cuthbert is the patron Saint of Durham, Langley was Bishop of Durham when the window was commissioned hence his portrayal in the window. It is also possible that the window is Langley's penance for his role in the execution of arch bishop Scrope which is dealt with in the next chapter. Verses 13 to 17 are omitted:-

13. "But I, as a deaf man, heard not; and I was as a dumb man that openeth not his mouth.
14. Thus I was a man that heareth not, and in whose mouth are no reproofs.
15. For in the, O Lord, do I hope: thou wilt hear, O Lord my God.
16. For I said, Hear me, lest otherwise they should rejoice over me: when my foot slippeth, they magnify themselves against me.
17. For I am ready to halt, and my sorrow is continually before me''.

By placing the Duke of Lancaster in the window Langley could, by allegorical reference, be explaining why he took no steps to save Scrope. Given the wording, either explanation is possible. Langley was with Gaunt in the last days of his life could Gaunt have elicited a promise from Langley that he would assist the son as he had served the father? Do the missing verses obliquely refer to the fact that, amongst certain of the monks of York, Langley's complicity in Scrope's execution was being discussed? The slipping of the foot is telling, I offer this thought as a matter for further debate as only the religious would be able to read and understand the psalm on the window when it was first installed, the majority of the populace being still illiterate. Words left unsaid but alluded to can be as telling as any written words. There is no doubt that Langley never publicly commented on Scropes death. The fact that he directly benefited, and that the monks of York had been cowed into accepting Langley as Dean, leads one to the conclusion that there is some form of personal atonement in the window.

Is it possible that, due to the limitations of the amount of wording, the size of the window dictated the inscription. However, given the allegorical trends that prevailed during the 15th century, the hypothesis is worthy of consideration. The Dukes of Bedford and Gloucester, grandsons of Gaunt were also included in the window. There were political reasons for this, *see section four*. Richard compounded his mistake by ordering all those who were associated with the appellant earls in 1387–8 to seek pardons, the price for this *pleasaunce* being £1,000 or 1,000 marks per county. Richard embarked on a spending spree that would be equivalent to a lottery winner scooping a roll-over jackpot, with tournaments, spending on palaces, furniture, food and clothes, "ostentation, pomp and vainglory" all in no small measure (**31**).

Writs were issued demanding that all subjects swear a special pledge to maintain the acts of the last parliament which included the grant for life of subsidies on wool and leather exports (**32**). There is no record of Langley attesting the special pledge. When Richard later went to Ireland Langley was appointed attorney to one of his retainers.

Just forty-six days after Gaunt's death, Richard II revoked Bolingbroke's right to appoint attorneys and extended his banishment to life, Gaunt's bequests to retainers being confirmed but his estates were forfeited and divided by the kings cronies, principally Exeter, Aumale and Surrey. This placed Langley in an invidious position, and there was widespread alarm amongst the rest of the baronage as they realised that no one's inheritance was safe. The king, unwisely, decided to embark for Ireland where revolt had once more broken out, landing in Ireland on June 1st. As a precaution he had taken Henry of Monmouth, Bolingbroke's son with him. Langley's relationship with Henry will be dealt with in a later chapter.

It is clear from the way that Bolingbroke's retainers joined him so quickly that men such as Langley and John Leventhorpe who was receiver general of the Duchy and another of Gaunt's executors, had been in close contact with the exiled Earl for some time. During the period from 18th March to June 1st, Langley had been receiving correspondence from the exiled archbishop of Canterbury, Arundal, as well as from Bolingbroke who were now together in Paris. Through Langley, who, owing to his duties as Gaunt's executor was in contact with all the Duchy retainers, preparations were laid for Bolingbroke's return. Langley, like many others, had realised that Richard II would have to be removed. This is the first instance where Langley's loyalty to the house of Lancaster over-road his neutrality; like many other retainers he had been forced to choose. The decision would not have been taken lightly. The removal of a king, particularly one who was the rightful heir of Edward III, would have caused someone like Langley, with his legal and religious training, a considerable amount of soul searching. Richard had been anointed, no matter his many faults, and legally he was the ruler of the kingdom. Had Langley and his clique taken their decision on the basis of the legal correctness of Richard's position, they would not, and could not, have supported the usurpation. His position both as executor and at court meant that he was well aware of the prevailing mood of the country. His contacts in the Commons ensured that he was able to lay the foundations for Bolingbroke's return.

Sometime between the end of May and the second week in June, Langley travelled to Lancaster and from there to Pontefract, where he joined Bolingbroke. The invading force numbered no more than 300, but within the space of a few weeks this had swollen to well over 30,000. The fervour that greeted his return bears comparison with Labour's landslide victory in the 1997 election, the country having grown tired of Richard II's regime of oppression. His treatment of the heir to the Duchy was an act too far. The mood of the country was one of unease and tension, and people felt a general insecurity just as they did nearly 600 years later. The majority of the northern lords joined Bolingbroke, significantly so Hotspur and Ralph Neville. York, Regent in the King's absence, surrendered at Bristol, the usual round of executions taking place immediately afterwards.

Richard returned landing at Haverfordwest from where he marched to North Wales. Bolingbroke arrived before him entering Chester on 9th August cornering the king in Conwy castle where he was offered terms. The terms were drawn up by Bolingbroke and his closest advisors, Langley amongst them. The problem facing Henry and his councillors was how to put a veneer of legitimacy on his actions. Legally Henry was not the rightful heir to the throne, the Earl of March was next in line. A further problem was that the Lancastrians could not risk embarking on wholesale changes to the composition of the council, as this would have alienated too many Lords and would have led to further unrest. The only way forward was one of prudence and gradual change. The first problem was to remove Richard in a way that did not disenfranchise the upper echelons of society. Pragmatism had to come to the forefront. The speed with which supposedly loyal Lords came over to Henry showed that allegiances could shift if matters were not conducted with tact and diplomacy. Caution was the watchword, the settling of scores would have to wait.

Notes and References

(1) Shakespeare, W. "Henry The Fourth, Part 1", act 5, scene 4, 115–121.
(2) McFarlane, K. B, "The Nobility of Later Medieval England", (Oxford, 1973).
(3) Hutchinson, "History of Durham", p. 332.
(4) McFarlane, K. B. "The Nobility of Later Medieval England", (Oxford, 1973)
(5) Goodman, A. "John of Gaunt, The Excercise of Princely Power in Fourteenth-Century Europe". (Longman 1992).
(6) Fowler, K. "The King's Lieutenant", (Martin Elek, London, 1969).
(7) Rymer, T, (ed), "Feodera Conventiones Literae et cujuscunque generis Acta Publicae", (London 1704–32).
(8) Goodman, A, "John of Gaunt, The Exercise of Princely Power in Fourteenth-Century Europe" (Longman 1992) p 304–5.
(9) Armitage-Smith, J. "John of Gaunt" (Westminster 1904) p 448.
(10) Legge, M. D, "Anglo-Norman Letters and Petitions", no. 29, (Basil Blackwell, Oxford).
(11) Goodman, A. "John of Gaunt, The Exercise of Princely Power in Fourteenth-Century Europe", (Longman 1992) p 155 and note 55 p 172.
(12) C. P. R. 1391–96, p 609.

(13)   Hennessy, G, "Novum Repertorium Ecclesiasticum Parochiale Londinense", (London 1898), p 86.

(14)   Lichfield, Act Books, no. 6, fo. 156.

(15)   McKisack, M, "The Fourteenth Century, 1307–1399, (Oxford 1959), pp 302–4.

(16)   Roskell, J. S, "Knights of the Shire for the County Palatine of Lancaster", (Chetham Society, 1937), pp 72–4.

(17)   Myers, A. D. (ed), E. H. D. , vol IV, p 169, doc. no. 70.

(18)   Froissart, J. "Ouvres", (ed), K. de Lettenhoven, 25 vols. , (Brussels, 1867–77).

(19)   Steel, A. "Richard II", (Cambridge 1941), pp 237–9.

(20)   Goodman, A. "The Loyal Conspiracy", (Routledge & Kegan Paul, London 1971).

(21)   Thompson, E. M. "Adam of Usk, Chronicon", (Oxford 1904).

(22)   Bain, J. (ed), "Calendar of Documents Relating to Scotland", vol. 4, (Register House, Edinburgh, 1888) R. S. , vol. 2, p 138.

(23)   R. P. , vol. 3, p 383.

(24)   Legge, M. D. "Anglo-Norman Letters and Petitions", (Basil Blackwell, Oxford 1941), no. 41.

(25)   C. P. R. 1396–9, p 547, R. P. vol. 3, p 383.

(26)   Steel, A. "Richard II", (Cambridge, 1941).

(27)   Froissart, J, "Ouvres", (ed), K. de Lettenhoven, (Brussels 1867–77).

(28)   York, "Register of Archbishop Scrope", fo. 17.

(29)   Post, J. B. "The Obsequies of John of Gaunt", (Guildhall Studies in London History, History 5, 1981).

(30)   Riley, H. T, (ed), "Gesta Abbatum Monasterii Sancti Albini", 3 vols, (Rolls Series, London, 1867–8).

(31)   Thompson, E, M, (ed), "Adam of Usk, Chronicum", (Oxford 1904); Clarke, M, V. "Fourteenth Century Studies", (ed), Sutherland, L, S. and McKisack, M. (Oxford, 1937).

(32)   Rot. Parl iii, p 419.

(33)   Keen, M, H, "England in the Later Middle Ages", (Routledge 1975), pp 291.

HENRY IV and LANGLEY, 1400–1407

"Uneasy lies the head that wears a crown" **(1)**.

Promotion and Power

The Crisis of the Early Years

The events of 1399 have been the subject of many studies and speculation. The Lancastrians could not allow Richard to remain on the throne even with

Henry acting as Regent. History had taught that so long as Richard was alive they ran the risk that should their administration create a climate of dissatisfaction civil war would again break out. The council would in effect be semi-crippled. A coalition government, particularly in the middle ages, would not be able to govern the country, concensual politics being the only way to bring peace and stabilisation. The feeling of animosity against Richard's administration would permit the removal of the King, the Lords could be bought off, and there was a pool of titles and estates with which to placate those who were neutral. In order to bring about as peaceful a transition as possible two things had to happen; Richard had to abdicate and Henry had to be crowned. For Henry to be universally recognised as the true king he would have to have the blessing of the church, the Bishops would have to be won over.

In the case of the see of Canterbury this was a simple matter: Arundel was reinstated, something the Papacy approved off. Those whom Henry charged with bringing about the transition had to be acceptable to a wide cross-section of the Lords, both temporal and spiritual; any perception of self-interest would not bring about the desired result. Langley, whilst clearly in the Lancastrian camp, could not be perceived as overtly over-ambitiousness, as at this time he was not a significant holder of either land or spiritual office. The general perception of him was one of an able, conscientious, professional administrator. This very lack of ambition, service being his raison d'être, was the reason why Henry quickly brought him into the inner circle of advisers that he gathered about him.

The terms offered to Richard were not unreasonable. Henry was to regain his Lancastrian inheritance, the reasoning behind this being both to allow him access to the wealth of the Duchy and also to re-establish Henry's position as the premier Lord in England. To the neutral observer these terms only sought to redress the injustices done to Henry. Regaining his lands and titles was merely righting a wrong, and those who had benefited from the confiscation's, Aumale, Exeter and Surrey, had already deserted Richard, having had the good sense to take the path of pragmatism. Richard was brought to Chester where writs dated 19th August were sent out Sending the writs out under Richard's name was a prudent move, as until parliament could be gathered, the mood of the country could not properly be assessed. Langley and Henry's other advisers needed time to ensure as peaceful a transition as possible. At this time it is difficult to believe that the Lancastrians had not begun to plot the formal deposition of Richard (2), leaving him alive was not really an option. Many commentators have cast doubt on this point of view. I find it difficult to believe that from the outset Henry only returned to claim his inheritance. Given the actions of Richard and the clique around him only the permanent removal of the king would give the Lancastrians the security they needed. They needed the sanction of parliament to achieve their ultimate ambitions. The reconciliation of parliament lay in the hands of Archbishop Arundel the ablest of Henry's councillors, and Langley, the most unobtrusive.

The purpose behind the Lancastrian's policy in parliament was to establish the dynasty's future, and this would clearly entail the removal of Richard and the disenfranchisement of anyone who could, in the future, stake a claim to the throne. Richard's fate had to have been agreed before parliament met, but how Langley as a churchman reconciled this with his Christian beliefs, only his confessor knew. This was not to be the first time that his loyalty to the house of Lancaster was to take precedence over his Christian upbringing. Exiling the king would create the possibility that in the future another coup could be mounted, as those who would inevitably lose their positions formed factions that would group around someone who could restore them. Langley could have decided to pursue his career in the church; Henry would have rewarded him with a benefice of substance. If he had taken this course Henry would not have viewed him as a potential threat or source of embarrassment, his national standing at this time being not that great. In any event it is most unlikely that he would have voiced any dissension or criticism.

Langley's decision to accompany Henry to London and accept one of the highest positions in his council shows where Langley's ambitions were. The Pope's refusal to agree to his induction into prominent positions within the church in the next few years has often been viewed as more a question of the Papacy's disapproval of royal policy at the time. One of the considerations behind the later Papal decisions will have been Langley's character and his part in the course of actions seen in the early years of Henry's reign. It could be argued that Langley's prime aim was the stabilisation of the country that only a more pluralistic form of governance would give. Clearly Henry would inevitably surround himself principally with Lancastrian supporters, thereby alienating others. The difference in the policies of the reigns was that Henry endeavoured to raise money and enact policy with the agreement of parliament rather than impose his will. This was done out of pragmatism as the country would not have accepted another despotic reign.

One of the reasons cited for the removal of the king was that he had lost the confidence of the people and that his actions had made him unfit to rule. Henry would not have dared to leave himself open to the same criticisms. Langley, who, as will be seen, was already close to the future Prince of Wales, would have viewed the true beneficiary of the usurpation to be Henry's son. The Prince's position as the anointed son who would automatically be, on his ascension, the legitimate king, the son of one who was by spiritual and temporal consent the rightful ruler. Bolingbroke's usurpation debarred him from this. This in turn would establish the family of Lancaster as the ruling house for the future, and any challenge to their position in the future would have to be based upon the actions and precedents set with the usurpation. Accordingly, the methodology employed to achieve the aims of the Lancastrians in 1399 would have far-reaching consequences. Langley will have weighed all these considerations in his decision to coalesce with and take part in the actions that were undertaken. Once Langley entered London with Henry he became inextricably bound to the events that were to follow, the option of the Pontius Pilate school of politics being removed. Langley will have studiously considered all the variations. His actions demonstrated his beliefs, and like many, his fate and future became dependent upon the continuation and perpetuation of the Lancastrian dynasty. Master and servant became joined by an invisible thread one to the other, each dependent upon the other for the rest of their lives. Each had to rely on their future well-being to ensure that their lives would continue and that they would prosper. Had Langley followed another course he would have led the life of a cleric tending to the spiritual needs of his fellow man. Langley was, to some extent, at a cross-roads in his life. Was it to be church or political life only later was he able to reconcile the two career options. This one instance epitomises his life and the thinking behind the man's actions; loyalty over-rode any other considerations.

To stake one's promising career and life on the, by no means assured, triumph of Henry and the Lancastrians was a big step to take. This, in part, explains why Langley supported the Lancastrians throughout the rest of his life. Not for the first time did a prominent civil servant's career become entirely reliant upon the continuance in government of one particular king and his family. Such factors naturally brought about a certain ruthlessness and intolerance which was directed against anyone who challenged or voiced any dissent that threatened the stability of the House of Lancaster and therefore of Henry and his son. It also explains why he occupied a place at the centre of political life for the next thirty-eight years, both the ruling house and Langley having a mutuality of interest in the continuance in power of the family of John of Gaunt. This ethos applied to a wide sphere of people, notably the Beauforts; self-preservation is a remarkably unifying force. Provided that this ethos is the fulcrum upon which the continuance in government depends then the only way to maintain this balance is by the politics of consensus. Langley's duty was to ensure that the advice he gave would continue this stability. Any dissension from the country against the monarchy would rebound on the crown's ministers. Langley's acceptance of high office was to mean that he inherited a department that was already staffed. The appointment to office carried with it the power to advance worthy candidates. Patronage and a mutuality of purpose were the twin gossamer threads that held the web of crown and civil service together in governance.

The first test was to be the presentation to parliament of the articles drawn up with the express intent of removing Richard. The tenuousness of Henry's position worked for the benefit of the country, and his councillors were mindful of this as they proceeded to deal with the mechanics of government the first stage of which involved dealing with and obtaining the formal approval of the Commons (3). Henry had allotted just 15 days for the articles to be drawn up and for parliament to assent to the abdication and his enthronement (4). Time was of the essence: any delay could allow the doubters to muster a counter-offensive.

The articles (5) that were placed before parliament were a masterpiece of "Sir Humphreyism", their ambiguity having raised questions throughout the study of history with a wide diversity of opinion (6). The contemporary chroniclers were also equally divided on the events surrounding the formal deposition. In order to create a climate of goodwill towards Henry, the Lancastrian propaganda machine let it be known that Richard had, at Chester, agreed to voluntarily abdicate. Langley the spin doctor was at work as the *de facto* keeper of Henry's Ducal signet. After the coronation his title was "the Kings clerk", which was applied to him when he resigned from his church at Castleford (7). In an order to the Keeper of the Great Wardrobe for the issuing of livery to Langley, on 22nd December 1399, he was noted as *notre secretaire*. Whilst Richard's holder of the privy seal was left in place the king's signet was given to Langley this was the most personal of all the seals available to the King. Henry used this seal as a counterbalance to the Privy Seal, he was more likely to entrust his personal thoughts and business to Langley than he was one of the former King's ministers.

The ring of Signet was handed by Richard to Henry on Monday 29th September around 8.00. p.m. in the Tower of London. The date of Langley being noted as "*notre*" provides an indication of just how involved he was in the usurpation and the events that preceded it. The 29th September to the 1st October was only eleven weeks before the aforementioned note, and no other secretary is mentioned. This infers that Langley was acting as the king's secretary from the moment that Henry landed at Ravenspur. This in turn demonstrates that Langley had been in contact with the exiles prior to the landing. A king's secretary placed the office holder in a position of intimacy in that he was privy to all the correspondence issued by Henry as well as being aware of the thinking behind the formal letters. Such a post would only be given to the most valued and trusted of the Duchy staff. This post was the most personal of all appointments clearly showing that Langley was regarded as one of Henry's closest, if not the closest, member of staff.

Langley had been involved in politics well before he appeared on the national stage, probably from the day that Bolingbroke was exiled, and certainly from the moment that the six-year period was extended to life. He choice between temporal and spiritual service was made when he was about thirty-five, his decision showing him as a man ambitious for higher governmental power. Someone hungry for the adrenaline rush that would accompany the power that a successful bid for the throne by the Lancastrians would give him. The office of the King's secretary would have been the office that issued the letters of propaganda regarding Richard's agreeing to voluntarily abdicate. The Lancastrians could not Richard to publicly disavow the rumours. The decision to imprison Richard in the tower was taken at Chester at the same time as the rumour machine was already being employed. Langley's career as the manipulative spin doctor of the Lancastrian Party had begun.

The First Parliament.

The status of *forma parliamenti of* the assembly of Commons which sat to hear the thirty-three articles that were headed *plura crimina et defectus*, was suspended. The *status et populus* unanimously agreed to accept Richard's resignation, the wording used being that he was "worthy to be deprived" (**8**). On the same day a composite deputation presented the articles (**9**) to Richard in the Tower. He signed that night as he had no option, and all he could hope for was that his life would be spared. With the signature, Langley's future was assured; the formal recognition by the commons the next day was the balm for Langley's conscience. The Lancastrian officials who drew up the articles would have had approximately four weeks to draw up this most important document, a tight timetable when one considers the complexities that were involved in the drafting. The gist of the articles was that Richard, by a recitation of his main acts since 1387, had shown himself unfit to hold the position of king, even the statutes of Magna Carta being included in clause 29. In a nutshell, its premise was that Richard had broken his coronation oath. The composite group who presented the document to Richard had been carefully chosen. It had to appear to be drawn from a cross-section of the

Lords Temporal and Spiritual as well as representatives from the Commons and the Judiciary.

Henry attended Richard on the evening, and his secretary Langley would have accompanied him. The next day, 30th September, the Commons heard the document that Richard had put his signature to. To avoid any doubt, the list of articles that were in effect a preamble to the document of abdication were also read out. This was done so that should anyone dissent in the future the Lancastrians would be able to say that parliament had been presented with all the facts. The throne was now legally vacant. Henry now rose and said, in English "... *God of his grace hath sent me wyth helpe of my kyn and of my friends to recover it (the throne)*". Note "my friends", clearly a reference to those such as Langley who was present in Westminster. As he witnessed this spectacle he would have been feeling a sense of pride in what he had a hand in. He was now in the very hall where the most important moments of his life would occur. All his training from the age of 12 had been in preparation for this moment. He was now at the pinnacle of power in this country, a far cry from the small farm in Middleton at the base of the Pennines.

For a third son who had left his home and family twenty-four years earlier this was a remarkable achievement. This had been accomplished by unstinting loyalty, education both lay and clerical, and luck. In the space of eight years he had risen from a chancery clerk to one of the most intimate of offices, a remarkable achievement. It should also be remembered that his promotion was due to his ability as a civil servant, unlike some of the Temporal Lords who were promoted because of their status. It was an opportunity grasped as it was presented. This was a defining moment in his life and career, the moment when he passed from relative obscurity to national prominence. He had stepped from the shadows into the light, his life to be public property from this day. The trappings of power were his reward, and all now depended on his ability to maintain the House of Lancaster's grip on the throne. A further point is that the parliament that offered the throne to Henry was not sitting under its usual auspices. This was not an authoritative body, and Henry had to avoid the perception that he had ascended the throne only through a grant by parliament, as this would have established a dangerous precedent (**10**). The fudged illusion that Henry created to the London populace was that a parliament in all but name, had ratified Richard's abdication and had accepted Henry as the rightful heir.

This acceptance was on the spurious precedent that Edmund of Lancaster's claim to the throne stood above Edward the First's claim. This was a the best excuse that could be concocted. Henry's claim was ratified by *"the said estates, with the whole people"*. Significantly Henry was offered the crown to

him and his heirs. Henry then showed the assembly the signet ring given him
by Richard. This was an intentional blurring around events, the illusion of an
acceptance by the Commons and the Londoners, but what precisely were they
accepting? Henry had wanted to occupy the throne by right of conquest, but
his advisers had warned against this. Arundel provided a solution; he put
forward the premise that the body now sitting in parliament would have to
curtail its sitting as the writs that had been issued by Richard had become
invalidated with the abdication. Professor E. F. Jacob has put forward the
view that the illusion of parliamentary approval was, in part, used to elicit the
agreement of the Londoners and confuse the chroniclers **(11)**. Langley the
spin-doctor at work again?

Henry was crowned on St. Edward's day (13 October), and a banquet in
Westminster Hall followed. The first parliament held on 6th October
contained 247 members representing 37 shires and 85 cities and boroughs.
The main purpose of calling parliament was to repeal the acts of 1397–8. The
Lords sitting on 23rd October sentenced Richard to perpetual imprisonment.
He was removed from the Tower to Pontefract Castle whose keeper was Sir
Thomas Swynford the legitimate son of Catherine from her first marriage.
Richard was never seen alive again in public. He was probably starved to
death. He was most certainly dead by mid-January 1400. The minor rebellion
of that Christmas, by, amongst others, the Hollands, Salisbury and Aumale,
caused consternation coming as it did so soon after the coronation. Henry and
his court, including Langley had to flee from Windsor. Support for the rebels
quickly faded, and all but Aumale were executed. Langley received the bed
of Sir Thomas Shelley one of the rebels who was executed **(12)**. Rather than
save Richard the rebels hastened his death. His body was brought by stages to
St. Paul's where it remained for two days before being interred at Kings
Langley.

Henry's son was invested as Prince of Wales, Duke of Cornwall and Earl
of Chester, and on 23rd October he was invested as Duke of Aquitaine. Those
of Richard's councillors who were charged by a deputation of the Lords with
a variety of crimes were all dealt with leniently, a prudent move. On 29th
October Langley was rewarded with the archdeaconry of Norfolk, which
included Thetford. It seems likely that he requested this office due to his early
educational connections with the shire. The duties of an archdeacon were, by
tradition, performed by a deputy, the office being a sinecure designed to
provide the recipient with an additional income. It was to be nearly seven
years before Langley formally visited Norfolk. The duties of an archdeacon
were mainly administrative. Usually the rights of the diocesan Bishop were
reserved in respect of the discipline, and appointment of clerics, except in

certain specified instances. The archdeacon's responsibilities covered disputes over wills, goods etc., clerical judicial appointments also falling under the archdeacon's jurisdiction. The appointment of teachers in diocesan schools fell within his orbit as did the appointment of priests to chapels and chantries **(13)**.

During the period of Richard's reign the crown's receipts from the customs and subsidy on wool dropped from the average figure of £47,000 during the years 1377–95 to £43,000 during the last three years. In the first three years of Henry's reign this reduced to £39,000, a drop of 16. 05% on the average yield, and further, these revenues dropped as low as £26,000 during part of his reign due to some very inclement summers. The loss of revenue obviously proved a great hindrance to Henry and his minister's ability to govern the country. Henry also had to promise not to tax the clergy by foregoing the immediate collection of the tenth *"nisi magna necessitate geurrarum et inevitabili neccessitate ingruente"*. This created considerable problems for him later in his reign. One of the principal reasons for this was that Henry, on his ascension to the throne, had awarded a number of pensions and grants to those who had supported him. The income from church benefices was a valued source to bolster the incomes of crown officials **(14)**.

The Office of the Royal Signet and Privy Seal

The role of the senior civil servants today is somewhat different to what it was in the middle ages. The functions of each particular office, whilst more sophisticated today, are still fundamentally the same. The significant difference between the periods is that the impartiality that the senior members of today's civil service are supposed to exercise did not exist in the middle ages. The senior ministers, and in turn the staff subsequently appointed, were not, up to 1377, generally open to the approval of parliament. Whilst parliament was the legislative body and increasingly drew more power to itself during the 15th century, the crown still controlled the ultimate reins of power. War could only be declared by the King, something that bound the hereditary Lords to the ruling house. The aristocracy still believed that their raison d'être was to wage war. Just as we have seen in the Falklands War and Serbia, warfare has a unifying effect on the people of this country. There are of course voices of dissension, but this was less marked in the middle ages. As it became more expensive to wage war so the crown became more reliant on parliament in terms of the financing of warfare. Hereditary right no longer counted when the King selected his ministers, political "nous" becoming the prime consideration. This generally produced a better form and tenor of government. When Richard II endeavoured to take control of the machinery of government it was this very lack of accountability that led to his downfall.

On Henry's ascension it became important that the appearance of continuity of service was maintained in the governmental posts. The judicial and shire office holders were all re-appointed. John Norbury, who had shared Henry's exile, was appointed Treasurer, Sir Thomas Erpington became Chamberlain, and Richard Clifford was retained as the keeper of the Privy Seal. How much Clifford was trusted, given that he served the previous hostile regime is open to question, but by keeping Langley close to him Henry could exercise some control over the office of Privy Seal. The office of Speaker was given to John Doreward an experienced man from Essex who had served in Richard's council but had the respect of the Commons. These were the officials who were the public face of the government, the back room staff being drawn from the pool of Duchy civil servants.

Langley at this time was constantly by Henry's side and travelled everywhere with him. The year of 1401 was a year of promotions and rebuffs. He was granted prebends in both York Minster **(15)** and the Royal Free Chapel of Bridgnorth and on July 1st he was given the Deanery of York **(16)**. His appointment was confirmed by Richard le Scrope, Archbishop of York, on 20th January 1402, being installed by proxy five days later. The Pope Boniface IX claimed the deanery and awarded it to a cardinal, Henry refused this provision. Eventually a bargain was made whereby the cardinal was awarded the archdeaconry of Exeter and Langley was allowed to take up his post at York, being installed for a second time in 1403 **(17)**.

Whilst the argument rumbled on he was awarded a second prebend at York together with prebends at Lincoln, Salisbury and Wells being described as *benebeneficiatus* **(18)**. The Deanery of York was one of the significant posts in the English church, and as a benefice it was the next rank below that of episcopate. By the age of thirty-eight he had received 14 positions in the church, each one a step up the ladder of preferment. So why did the Pope refuse to allow Langley the deanery of York?

On June 28th 1401, the eleven-year-old Isabelle, widow of Richard II, returned to France. The negotiations for her return had been protracted and bitter. The delegation from England, which included Langley, met the French at Leulinghen and countered the French demands for the return of the 200,000 franc dower with demands for the outstanding money owed for the ransom of King John together with some redress for the infringements of his rights that Henry was suffering in Guienne. Adam of Usk described her appearance on her journey as *"clad in mourning weeds and showing a countenance of lowering and evil aspect to King Henry"*. She died in childbirth in 1409 aged nineteen. Henry refused to return her dowry, he needed the money. Langley, as keeper of the royal signet, will have had a significant part in the negotiations for her return. The French, Isabelle in particular, felt that Henry had ordered the murder of Richard. Louis of Orleans was scathing of Henry and his treatment of the young widow. The chronicle of Enguerrand de Monstrelet contains a letter from Louis in which he says *"... How could you suffer my much redoubted lady the Queen of England to return so desolate to this country after the death of her lord, despoiled by your rigour and cruelty of her dower, which you detain from her and likewise the portion she carried here on her marriage"*. Henry's reply was written by Langley *"God knows from whom nothing can be concealed that so far from acting towards her harshly we have ever shown her kindness and friendship and whoever shall dare say otherwise lies wickedly ... on leaving this kingdom I have made her such restitution of jewels and money, much more than she brought here, we hold ourselves acquitted"*. This situation was naturally exploited by the French who began to commit acts of piracy in the channel. The French held more influence in Europe at this time, therefore the Pope supported their cause.

The rebuff to Henry over Langley's appointment would also have been intended as a sign of disapproval of the keeper of the royal signet, Thomas Langley the author of the letter. Should Henry's nominee have been someone who was not as close to the King I doubt that the Pope would have objected. He was formally recognised as keeper of the Privy Seal at Hertford Castle on 3rd November 1401 (19). Clifford the previous incumbent received the usual reward for someone who had occupied the office and was consecrated Bishop of Worcester (20). The use of the Royal signet was the most personal of all the official seals available to the monarch. Under Richard II, particularly in the later years of the reign, the office had been misused and had become a device to circumvent the authority of parliament. As a consequence of this the department was, at the beginning of Henry IV's reign, mistrusted. Henry sensibly formalised the office in that a proper department was constituted with a hierarchical structure. Under Langley the importance of the office grew, partially dictated by the events surrounding Henry's ascension. Langley's official appointment was the first high office to be awarded to someone who was overtly a Lancastrian.

The office of the keeper of the Privy Seal became, under Langley, the prime department of government. As the art of diplomacy became increasingly refined owing to the schism and the need for renewed initiatives towards France, so the functions of the office expanded. A significant increase in the need for public relations had come about due, in part, to the Poll Tax revolts. The consent of the people, through parliament, meant that greater thought had to be given to the presentation of policy. Parliament was able to exert greater powers, the monarch could no longer cow the Commons into submission. One way to circumvent parliament was to create a climate in the country whereby public opinion became fundamental to the pursuit of royal policy.

The burgeoning merchant class and the various gilds that were created also had to be courted. As the wealth of the people through the export of wool became essential to the prosperity of society, the opinions of this new class had to be considered. With commerce and the balance of trade, a quasi common market, England was about to embark on a whole new form of governance. The beginnings of the birth of a more pluralistic society with a greater degree of dependence on commerce to create a diversity of wealth-spread embraced the populace and in turn the country. The characters so well depicted in the Canterbury Tales clearly reflect this. Langley showed by the way that he traversed the minefield of politics that surrounded the royal court that he, like Chaucer, was a keen student and observer of his fellow man, both high-born and commoner, Lord and Peasant, Bishop and Monk. During his career he dealt with all manner of men through the offices that he came to.

Chaucer's work was primarily written for speech, and Langley will have heard both "The Boke of the Duchess" and "The Canterbury Tales" read aloud at both Gaunt's and his son's courts. His travelling with Henry IV's entourage will have brought him into contact with all stratums of society, and the soundness of the judgements he handed down, particularly as chancellor, shows that he was attuned to the nuances of public opinion. His ability to dissimulate the mood of the country through the crisis that became the constant companion of Henry IV's reign can in part be attributed to his humble origins. No high-born courtier had the access to the varying strands of society that he had. The ability to harness public opinion to the Royal cause was a prerequisite for the offices that he was to hold. Langley understood this. His prime aim during his first years in office was to present the image of Henry as the rightful king, anointed by the church, chosen by common consent, a unifying force after the previous turbulent reign. This was a difficult task as the basic premise of Henry being, in law, the lawful holder of the throne was fundamentally flawed. No amount of doctoring could legitimise his claim to the throne through hereditary right, and a good constitutional lawyer would have demolished any case that was put forward. The unpalatable fact was that Henry was a usurper, no veneer could cover this tenet. Henry became the first monarch to employ a public relations department which was incorporated in the office of the Privy Seal, its first exponent being, Thomas Langley; the first spin-doctor.

Langley's closeness to the King as keeper of the Royal signet brought him into contact with a variety of people drawn from many different backgrounds, just as today, a change in government meant that those who had business dealings with the new regime were the ones who jockeyed for favour. He became the conduit through which the King transmitted his private personal correspondence, and conversely, those who wished to write to the King on private matters would pass the letters through Langley. The royal signet was sometimes used to "prompt" the privy seal, an indication that Henry used Langley to control the privy seal office. This gave the keeper of this office unparalleled access to the King; all Royal policy would be discussed between the two men. Langley's position was one of the most influential of all the governmental posts. There is no recorded scandal or gossip in any of the contemporary chronicles. Had Langley been corrupt there would have been some hints. After the upheavals of the previous reign the Commons were particularly judicious in their scrutiny of the workings of the departments of the senior officials. The King's need for loans would have placed Langley in a good position to elicit bribes in return for titles and favours. Any wealth or promotions he obtained was earned from the crown or the church. This is remarkable when one considers the increase in wealth that a good many speculators accumulated.

There were three notable additions to the council in the early years of Henry IV's reign: John Shadworth, William Brampton and Richard Whittington, all wealthy merchants based in London, all three being appointed on 1st November 1400. Whittington was the son of a minor Gloucestershire landowner, and arrived in London with little money. By the 1390's he was supplying the Great Wardrobe with a considerable variety of goods, and in 1403 Henry IV owed him £1,000 **(21)**. He was appointed to the King's council in November 1399 **(22)** and worked closely with Langley who would have learnt much from this clever merchant. Whittington's export business will have afforded Langley with a rich source of insights into the commercial world. He continued to lend money to the crown for the next twenty years, and the fact that he rarely charged interest on the loans he made to the crown would have made him a firm favourite of Langley's.

The similarity of their childhood backgrounds would have created a bond between the two men. New men whose time was ushered in by the dawning of a new century and a new dynasty, the Lancastrians. The continuance of the reward of Royal patronage binding them together, role models for the class of society they rose influence and role in Royal policy linked to Whittington's wealth and the loans it produced. Langley's payment to Whittington being the procurement of Royal favours which resulted in Whittington being appointed to a number of official posts that enabled him to accumulate greater wealth which in turn enabled the crown to finance its policy objectives, principally its ambitions in France. These men together with others were the founders of the mercantile and professional middle class.

The office of Privy Seal contained its own staff of clerks, the keeper being paid 20 shillings a day. One of Langley's clerks was the poet Hoccleve, who has given a fascinating insight into life in the office of the privy seal:-

This (these) artificers, se I day by day,
In the hotteste of al hir bysynesse
Talken and syng, and make game and play,
And forth hir labour passith with gladnesse.
But we labour in trauaillous stilnesse;
We stowpe and stare up-on the shepes skyn,
And keepe muste our song and wordes in (**23**).

Silence in a sometimes hot and oppressive atmosphere, labouring for long hours transcribing and copying the copious amounts of correspondence generated by Langley on behalf of the King, this was the life of a clerk in the Privy Seals office. The hub of government, was austere and dedicated, fading light lit by the glow of candles. Fingerless mittens were worn in the winter during days sometimes 14 hours long beginning with matins. The scratch of the quill was the only sound that broke the silence, the clerks hunched over their small desks oblivious to the world outside. This was a world that Langley was conversant with from his time at Thetford and Cambridge. The world of the cleric in the civil service, a vocation of dedication and assiduousness, orderly and precise, overseen by Langley. There was an ethos of monasticism, the clerks taking their transcriptions to Langley for him to check, approve and seal before being despatched to all parts of the kingdom. A posse of messengers attached to the office would be waiting to carry the missives to all parts of the realm. Ostlers and grooms tending to the stables, cooks and servants, washerwomen and butlers, these would all be engaged to ensure the smooth working of this key department, all under Langley's control. It was a separate world attached to the king's court. Trappist in its existence, a world of precision and perfection, the correctness of grammar and syntax the ideals to be aimed for. It was the written word controlling the affairs of state, a world of orderliness, a dour existence, oblivious to the comings and goings of the 35,000 citizens of

London. You can picture Langley with a posse of clerks scurrying behind him, arms laden with bundles of letters and writs as they made their way from Westminster to his inn in Holborn.

Warrants under its seal were sent to every department. In essence it was a semi-autonomous department, its letters were not enrolled. As keeper he was an *ex officio* member of the council. The early development of the office can be traced through the chancery warrants. From the 3rd November 1401 when Langley's appointment was formally announced to 2nd March 1405, warrants were issued to virtually all the crown officers in all parts of the country. Every facet of government received instructions from the Privy Seal's Office, both in the capital and the provinces. 1,340 warrants survive for the first three and a half years of Langley's Stewardship. The majority of petitions for grants of land, money and pardons were made directly to the king, and the privy seal was the instrument under which the king signified his ruling. The privy seal then sent notice of any decision to the relevant department for action, principally Chancery. During the year 1404–5, 3.2% of the chancery warrants were considered by the council whilst 36.6% of the privy seal warrants to chancery are know to have been considered without reference to the king. This clearly indicates the trust that Henry placed in Langley's judgement, it also indicates the power that Langley was able to exercise. The office of privy seal also dealt with diplomatic correspondence, both the issuing of and the receipt of letters **(24)**. This was a wider stage with more power for Langley. Although Langley is not often mentioned by name in works on the period, the fact that he was the holder of the office enables us to chart his career, and by his actions we can trace the policies he was pursuing on behalf of the crown. Henry and his councillors will have debated issues before leaving Langley and the other crown ministers to deal with the details once a course of action had been agreed. Henry and his son put great store on government by consent, i. e. with the acquiescence of the Commons, witness the Commons requesting that the king's councillors be named, something Henry agreed to. At this time Langley rented the London house of the Bishop of Coventry and Lichfield **(25),** and he also had rooms at the king's manor of Eltham **(26)**. During the Christmas of 1401, Langley was present at Eltham when Henry entertained Emperor Manuell II of Palaeologus of Constantinople.

Rebellions

It is no coincidence that rebellions broke out in both Scotland and Wales within the space of six months. Both countries were aware that the new administration was strapped for cash and that the king would have difficulty raising the finance to mount a campaign against them. The insurrections created tensions between the king, Commons and lords that plagued Henry throughout his reign. The enthusiasm that greeted Henry's ascension quickly disappeared. The Royal coffers had been emptied by Richard's profligacy, and the constant demand for additional finance raised through taxation began to alienate the Lancastrian supporters. The problems that came to the fore from Ireland, Scotland, Wales and France all required a military solution.

Military campaigns were expensive, only justifiable if a campaign produced additional territories. Merely maintaining the status quo was not an attractive proposition to the bankers and leading Lords who were the main source of funding. Those magnates who felt that they had not recognised by Henry began to feel disenfranchised as he, and his council, started to exert their own prerogative.

The first problem came from Scotland. The French were actively courting an alliance with the Scots, and keeping England preoccupied with the Scots would allow the French to exert their dominance over their regions still under English control. In 1399, Langley wrote to Robert III on the King's behalf complaining of "... *the great and horrible outrages committed by the sons of Scottish Wardens*". Robert's reply was addressed to "*Duke of Lancaster, Count of Derby and Seyeschal of England*", clearly intended to goad Henry. The King's council met at Westminster on the 9th February 1400 to arrange the financing of an expedition to Scotland. Henry's councillors had also been trawling through the royal archives to justify Henry's demand for homage from Robert III. On 15th July, John Norbury the treasurer presented Henry with a dossier supporting Henry's historical right to homage. Langley's public relations department was at work again to justify the expedition to both the Commons and the country.

As keeper of the royal signet he had been busy eliciting loans to finance the expedition, and it is no coincidence that Richard Whittington was in attendance in the council at this time. Langley travelled with the King to Pontefract and on to York. The Scots offered a peace treaty based on the treaty of Northampton of 1328. This would have given the Scots control of a number of the border towns, something that was obviously unacceptable. From York the King moved on to Newcastle where he issued a proclamation on the 7th August appealing to all Scots to induce Robert III to do homage at Edinburgh on the 23rd August. Langley advanced as far as Leith, and then he issued a warrant dated the 12th August before retiring to Newcastle (27). The Scots would not offer battle and Henry was forced to retire to Newcastle.

Negotiations continued in the following year with Henry Percy and the Earl of March undertaking a series of raids into Scotland.

On his way south Henry was brought the news that a quarrel had broken out between Owain Glyn Dwr and Reginald Grey of Ruthin. The origins of the dispute are unclear. However, on the 18th September, Philip Hamer, brother-in-law of Glyn Dwr, was proclaimed prince of Wales and celebrated by burning Ruthin and pillaging as far as Holt. The insurgents were defeated near Welshpool by a combined force from Shropshire, Warwickshire and Staffordshire. The old tribal loyalties and land holdings of Wales had been gradually eroded as the feudalism introduced by Edward I supplanted the old regimes. Consequently Wales became a more unified principality.

Henry acted decisively and marched to Shrewsbury joining the Prince of Wales. From here he moved to Rhos Faror where one of Owain's followers attacked the royal family. In retaliation Henry destroyed the Franciscan house of Llanfaes. The Franciscans had been highly critical of Henry since the usurpation, even spreading rumours that Richard was still alive. There is no record of Langley admonishing the King for his attack on fellow clergymen; yet again his loyalty to Lancaster over-rode his cloth. Two years later Henry had a Franciscan friar from Aylesbury who showed dissent beheaded – again silence from Langley.

There was an incidence that occurred early in 1400 that points to Langley's intolerance of disloyal and heretical clergy. A Lollard Priest from Langley's archdeaconary of Norfolk, one William Sautre had been examined in 1399 by Archbishop Arundel, after which he renounced his beliefs. Subsequently he resumed his teachings and was arrested and brought before Arundel who condemned him to be *"chained standing to a post in a barrel packed round with blazing faggots"*. As archdeacon Arundel would have consulted Langley in regards to the punishment, further intolerance towards dissent demonstrates his orthodoxy in religious matters.

There is one further incident concerning the Franciscans that exemplifies tacit approval of Henry's firm dealings with the order. Henry had received word that an assembly of those who still believed that Richard was alive was to be called at Oxford. The principals in this movement were ten friars of the Leicester convent led by Roger and Richard Frisby. One member of the group, Walter Walton, got cold feet and denounced the conspirators to the king. On 15th August 1402 a trial was held appropriately at Leicester, Langley attending with the king. The dialogue between the king and Richard Frisby is worth recording as it exemplifies some of the undercurrents that were a permanent feature of Henry's reign. These undercurrents created difficulties for Langley and the rest of the king's ministers. The dialogue is also interesting in that it shows that the Lancastrians were never able to govern England in complete security.

The King	*Did you say that King Richard is still alive?*
Frisby	*I do not say that he is alive, but I do say that if he is alive he is the true King of England.*
King	*He abdicated.*
Frisby	*He did abdicate; but under compulsion while in prison, and that is not a valid abdication.*
King	*He abdicated right willingly.*
Frisby	*He would never have resigned had he been at liberty. And a resignation made in prison is not a free resignation.*
King	*Even so, he was deposed.*
Frisby	*While he was King, he was captured by force of arms, thrown into prison, and despoiled of his realm, while you usurped his crown.*
King	*I did not usurp the crown, but was duly elected.*
Frisby	*An election is null and void while the legitimate possessor is alive. And if he is dead you killed him. And if you are the cause of his death, you forfeit all title and any right which you may have to the kingdom.*
King	*By this head of mine, thou shalt lose thine!* **(28)**

Frisby was indeed brave. Langley and the rest of the council will have viewed the proceedings with alarm. These undercurrents had to be vigilantly guarded against. Shakespeare was right, the crown did rest uneasy. Should the king fall then so to would Langley. Any sympathy that he may have felt for a fellow cleric would have evaporated with this thought. Underlying tension was a constant companion to Henry's reign, Langley had to be constantly alert. This was a pressure that was unremitting not only during Henry IV's reign but also during the early years of his son's rule, and only the victory at Agincourt brought any relief. Professional civil servants like Langley had to perform a balancing act between the Commons, who increasingly expressed the displeasure of the people, and the excesses of royal policy

To alienate the king from his people would have spelt disaster for the monarch and his family. As will be seen, Langley's ability to keep his finger on the pulse of public opinion enabled Henry V to pursue and continue his continental ambitions when he ascended the throne. In fact it was this affinity that made Langley so invaluable to the Lancastrians; his humble origins meant that he remained conversant with the feelings of the populace, and he never lost touch with his roots. This was one of his best traits, the art of giving honest, sincere council. His sound reasoning meant that, during all his time at the centre of government, he never received any public criticism. A significant factor in this was that as a professional civil servant he did not seek or expect to collect the plethora of rewards that often created envy in others. The country had suffered enough from overmighty subjects whose only purpose in council was self-aggrandisement. Langley, one of the first truly professional civil servants was a rarity, a quality that made him indispensable to Henry V. It also follows that there is little point in employing councillors if one does not take cognisance of their advice. At times this advice may not always be what one wishes to hear, this being especially true in the middle ages when the power vested in the monarchy was greater than it is today.

A councillor would often have to urge restraint to preserve the throne; a sensible monarch would heed advice, especially if it was given by someone whose loyalty was unquestionable and who did not have an ulterior motive. Surrounding oneself with sycophants could sound the death-knell for a king, this being the case in Richard's reign when during the later years no one exercised any restraint. Langley will not always have told Henry what he wanted to hear, but nevertheless he remained by the king's side throughout his reign, a sure sign that he was indeed utterly trusted and indispensable. This is one of the prime reasons behind my calling him the first spin-doctor.

Conwy was captured on Good Friday (1st April) 1401 by Rhys and Gwilyn ap Tudor cousins of Glyn Dwr. The castle was commanded by John Massy of Pudington who had fifteen men at arms and sixty archers under him. Whilst the garrison was at mass, the brothers together with forty men entered the castle and barricaded themselves in. Hotspur and four hundred and twenty men laid siege to the castle, eventually obtaining the rebel's submission. The cousins were spared but nine of their men were beheaded and quartered. Langley sent a payment of £200 to Hotspur to meet the expense of the siege. The Welsh insurrections were beginning to drain the crown's resources. Langley and certain others of the council had, through Northumberland, hinted to Glyn Dwr that should he apologise he would be treated with leniency; financial expediency came to the fore, "real politick". As a canon of St. Asaph, Langley was well placed to advise on the mood of the people of Wales. Not for the first time Glyn Dwr did not trust the baronial clique that controlled the Commons, and he declined the offer. The problem rumbled on. Henry mounted expeditions but a combination of bad weather and the terrain prevented any progress being made.

In tandem with the Welsh problem a more serious dispute came to a head. Northumberland, his son Henry Percy and the Earl of March, had captured a number of Scottish nobles at the battle of Homildon Hill. A handful of the prisoners were delivered to Henry but Percy declined to give up Douglas claiming that he was considerably out of pocket and would use the ransom to defray his expenses, not an unreasonable standpoint. Henry was endeavouring to exert his kingship over his most powerful lord who had only four years previously, supported his bid for the throne. The combination of Wales, Scotland, the Percies and the persistent rumours that Richard was still alive, came to a head.

During this period Langley had spent most of his time at Westminster. Henry had been a widower for eight years; he was now thirty-six. On 3rd April 1402 he was married by proxy to Joanna of Navarre widow of Duke John IV of Brittany. She was thirty-three and was represented at Eltham by her envoy Anthony Ricz. Henry Beaufort performed the ceremony in Winchester Cathedral. It is noteworthy that the negotiations for the union were carried out at Eltham where Langley had rooms, and where as keeper of the Privy Seal he will have dealt with the diplomatic correspondence concerning the marriage. Two orders from the Privy Seal's office to chancery authorised the expenditure of £433.6.8 for the cost of the ceremony and £333. six shillings and eight pence for a collar for the bride were signed by Langley.

Katherine Swynford died on the 10 May 1403 in the house she occupied in Lincoln (**29**). She had been treated generously by Henry who had granted her a pension of £1,000 marks a year from the revenues of the Duchy. Langley, together with the Beauforts, Henry and a number of the Lancastrian lords, attended her funeral in Lincoln Cathedral. There is no evidence that she was particularly close to Langley even though both owed the other a good deal.

The financial crisis affected Langley's department more than any other. All expenditure from the Royal Wardrobe passed through the office of the Privy Seal. Langley was forced to negotiate loans, principally from the London merchants, to stem the financial crisis. They started to find this difficult as they began to question the wisdom of supporting Henry and the Lancastrians. Power blocks came to be formed around the Percies and their allies. The dilemma those opposed to Henry faced was that there was not a credible alternative candidate, a proposition that Langley the spin-doctor spread around the Commons. A further problem for the Commons was that they had assented to Richard's deposition. Great care had been taken in the framing of the document that was presented to the Commons regarding the deposition. Langley sensibly realised that the representatives in the Commons who owed their positions to the Percies or who owned land adjacent to, or in,

Wales and Scotland, would side with the rebels. He concentrated on eliciting loans to finance the raising of an army. It was at this tome that Whittington lent the sum of £1,000. Langley's tactics were to woo the merchants, his main tool being the power of patronage. Fortescue, the eminent lawyer, was to remark on royal poverty during the reign of Henry's grandson: *"his subjects will rather go to with a lord that is rich, and may pay their wages and expenses, than with a King that hath nought in his purse"*. On patronage, he remarked: *"The knights, barons, and the greatest nobility of the kingdom often place their children in the Inns of Court"*. Langley, the recipient of considerable patronage understood how to manipulate the snobbishness of those who sought preferment. Fortescue's remarks were just as pertinent to the situation in 1401 as they were in the reign of Henry VI.

The pool of positions at court and the land and titles in the king's gift far exceeded the number of positions available to the rebels. The power of patronage became a finely honed tool in the hands of the Lancastrian officials. They were never erratic in their awards, and it can be seen from the numbers of persons from the mercantile classes who received appointments, that the Lancastrians pioneered the policy of commercial patronage as a tool of government. After Agincourt Langley used this additional tool to raise considerable sums to finance the later expeditions to France. The rise in the representation of the mercantile classes in the Commons also assisted Langley in his policy of tying the upper echelons of society to the ruling house. His time at Westminster during 1400–1 was well spent.

1403, the First Denouement

Henry was at Leicester when he heard of the Percy's rebellion. On 12th July he was at Lichfield when he issued an order to the council to join him (**30**). On 16th July, he asked all the midlands sheriffs to join him with as many men as they could muster. The order to the council came first showing that Henry felt the need to summon Langley before the sheriffs. By July 21st, Langley was with him at Shrewsbury (**31**), the speed with which Langley joined the king showing the alarm he felt. Hotspur's rebellion had been brewing for some time and he had two major grievances. Hotspur and his father harboured the feeling that they had not received the rewards that they were entitled to for their support in 1399. Secondly they felt that they were being overlooked in favour of Ralph Neville, Earl of Westmorland, who was married to Joan Beaufort, Henry's half-sister. Already the legitimisation that Langley had brokered was causing problems for the ruling house, and this was not to be the only problem the Beauforts brought to the house of Lancaster. As a precursor to the rebellion, the Prince of Wales, who had been appointed Lieutenant of Wales earlier in the year, wrote to his father from Shrewsbury that his campaigning in Wales had left him short of money. Henry wrote to Langley from Higham Ferrers requesting him to arrange the immediate payment of £1,000 to relieve the Prince's plight.

It could be viewed that by openly rebelling Hotspur had brought to a head the simmering discontent that had hampered the smooth running of the kingdom. Clearly Henry and his councillors had experienced considerable difficulties in maintaining any stability since 1399. They had been constantly hamstrung by the various factions who had sought, through the commons, to exert a degree of control over the new regime. Rather than ushering in a period of peace and stability Henry's brief kingship had been plagued by a variety of problems. The fact that Langley and other senior councillors hurried to Henry's side suggests that they had come to the corporate decision that until such time as matters with Hotspur were finally resolved they could not make any progress in the governance of the kingdom. History had shown that the backing of parliament and the City of London was fundamental to any monarch's retention of the crown. By leaving London, Langley must have felt reasonably secure that the Commons would not turn the capital and its inhabitants against them. They would be hoping that by defeating Hotspur they could put an end to the rumours surrounding the late king and the legitimacy of Henry's right to the throne. Tellingly, Hotspur and his supporters were promulgating the rumour that Henry had sworn that, prior to his meeting Richard at Chester, he did not wish to seize the throne for himself. Hotspur was reported to be openly saying that Henry had pledged at Doncaster to keep Richard on the throne. The chroniclers are divided on this. I do not believe that Langley and Henry's other advisers would have allowed him to state this so openly.

Clearly if this had been the case Richard would, over a period of time, have gathered enough support to reassert his authority. Langley the spin-doctor would not have been comfortable with Henry publicly stating this as his avowed intent. Hotspur needed to draw the waverers to his cause which is why he stated that Henry had, in his hearing, stated that he merely sought, in 1399, to bring peace and harmony to the realm. Significantly he had remained silent on this point up until now, a fact that was not lost on the Commons who, in the main, did not voice a great deal of support for Hotspur and his supporters. Langley, Arundel and the Beauforts had been busy in Westminster making these points to the more influential members. This would have been done through the Lancastrian retainers in the Commons.

Hotspur's impetuosity was to prove his downfall, Henry was progressing to the north with a sizeable force to assist the Percys in subduing the Scots. Henry acted decisively: the rebels must be prevented from joining Glyn Dwr, Mortimer and the Cheshire archers who were commanded by Hotspur's uncle, Thomas Percy. These three had begun canvassing support by using the same excuse for rebellion that Henry had used. A manifesto was issued at the beginning of May. The public interest argument was the main plank of their propaganda together with an accusation that the treasury had mis-managed the crown's finances. The precise amounts that the Percys had received are a matter of interpretation. Just as today, the figures were manipulated by both sides, Langley pointed out that the Percys had received by far the largest amounts of money from a cash-strapped crown for the defence of the borders. Various other charges were made in the manifesto issued by the rebels. Langley countered this by sending a commission to the Bishop of Carlisle, William Barrow the sheriff of Cumberland and Westmoreland, and Henry Percy, ordering them to arrest and imprison all persons who asserted that Richard II was still alive. A further order was sent out to the leading magnates in each county. This ordered them to the arrest of all those who were spreading the rumours, including preaching that "... *the King had not kept his promises that he had made at his advent into the realm and at his coronation and in parliament and councils, that the laws and customs of the realm shall be observed"* **(32)**. The document was cleverly worded, it covered parliament, "preaching" (the friars) and the coronation that had been unanimously agreed. By addressing the writ to all the leading magnates in every shire, Langley would be able to weed out those who, by ignoring the order, were Percy supporters. Compared with the manifesto from the rebels it showed that Percy and his advisors were not as skilled as Langley in the art of public propaganda.

The wording of this document was a master-stroke of public relations, Langley at his best. Henry must have been expecting some sort of uprising to follow. Indeed it could be argued that by the issuing of the orders to the shire magnates Langley and the council hoped to provoke the Percys into open rebellion. The orders for the army to muster for the expedition to the north will have been sent out well before July. Was Henry's real purpose in going north to confront the Percys? It seems possible that by confronting them in the north, he would have been able to stop them from joining with the rebels in Wales. The forces of the Prince of Wales from a base at Shrewsbury could have checked any attempt by Glyn Dwr to march to the Percies aid. His intelligence network would have made him aware of the Percy's alignment with the Welsh rebels.

Shrewsbury

Hotspur left Chester, striking towards Shrewsbury in an attempt to capture the 16 year old Prince of Wales. Henry arrived with a force of 14,000 men, reaching the town on Friday 20th July. Hotspur's haste to capture the Prince and Henry's decisiveness in marching to the aid of his son meant that Hotspur was left to face the King without the support of his fellow rebels, principally Glyn Dwr. His father, Northumberland, was taken ill at Tadcaster and was unable to join his son. The speed with which Henry had moved had taken the rebels by surprise and had given him the initiative. Henry's advisers urged him to confront Hotspur before reinforcements could join him, which was good advice given that Glyn Dwr's whereabouts were unknown. Henry was not inexperienced in warfare as he had fought in Prussia with the Teutonic Knights against the Lithuanians where he gained a high reputation for his chivalrous conduct. Henry, accompanied by Langley, moved out of the town on Saturday 21st July, halting at the village of Berwick two miles to the north-west of the town.

The army formed into three battle divisions, the centre being commanded by Humphrey, Earl of Stafford, with Henry on the right and the Prince of Wales on the other flank. Hotspur faced him having taken a position at the top of a slope in Hayteley Field, where a thick crop of peas and vetches were ripening. The slope and the density of the vegetation proved a serious hindrance to the Royal forces. Henry sent Langley, *Clericus de privato sigillo* (**33**), and the abbot of Shrewsbury, Thomas Prestbury, to the rebels with an offer to consider any statement of grievances they might have if they would disperse. Alternatively, Henry offered to receive a confidential envoy. Langley, as Privy Seal, would have acted as the spokesperson for the King. Ever mindful of the wider picture, Langley and the King had to be seen to be observing the proprieties. By offering to consider any grievances, Henry was portraying himself as a reasonable monarch who wished to avoid bloodshed. The offer was also intended to appeal to both the waverers and Glyn Dwr's followers. Langley's closeness to the king, together with his civil and clerical rank, lent gravitas to the offer. It is significant that, of all the Lords with the King, he should choose Langley as his emissary. To the rebels Langley would be perceived as Henry's man, and as such he represented the regime that was the focus of their discontent. It has been stated that the parleying continued for three hours. There is no doubt that Thomas Percy was sent to speak with the King but the precise details are clouded by bias. The main sources, John Capgrave and Ralph Holinshead were writing many years after the battle, and Capgrave was just ten in 1403. They were compiling their histories at a time when the house of Lancaster was in the ascendancy, and some of their observations, particularly the alleged words spoken by Henry to Thomas Percy, should be treated with a high degree of caution. What is clear is that the rebels felt that they could not trust Henry to properly consider their grievances.

The battle itself lasted until nightfall, the Cheshire archers initially causing mayhem within the Lancastrian ranks, but after three hours the rebels were routed. Hotspur had been surrounded and killed, and the Earl of Douglas was captured when his horse threw him as he fled the field; Worcester was captured on the field. Casualties were high, Hollinshead puts the number of dead at 1,600 on Henry's side with a further 4,000 wounded, 35% of his total force. This high figure can be accounted for by the ground conditions, as Henry had to attack against a steep gradient, the density of the crops and the Cheshire archers. The rebel casualties were put at 5,000, and the majority of the wounded were murdered by pillagers. Henry initially gave permission for Hotspur's body to be taken to Whitchurch. He later ordered the body be brought to Shrewsbury where it was tied between two millstones. There was to be no repeating of the rumours that surrounded the late King Richard. Thomas Percy, Sir Richard Venables and Richard de Vernon, were tried on the following Monday, and both were beheaded on the same day. As Privy Seal, Langley would have been present at the summary trials. The heads were taken to the capital and spiked on London Bridge. Hotspur's head was sent to York where it was placed on Micklegate Bar. This was the first time that Langley had witnessed the horror of battle; medieval warfare was not the glorious field depicted by the troubadours. Twelve years later he was to provide the wherewithal for an even greater slaughter.

Langley moved with the King to Lichfield from where, on the 25th July, he wrote to the Exchequer ordering that arms were to be brought to Pontefract as the King was moving northwards to deal with Northumberland **(34)**. From here he travelled to Nottingham and then Doncaster, arriving at Pontefract on the 4th August. Langley moved onto York with Henry reaching the City by August 8th, when he took the opportunity to be installed as Dean after which he officiated together with Archbishop Scrope at the mass held in honour of the king **(35)**. Henry had moved to York to receive the formal submission of Northumberland who realised that further resistance was futile. Langley had drafted a letter from the King offering to take Northumberland back into favour if he came to York. The wording, *"back into favour"*, came to mean that his life was spared, but he was stripped of his office as Constable and Warden of the West March, this post going to Neville. A number of his castles were confiscated whilst Thomas Percy's estates were distributed amongst the king's supporters. Langley went to Pontefract where he made the formal arrangements for the distribution of the confiscated estates **(36)**, before returning to Westminster. There was a good reason for sending Hotspur's head to York. Henry was rightly suspicious of Scrope, he believed that he had secretly assisted the rebels, and his suspicions were to be proven well-founded. The site of his son's head atop the Micklegate Bar would have been particularly distressing for Northumberland.

On 3rd September, Langley joined the king at Worcester and travelled with him to Wales. Glyn Dwr had been taking advantage of events in England and had captured a number of castles. Henry was desperately short of funds. At Carmarthen he had to borrow ten marks from Langley to pay some of the arrears of pay owing to the garrison **(37)**. Glyn Dwr had been receiving support from the French, particularly ships which assisted him in capturing the castles on the coast. Henry withdrew to London, Glyn Dwr was to continue his advance in Wales during the next year. The mounting demands brought about by the almost constant state of crisis meant that Henry had to constantly raise loans against customs, taxes (subsidies, lay and clerical), and land. Between the years 1400 and 1407, extraordinary expenditure had to be found for Calais, the Isle of White, Ireland, Scotland, The Percy Rebellion, and the Welsh Revolt. The crown's financial plight, caused principally by the drain on its resources caused by Glyn Dwr's success, had at least one beneficial consequence. The Commons were able to gain greater degrees of control over Royal expenditure and the composition of the kings council.

The parliament that met in the refectory of Westminster Abbey on the 14th January 1404 was a particularly difficult one for Langley **(38)**, sitting for sixty-seven days and starting at 8 o'clock every morning. His time was spent trying to mediate between the king's wishes, the treasury and parliament. He and the Chancellor, Henry Beaufort, Bishop of Winchester, spent a good deal of time impressing on the Commons the need to surpress the rebellion in Wales. The Commons were not in a conciliatory mood, and they insisted that four members of the king's council be removed. They also extracted a promise from Henry that he would not use the office of the Privy Seal too circumvent the judicial process. It appears that the commons felt that Langley had to much autonomy, a clear sign of the control he was able to exert **(39)**.

Northumberland appeared before the Lords who determined that his conduct amounted to trespass not treason, and he was set free. The consequences of this action were to manifest themselves in the next year. Langley remained in London until 20th June **(40)** when he travelled to Pontefract, where he drew up the agreement whereby the Earl of North-umberland surrendered his border castles **(41)**. Whilst he was at Pontefract he also drew up a peace treaty with the Scottish embassy for a defence of the Marches **(42)**. Langley briefly returned to London before accompanying the King on a perambulation around his midlands estates **(43)**. Langley was the only member of the council with the King at this time, and he, and he alone dealt with the business of government with the King, no reference being made to the council. So much for the complaints of parliament earlier in the year **(44)**.

Glyn Dwr was receiving increasing amounts of aid from the French, and had penetrated as far as the outskirts of Worcester. Henry continued to endeavour to mount a campaign against the Welsh and their allies. In September whilst he was besieging Coety Castle, flooding caused him to retreat. Glyn Dwr captured forty of his wagons which contained a significant amount of his jewels. Fate was not on his side. Langley had occupied the office of Privy Seal for three years. During this time he had been the closest minister to the King, and it was now time for further reward. The Bishop of London, Robert Braybrook, died on the 27th August, and Henry issued the licence for the election to the chapter on the 10th September. Henry had let it be known that he wanted Langley appointed to the post. He was formally elected by the chapter on 10th October **(45)**. Previously, the Archbishop of Canterbury had written to Pope Innocent VII recommending the Chancellor of Oxford, Robert Hallam. He now wrote another letter recommending "... *our dear friend, ... whose virtues as well as his long service to John of Gaunt and King Henry made him a worthy candidate*" **(46)**. On the 10th December, the Pope imposed Roger Walden the former Archbishop of Canterbury, who had occupied a number of positions in the council of Richard II, including secretary. A second rebuttal. The Pope would have taken a number of points into consideration in refusing Langley's candidature. Langley's current position in the church was archdeacon of Norfolk, but since taking up the post he had not visited his diocese. He had been complicit in the deposition and murder of Richard II, allowing the death by burning of members of his fellow clergy. He had been the closest councillor to Henry since his landing at Ravenspur.

Whatever the feelings and relationship at that time between the Papacy and Henry, Langley would not have been viewed by Innocent as someone who should benefit from Papal approval. Another telling point is that Innocent's candidate was closely associated with Richard II, both as a member of his council and also as Archbishop of Canterbury. This incident was the clearest sign that Rome viewed Henry as a usurper and did not approve of his occupation of the throne or of Langley's role as his closest confidant.

1405, the Second Denouement and Promotion

Langley did not have to wait long for promotion. Henry Beaufort, Bishop of Lincoln, and Henry's half-brother, had been Chancellor for the past two years. The see of Winchester had become vacant and he was translated to the vacancy. Two weeks prior to this he had resigned the Great Seal. Langley was appointed Chancellor of England on the 2nd of March 1405 (**47**). He was now about forty-two years of age, and he had served in the civil service of the Lancastrians for twenty-four years. He was one of the few medieval chancellors who was not either related to the monarch, came from a titled family, or occupied a Bishopric. He owed his place to assiduous hard work and an ability to maintain Henry on the throne despite the undercurrents of unrest which had provided his office with numerous problems. His support, especially during the crisis of 1403, was rewarded by a king who valued loyalty above political expediency. Langley had now attained access to the greatest pool of Patronage and influence available to a civil servant. He remained at his inn in Holborn but his household doubled in size. Within eight weeks he was to face the hardest choice of his life, an event that was to haunt him during all the remaining years of his life. His first weeks in office were spent in daily council, whilst Henry was absent from London. Langley, the Treasurer and the Keeper of the Privy Seal, were the most regular attendees (**48**).

The great council met at St. Albans from 1st to the 6th April, after which Langley took the opportunity to visit his archdeaconry. Langley had been acting as one of the attorneys at court for the Bishop of Norwich, Henry Despenser (**49**). His perambulations through Norfolk took him to Baldock on the 7th April, Babraham the next day, and Shouldham near Kings Lynn on the 11th. The 18th saw him at Corton near Great Yarmouth, finally arriving at his first place of clerical training, Thetford. The first and only chancellor ever to have been at the abbey, his reception was the highpoint of Thetford's history. From here he returned to London. The main features of Langley's Chancellorship were the award by the commons of the tax of 20s on each knights fee valued at £20 or more, a tenth was granted by the Canterbury convention and the revenue from the customs and subsidy was granted for one year. The argument regarding the taxation of the clergy had rumbled on since 1404. Henry had asked for a subsidy as well as a tenth from the clergy. At this time Langley was Dean of York in which capacity he attended the Convocation of Canterbury held on the 21st of April, the church granted the request.

However, at a further Convocation held at St. Paul's on the 24th of November in the same year the clergy refused to grant the subsidy when it applied to the clergy who did not contribute to the tenth. The argument continued until 1406, the year that Langley was appointed Chancellor. The outcome of the debate was that a levy was placed on the church. The sees of Durham and Hereford paid the highest levy, £40 each. It is not unreasonable to surmise that given the reluctance of the clergy, and to a degree parliament, the King would seek to appoint a minister who would deliver the subsidies to the royal coffers. When one considers this, Langley's appointment as Chancellor clearly shows that the King, prior to the appointment had determined that with Langley he stood the best chance of gaining the extra revenues that he needed to replete the coffers. Langley's delivery of the levy shows where his prime loyalties lay (**50**). Food prices remained stable during his Chancellorship as did the average real wages. The price of all foodstuffs except butter and barley rose slightly before reverting, in 1411, to the levels they were at in 1400. Wages remained generally stable, the levy affected the real incomes of those who had to pay but this was inevitable. It was specified that the money raised had to be used for defence purposes only, and it was stated that this grant was not to create a precedent. This suited Langley who would have inserted this clause to assuage the concerns of the Commons. The politics of pragmatism. This money was principally used to pay the arrears owing to the troops in Wales. It is no coincidence that the Prince was able to make significant progress against the rebels following the receipt of this money. Langley was directing his energies towards creating stability on England's borders. The assistance that he was able to give to the Prince was to be rewarded when the Prince ascended the throne.

Archbishop Scrope had assisted at Henry's coronation, and he had also attended the Great Council held at St. Albans. He was suspected of being in league with and sympathetic to Hotspur and the Percys whom he was related to by marriage. In the summer a list of ten articles were published in the form of a manifesto by Thomas Mowbray the Earl Marshall, Lord Bardolf, and Sir William Plumpton. They were also joined by a large number of Yorkshire knights. The manifesto's were distributed throughout York and were pinned to the doors of the monasteries. Their grievances were similar to those published by Hotspur; taxation, bad governance and a request for the punishment of those who spent the nation's wealth. Its worse accusations were that Henry had usurped the throne and that he had connived in Richard's murder, the first time that such an accusation had been made publicly (**51**). The danger to the Lancastrians was that the accusations regarding Richard and the throne were true. The other alarming clause asked for help in placing the legal heir on the throne.

It pre-empted Langley's move to introduce a tax on land. This was introduced later at the Coventry parliament, a ten-per-cent on all income of £20 from land that was valued at 500 marks or more a year. This represented a doubling in the tax introduced in the previous parliament. Had Scrope been told about this proposal when he and Langley met at St. Albans? Henry was at Hereford on the 22nd of May when he issued orders for the shire levies from the midlands counties to be summoned **(52)**.

By the 28th May he had moved to Derby from where he asked his councillors to join him at Pontefract **(53)**, the council had been sitting at Westminster, the summons arriving to the 30th. Langley reached Nottingham, Henry's next stop, on the 1st of June, a journey of 119 miles completed in three days. Langley must have been particularly perturbed. Clearly whilst the King had asked the council to meet him at Pontefract, he had sent a separate letter to Langley to meet him as soon as possible – yet more evidence of his place as Henry's closest adviser. Langley's haste could well have been because of the archbishop's position. How could they deal with such a high-standing churchman? To banish him would just create a focal point for the disenfranchised.

Any punishment would have to consider the views of the Papacy. Innocent's imposition of Roger Walden probably influenced Scrope's decision. The key question regarding any punishment had to start with the determination of which sphere of the judicial system could he be tried in. To try him in a Lay court he would first have to be stripped of his office, something the King could not do without the acquiescence of the Pope. No Clerical court would hand down a severe punishment and this supposed that Henry would be able to bring charges in a Clerical court. The rest of the council joined the king at Pontefract on June the 3rd. The involvement of the second-highest churchman in the land would have been viewed by Langley as of particular concern.

The involvement of the lords and shire knights could be explained by their affiliation with the Percys. Scrope's position and standing was different. This was the Church turning against the anointed king. Removal of its sanction for the reign would attract the non-committed and would split the church between Canterbury and York. The surprising thing is that Scrope chose now to support what was in effect a localised rebellion. Was he gambling on his rank being a protection against the worst penalties?

There is no record from the Great Council meeting at St. Albans that

Scrope had been dissenting. Langley would have detected any animosity, even though Scrope had disguised his beliefs well. As Chancellor, Langley would be the prime target of those discontent with the governmental officials, and it would be Langley who would have to manage the prosecution of Scrope on behalf of the crown. Which hat was he to wear? Chancellor or Cleric, he would still be mindful of the Pope's rebuttal over the London See. Was there an element of revenge in his part in Scrope's downfall? His twin loyalties were to be examined again. Scrope was reported as stating to his followers that their sins would be forgiven "*... to all them whose hap was to die in the quarrel*" (**54**). This gave the rebellion the ethos of a crusade, a holy war against a usurper and murderer assisted by corrupt officials who, by dint of their bad governance were guilty of treason to the people of England. A further clause in the manifesto showed that Scrope was in close contact with Glyn Dwr. Part of the clause stated "*... if these matters be remedied, we have full information and promise from those now in revolt in Wales, they will be content as they were in the days of King Edward and King Richard*" (**55**). This clearly showed that Scrope and certain of the other rebels had been in contact with the rebels in Wales for some time. The collusion was obvious, this presented a *prima facia* case of treason against Scrope. Only two archbishops had been tried for treason, Alexander Neville, Archbishop of York in 1388, and Archbishop Arundal in 1397, neither having received the death sentence. These were the dilemmas that Langley had to confront.

The Earl of Westmorland moved south to drive a wedge between the rebel groups marching from Cleveland led by Scrope, Clifton and Marsham. The Cleveland rebels were waiting at Topcliffe for the Earl of Northumberland to join them, and they outnumbered Westmorland when he took up position at Shipton Moor. The two groups faced each other for three days starting from the 29th May to the 31st May. Westmorland began parlaying with the rebels. As the talks entered their third day Scrope's followers began to disperse, disenchanted with the lack of progress. Westmorland, unexpectedly to Scrope, Mowbray and his nephew Sir William Plumpton, arrested them and took them to York. Henry and Langley stopped at Pontefract on the 4th June where a judicial commission was appointed under the Chief Justice of the King's Bench, Sir William Gascoigne. Arundel had arrived on the 5th, and he urged caution, obviously concerned about the judicial consequences. Henry instructed Gascoigne to bring in the death sentence on Scrope and his associates.

Gascoigne pointed out that a secular court could not prounounce the death sentence on the archbishop, and he refused to adhere to the King's instructions and resigned. Langley had more than enough experience to know that no secular court could try the archbishop, and even if it had tried the cleric it had no power in law to carry out any sentence. This could have been a case of Henry wishing to exert royal control over wayward clerics, and by inference Rome. Either the King was beyond pursausion or he and Langley had felt confident that Gascoigne would be amenable to their wishes. Gascoigne had at one time served on Henry's Council when he had been Earl of Derby. Arundel's arrival stiffened the Chief Justice's resolve. It would appear that Langley's relationship with Arundel was not as close as was previously the case. Arundal's position is understandable, Scrope was in effect his deputy in that the see of York was the second highest bishopric in England. Had he not supported Scrope then the Pope would have questioned Arundal's role in the affair. Yet again his position in government over-rode his loyalty to the church. They joined the rest of the council who had arrived at Bishopthorpe, the Archbishop's manor, on Saturday 6th June.

There is a telling remark attributed to Henry, which was made when he was in Nottingham on the 1st of June. John Tilton was granted a pension, to be paid by *"he who is next created archbishop of York"* (**56**). If these words were true, and given Henry's later actions it seems probable, Scrope's fate had already been decided by the King and Langley who was the only councillor with him at Nottingham. The gossip about this remark was widespread. Also when Langley's candidature was rebuffed by Innocent VII in October of the previous year, were the King and Langley aware at that time of Scrope's treason? The Schism had reduced the Papacys power to act, something most of Europe's monarchies were busy exploiting. It seems likely that they had agreed that Langley would receive the archbishopric in the not too distant future. They would have been aware that Scrope was already in contact with Glyn Dwr, and he had supported Hotspur. Was he backing both sides? It would explain Henry sending for Langley separately from the council. Scrope's fate had been sealed well before he openly rebelled.

Scrope was tried in a secular court despite the immunity his position in the church gave him. Sir William Fulthorpe was appointed as the new President of the Council. He, together with Sir Thomas Beaufort and two others found all three guilty, Mowbray and Plumpton were sentenced to beheading, and Scrope was sentenced to death. Langley was beside the King throughout the proceedings. Plumpton, Mowbray and Scrope were taken to a field of barley at Clementhorpe. Scrope suffered further humiliation when he was placed *"on a sorry nag not worth a nail"*. The executioner took six strokes to remove the archbishop's head. Plumpton's head was set on Micklegate, Mowbray's on Botham Bar, and the archbishops body was taken to the Minster. Allowing Scrope's body to lie in the Minster may have seemed unwise, but where else could it have been taken to? Henry and Langley had slighted the archbishop enough and they could not risk compounding matters. In any event Arundel would have insisted on it and they could not chance a public argument. Scrope had received a great deal of support from the local clergy when he rebelled. Four of the mendicant orders had members at Shipton Moor and another insult would only fuel their animosity.

When a royal pardon was granted on the 24th August 1405 a number of people from a variety of social classes were marked *"of York"*. Langley will also have been aware that the support for Scrope quickly melted away at Shipton Moor. The customary miracles began to be attributed to Scrope's tomb situated in St. Stephen's Chapel. So popular had Scrope been that the monks erected a wooden parclose. Henry ordered its removal. He also issued instructions forbidding veneration at Scrope's tomb. The handling of the affair was nearly a public relations disaster for the ruling clique. Either Henry would not listen or he felt that only firm action would quell any further unrest. Northumberland and Bardolf had scuttled over the border, and there was no one to lead any further resistance movement in the North. It became apparent that Henry and his ministers were following a policy designed to utterly subdue the north and York in particular. The cost of continually having to deal with rebellions in the north, three in the last few years, were proving such a drain on the Chancery that the campaigning against Glyn Dwr could not be properly conducted. Previous reference has been made to the loans that the crown was continually having to raise. Langley had also been looking at taxation of the clergy, was bitterly opposed by, amongst others, Scrope. Scrope's rebellion had presented Langley with the opportunity to remove this drain on resources once and for all. As part of an overall strategy, to create the financial climate whereby the twin sources of discontent could be dealt with, was prudent. From the crown's viewpoint this strategy made sense, short-term difficulties for long-term gain. It was unusual for the monarchy to plan policy in this way, and viewed like this, the way that Scrope was dealt with is understandable and even masterful.

William the Conqueror embarked on the harrying of the north for the same policy reasons as Henry. Following his sweep through the north he was able to turn his attention to Wales. Henry was mirroring the same policy. The surprising thing is that Langley, as Chancellor, chose to ignore the fact that he was also a cleric. The chroniclers openly wrote about Arundels protestations on behalf of the archbishop, but they are silent on Langley's role. Langley was to remain one of the most senior members of the king's council for many more years, so it is hardly surprising that the chroniclers remained silent. Having seen what happened to Scrope it is not unsurprising that they refrained from any criticism. That was reserved for the king, and then mainly after his death. His illnesses, coming so soon after the executions, provided them with enough ammunition. Viewed with the benefit of hindsight the crown's reaction to Scrope's rebellion taken in context was understandable.

The early optimism that had accompanied Henry's landing in 1399 quickly evaporated when those who supported him realised that they would not gain as they had expected to. For the past five years the government had been faced with a constant state of flux. A good number of the Commons recognised this, and the situation had actually brought about changes in the status of the Commons. Anyone considering the situation dispassionately would have concluded that there was a certain justification in Henry's actions. Politically Langley did not suffer any damage to his career, but much has been made about his replacement the next year as Chancellor. As will be discussed in the next section, the reason for his replacement was due to a change in direction of royal policy towards France and Europe. The constant undercurrents of discontent principally fostered by the Percys and their allies had worn the patience of those in the south who were more concerned with the effect this unrest was having on the country's trade both internally and externally. Tying up the resources of the crown on internal matters had badly affected the government's ability to carry out its foreign policy to the detriment of the country as a whole. French privateers were acting with impunity and the Calais garrison was in a state of near-permanent mutiny due to lack of pay. Langley had been stressing the drain on resources that the rebellions had caused. He had argued his case well, he had ''spun'' public opinion behind the crown. The mistake of the English rebels was that they had failed to put their case to the Commons, thereby isolating themselves from the mainstream of public opinion. Langley had outflanked them. Not for the last time were troubles in the north to be blamed for England's financial plight, remember the miners strike.

The fact that the wealthy merchants continued to make loans available to the crown exemplifies the feelings in the capital. The opinions of the mercantile classes were increasing in importance, something that Langley for one fully appreciated. This factor would have formed part of the reasoning behind Langley's advice to the king. A replacement for Scrope now had to be found, someone who would remain loyal and who would quell any further support for Northumberland and Bardolf. The King gave his licence for an election on the 17th June, and Langley, who was Dean of the Minster was his nominee. He was formerly elected by the members of the chapter on the 8th August. There is evidence that the Lord Mayor of York, William Frost, openly disapproved of Langley **(57)**. Whilst the formalities of the election process were being observed, Henry sent John Catrick to Rome to explain the reasons behind the execution. He also took with him a bribe in the form of letters to the Cardinals of Florence and Naples. On the 18th June Henry had granted that they would be able to obtain provision to some English benefices which totalled £200 in value (**58**). It could be viewed that this was a cheap price to pay for the archbishop's death. The letters were issued by Langley's office, Chancery, hardly the act of a man who was feeling any remorse. The contents of the letters were clearly a bribe, so it would appear that Langley had no scruples. Conversely, he was only following what had become custom and practice. Henry had also conceded on the 24th of June that Walden could enter his post as Bishop of London (**59**), hardly subtle. Storey is of the opinion that the see had remained vacant because Henry was pushing Langley's claims (**60**). I find this difficult to believe for the reasons that have been outlined.

Innocent refused to accept Langley and nominated Robert Hallam to the see (**61**). The Pope went further in that he excommunicated all those involved in Scrope's execution. Henry refused to publish the sentence or Hallum's provision to the vacancy. The chroniclers were silent on this matter, due in part to the fact that the sentence was not public knowledge. During the coming months both the King and Langley were to continue fulfilling their duties, not the actions of men troubled by being excommunicants. The Schism had made the implementation of the sentence virtually impossible. Within seven years Langley had paid for the Middleton parish church where he had recived his first introduction to education and God. Was this act one of penance for his part in the execution? (See also the section on Gaunts window pp). With two rebuffs in the space of ten months, it appears that the Papacy viewed Langley as a politician first and a cleric second, and it also shows that he was viewed as being too close to the king and too involved in Scrope's downfall. Putting him forward for the see of York has the appearance of arrogance and insensitivity. At home, the message to York and its clergy was that they either accept Langley, a Lancastrian, or they suffer more penalties. It was clear that the King was determined to put an end to the pernicious gossip that seemed to originate in the City. Henry's nomination of Langley was the clearest public statement of the role that Langley had played in the affair. By accepting the nomination, Langley was clearly showing his approval of the King's actions. Storey attributes the delay between Scrope's death and Langley's formal candidature to Langley's reluctance in accepting the vacancy. I believe that the delay was to give the appearance of observing the proprieties and cowing the chapter into agreement, as they would hardly welcome someone who had a fundamental part in their archbishop's execution.

Langley continued to carry out his duties as archdeacon of Norfolk, and from 4th to 18th April he travelled around the shire. During this visitation he carried out a number of duties, hardly what an excommunicant should do. Langley may have taken the view that the excommunication applied to all those involved in Scrope's death. He may have deemed that this meant all those involved in the trial and actual beheading, therefore not applying to him if so strictly interpreted. If this was his view, it was a fine distinction that he was making. Even though the Papal sentence had not been formally pronounced, it still applied. Langley obviously did not pay much heed to Rome's jurisdiction. The see remained vacant until the 12th April 1408 when Innocent's successor, Gregory XII, offered absolution to all those involved in the archbishop's death. Langley and the Bishop of Lincoln were appointed as his mandatories. Langley had regained favour, and his appointment as a mandatory was an insult to the archbishop's memory, there being no sentiment in politics either in Westminster or Rome. As will be seen there were other reasons for Gregory's *volte face*. This cannot be viewed as exonerating Langley from culpability.

The Aftermath

Langley returned to Westminster whilst Henry moved north to accept the surrender of the rebel's castles. By the 14th July he had captured Alnwick Castle, the last stronghold of the Percys. During this mopping up it was alleged that Henry found proof of the Baron's involvement in the earlier rebellions when he took Warkworth Castle. This "proof" was never actually produced – Langley the spin-doctor? This seems probable, who would get what had already been decided. This piece of propaganda served to further justify the confiscations. Whilst the King was taking control over the rebel's estates, Langley was busy at Westminster completing the formalities involved in the confiscation of the rebel's estates. Northumberland and Bardolf were declared traitors in parliament. Langley used the confiscated estates, and more importantly their revenues, to pay off the crown's debts. He also judiciously used the estates to cement alliances with a number of the leading families of the nobility. This distribution would have been one of the benefits of the rebellion that the King and Chancellor would have weighed prior to taking such decisive action when they arrived at York. This strengthening of the ties between the leading families and the House of Lancaster was the most significant consequence of the 1405 rebellion.

Judged after a period of time Henry's and Langley's handling of matters was impressive, further enhancing Langley's reputation in Lancastrian circles. The entire situation had been turned around to the extent that one of the prime sources of rebellion had been fundamentally removed by isolating the rebels from any support that they may have expected from the rest of the country. Henry's decisive military action and Langley's political adroitness had restored the King's grip on the throne. Bardolf's Norfolk estates went to the Earl of March and Mowbray's lands in Essex to Prince John together with a number of the Northumberland holdings in the north. The Prince of Wales received Mowbray's castle of Framlingham in Suffolk. The Queen was given a number of Bardolf's and Westmorland's possessions. This made up the arrears of £10,000 marks owing on her dower. The Isle of Man and Cockermouth Castle went to Westmorland, husband of Joan Beaufort the King's half-sister. The grant of the Isle of Man was cancelled as illegal and it passed instead to Sir John Stanley. The island's income was £400 per annum and came to found the bedrock of the Stanley fortunes. Henry and Thomas Beaufort, Henry's mother-in-law the Countess of Hereford, and his niece Constance, all received large grants from the pool of confiscation's. By awarding the northern lands of the rebels to his close family, Henry was able to bring large swathes of Yorkshire and the borders into his extended family's control. Politically Langley would have been mindful of the fact that the Beauforts needed to be seen to be as publicly associated with Henry as possible, as the country could not have stood another dynastic war. The family's loyalty had to be repaid and its dependence of the largesse of the Lancastrian regime reinforced. The apportionment's were very astutely handled. Yet again all the leading families had something to be grateful for, as Langley's position as the leading member of the council was reinforced. The Beauforts were becoming more closely associated with the Prince of Wales, and Langley needed to draw them closer to his circle.

Conclusions

The crisis created by Scrope and the Northern Earls had been mishandled by the rebels. Had Glyn Dwr gone to Hotspur's assistance at Shrewsbury the outcome would have been different. Welsh parochialism worked against the principality's long-term interest. The financial position that Henry had inherited placed his government in a no-win situation in terms of its ability

to satisfy all those who initially supported the usurption. Had Northumberland, his family and his supporters, taken a long term view and assisted
Henry, particularly against the Welsh, they would have gained more. They
had places in the Prince of Wale's Council, but impatience was their downfall
country was not ready for further upheaval. The rebel's chief mistake was
their not obtaining the backing of Parliament or the merchant classes.

The rebellions were viewed from London as being localised uprisings and
apart from Scrope and the local clergy they received no support from the
church. The Schism meant that Rome had no influence on affairs, a strong
Pope would have refused to sanction Henry's Kingship. The Lancastrians had
acted prudently on seizing power; there had been no initial changes to either
the chief ministers or the main positions in the church. Langley and Henry
Beaufort had cultivated both Parliament and the merchant classes, and both
had understood the need to garner the support of the non-military castes.

Henry, to his credit, had shown himself willing to rely on his councillor's
advice. Fortunately for him the advice he received was well thought out,
Langley clearly understanding the need to cultivate public opinion, unlike the
previous regime. His early background and the way the poll tax riots had
affected John of Gaunt had taught him lessons that he never forgot. The
rebellions had been quelled as much by a public relations campaign as by
military decisiveness. The events of the first five years had been "spun" to
the benefit of the Lancastrians. Langley's understanding of the mood of the
Commons meant that there was a more flexible attitude to the requests of the
Commons, the politics of pragmatism. I hope that this re-appraisal of events
of the early part of the reign of Henry IV causes a re-evaluation of Langley's
position within the Lancastrian circle. It is evident when one traces his
movements that it was his continued presence at the King's side that ensured
that the ruling clique suffered no long-term damage to the dynasty. Without
his careful planning in laying the foundations of stability, Henry V would not
have inherited the throne without further bloodshed. The peaceful transition
that followed the death of Henry IV was due in no small measure to
Langley's assiduous behind-the-scenes work. His role as the chief public
relations officer, the spin-doctor, was invaluable to the future of the dynasty
and its closest followers and supporters, chiefly the Beauforts.

The King's Health

Shortly after Henry's sweep around the north his health began to deteriorate.
The first record of his illness can be traced to his stay at Archbishop
Arundel's manor at Mortlake on the 19th June to the 12th of July. The

nature of the illness, pus-filled blotches and cramps, led many of the hostile chroniclers to announce that he had contracted leprosy. Not unsurprisingly this was credited to God, who had caused the affliction in revenge for the execution of Scrope. Much had been written about the precise nature of the King's periodic illnesses, but one thing is clear, he was not suffering from leprosy. He continued to mix with the court and the public, but had he been a leper he would not have done so. His first bout displayed all the symptoms of a nervous breakdown, hardly surprising considering what he had been faced with. What is clear is that the rest of his life was dogged with sometimes debilitating bouts of infirmity. The activities of the Prince of Wales in the principality meant that no one was able to take advantage of the King's spasmodic incapacity. He had recovered by 14th August when he met Langley and the rest of the council at Hereford. Langley had travelled by way of Leicester and Worcester, as he was raising loans to finance another expedition into Wales. Langley went to Coventry **(62)** before rejoining the King at Worcester on the 29th September **(63)**, from where they returned to London.

1406, The Long Parliament and Promotion

The Parliament that commenced on the 1st of March was to become the longest held during Henry IV's reign. It adjourned on the 3rd of April, resumed on the 25th of April and continued until the 19th of June. There was another adjournment until the 15th of October after which it sat until late December. A hundred and fifty four days altogether. Langley's opening address emphasised the king's love for his subjects and how his thoughts were constantly concerned with the health of his subjects. His words had been carefully chosen in view of events in York the previous year. No one in the Commons publicly voiced any comment on Scrope's execution, they had other matters on their mind.

Langley was present every day. It was a parliament of compromise for the council as the Commons sought to extract as many concessions as they could from an impoverished crown. The innovative Land Tax that Langley had introduced was one of their targets. They sought to obtain a personal guarantee from the members of the council that they would personally refund to the treasury any grants that were deemed to have been misspent. Henry came to Langley's aid by refusing to accept this intrusion into what he rightly regarded as his own prerogative. Earlier in the previous year, February 26th, they had asked if the Commons could have the right to reply to petitions before any grants were made **(64)**. Langley had a number of thorny problems to deal with, in particular the wishes of the Commons concerning the king's council. In this, the new speaker John Tiptoft, and John Rome the clerk of parliament, were to provide great help. The council was formerly nominated on the 22nd May and the Commons were presented with a compromise. Bills passed by the chamberlains or under the royal signet, together with mandates to the chancellor, treasurer, and keeper of the privy seal, would be endorsed by the council and noted as by "the advice of the council" **(65)**. The Commons had secured the principle that the members of the council had to be formally named before parliament, an important constitutional concession, the benefits of which the Commons felt many years later.

The other key underlying issue concerned the decision making process. The Commons obviously had reservations about the fact that it appeared that major decisions were being made by only the King and Langley without reference to any other members of the council. You can detect the hand of Arundel in this request. He still felt that Scrope's fate had been pre-determined, which it had, by a process that had denied Arundel the opportunity as a member of the council to argue on the archbishop's behalf. In a further attempt to exert some control on the King's personal expenditure, the Commons also sought to have an enquiry set up into value of all the manors, lordships, lands, tenements, alien priories, marriages, wardships, et al. The purpose of the inquiry was to determine if the value of the various gifts was greater than the revenue that they produced, and if this were the case, the Commons proposed that the council be given the power to increase the payments from these gifts. The hidden purpose behind this request was to curtail the access to the King and, following this, to control the power and access to royal patronage.

The key clause for this book concerned the request that nothing should pass under the Great Seal (Langley), or the Privy Seal **(66)** without having first been before the council. This was aimed at the way that the rebel's estates had been divided by Henry and Langley. The underlying feeling was that the King's officials were taking advantage of their positions to obtain preferment. Tellingly, the Commons also wanted all the councillors to swear that they would not take any additional income other than that from their salaried positions. These provisions were only to remain in place until the next parliament. It appears that the true purpose of the requests was to send out a signal of disapproval regarding those around the King **(67)**, principally Langley and the Beauforts. There is no record of anyone close to Langley, family for instance, receiving undue preferment. Any patronage that he afforded to either members of his family or friends came from the Duchy of Lancaster estates and, later, from Durham. (see recapitulation at the end of the book).

During the break in proceedings between the 3rd and 25th of April, Langley again visited Norfolk. By the 12th he was at Corton from where he went, via Norwich, to Kings Lynn, which he reached by the 18th. On the 20th he was at West Dereham **(68)** where a recognisance was taken. His visit to his archdeaconry could well have had another purpose.

Promotion to Durham

Fresh diplomatic initiatives were beginning in an effort to resolve the great schism. There was a movement to persuade Innocent VII and Benedict XIII to resign thereby allowing a new election to unify the Papacy. Henry had been privately petitioning Rome to have Langley translated to a see. As a matter of principal Henry was determined that his closest adviser should have a Bishopric. The two snubs to Langley were also aimed at the king. The death of Walter Skirlaw, Bishop of Durham, allowed a compromise to be broached whereby Henry would withdraw his nomination of Langley to the see of York in return for Langley's translation to the Bishopric of Durham. Innocent VII needed the King's support to maintain his position. He, for obvious reasons, was not inclined to resign. Langley received his Bishopric by way of a political trade-off, but not by virtue of his being manifestly the right candidate, religion did not play any part in his promotion. Note that there was no mention of the excommunication by Innocent; political survival over-ruled the memory of an executed archbishop. Langley's visit to Norfolk could well have been to discuss his translation. The vote of the Durham Chapter was 33 for and 12 against. He received his Papal Bull to the see on 14th May, with his consecration following on the 8th August. Archbishop Arundel together with Bishop Beaufort of Winchester and Bishop Clifford of London, officiated at the ceremony in St. Paul's Cathedral. Langley had requested that all three took part in the consecration, Beaufort and Arundal for political reasons (in Arundel's case as a public statement that they had buried their differences), Beaufort because he and the rest of his family were particularly close, and Clifford as a gesture to the Pope and also because he was Bishop of London. Henry attended the ceremony as did all the members of the council and a number of the leading members of the Lords and Commons. Langley's appointment to Durham enabled Henry to bolster the judicial system in the border country. The Bishopric of Durham had Palatinate powers, and by appointing Langley, Henry was able to impose a firmer grip on the tenants of the Percys both through the religious and secular power vested in the

Bishopric of Durham, and through the lordships that had been awarded to Henry's supporters following the previous year's rebellion. The diocese contained 130 parishes, some of which were covered large swathes of open moorland. The crown had completed the subjugation of the Northern Marcher lands.

Langley's early employment by John of Gaunt in the Duchy household enabled him to take up the reins of the Bishopric with ease. In many ways the powers of the two Duchies mirrored each other. He had a considerable amount of autonomy in the internal affairs of the see, and through his attendance with the King on his forays against Northumberland and the Scots, he was conversant with the politics of the region. The see clearly needed the appointment of a political Bishop, not a Bishop politic. Durham had a rich religious heritage based upon the cult of St. Cuthbert, and Gaunt had made many endowments to churches dedicated to the Saint. He was unable to take up his duties immediately and he appointed vicars-general on the 10th August **(69)**. Politically Henry could not allow his Chancellor to vacate his post during the Long Parliament; there were too many issues to deal with. Langley moved from the inn of the Bishop of Coventry and Lichfield to Durham House which was situated near where it joins the Strand. This was a substantial residence which had a chapel and a garden.

His income increased considerably, he now had revenues of over £30,000 a year at his disposal, a reflection of the size and status of the office he now held. He had his own Chancellor, Chamberlain and Treasurer as well as a sizeable household. In addition to his Town house he also had a house of his own at Old Ford **(70)** which was situated three miles north-east of the Tower, the area today is called Bethnal Green, and Old Ford Road runs parallel to the old Roman Road. He resigned his post as Chancellor on the 30th January 1407 **(71)**. Stubbs **(72)** is of the opinion that Langley was removed due to the criticism of the Long Parliament regarding the King's councillors. Storey had taken the view that the resignation was due to Langley wishing to attend to his duties in Durham **(73)**. Whilst I would partially agree with Storey's view there were other reasons for Langley's resignation. The new Bishop did not visit his Bishopric for a further sixteen months, hardly the action of one who wished to immediately take up his new office. Storey quite rightly points to his immediate appointment to the King's Council with a salary of 200 marks per year **(74)**, a sign that he was not out of favour.

The removal of the threat from the north and the Prince of Wales successes in the Principality allowed the Lancastrians to turn their attentions to Europe, and France in particular. Also Henry's continuing bouts of infirmity meant that the Prince of Wales began to take a more active part in the governance of the kingdom. Langley, together with the Beauforts formed a coterie around the Prince. It seems far more probable that Henry wanted Langley to lend his experience to his son's council to ensure that there were no divisions created between the heir and the present incumbent. Langley was to become in effect the Foreign Secretary, the country being now in a position to deal with issues in Rome and Paris.

Langley was now forty-four years old, and the last few years had been ones of strain and tension. The award of his Bishopric was a position that he had earned. He, together with and the Beauforts represented the inner circle of Lancastrian advisers. His greatest service to date had been the handling of the Scrope affair and the compromise-politics of the Long Parliament. His continual presence at Henry's side had allowed him to extend his influence to foreign affairs both in France and at the *Papal Curia*. The revival of the diplomatic negotiations to heal the Schism were to provide Langley with another challenge.

Notes and References

(1)   Shakespeare, W. "Henry The Fouth", part 2, act 3, scene 1, 26–31.
(2)   Riley, H. T, (ed), "Annalea Recundi Secundi et Henrici Quarti "in" Johannis de Trokelowe et Anon Chronica et Annales", (Rolls Series, 1866); also, Taylor, J, (ed), "Kirkstall Abbey Chronicles", (Thoresby Society, 1952); Post, J. B: and Hunnisett, R. F. (eds), "Courts, Councils and Arbitors in the Ladbroke Manor Dispute", 1382–1400, "Medieval Legal Records Edited in Memory of C. A. F. Meekings", (London 1978); Webb, (ed), "Metrical History" from Buchon, J. A. (ed), "Collection des Chroniques Nationales Francais", xxiii (Paris 1826).
(3)   Myers, D, C, (ed), E. H. D. vol iv, 1327–1485, pp 179–187; Sayles, G. O. "The Deposition of Richard II: three Lancastrian Narratives" from Corpus Christi College, Cambridge, MS, 59, ff. 230v-231, (Bulletin of the Institute of Historical Research, 1981); Thomas, A. H. (ed), "The Great Chronicle of London", (1983). R. P. iii 415–53.
(4)   Jacob, E. F, "The Fifteenth Century, 1339–1485", (Oxford 1961), p16.
(5)   McKisack, M, "The Fourteenth Century", 1307–1399, (Oxford, 1959). The views expressed on pp 496–98 are the most succinct analysis of Richard's reign.
(6)   C. P. R. 1399–1401, P 178.
(7)   Exchequer, K. R: Accounts, Various, box 649.
(8)   McKisack, M, "The Fourteenth Century, 1307–1399, (Oxford, 1959), pp 494–5.
(9)   Riley, H. T, (ed), "Annales Ricardi Secundi et Henrici Quarti", in, "Johannis de Trokelowe et Anon Chronica et Annales", (Rolls Series, 1866), also

reproduced in, Given-Wilson, C, "Chronicles of the Revolution, 1397–1400",
(Manchester 1993), pp172–183.
(10) Lapsley, G, "The Parliamentary Title of Henry IV", (E. H. R. xlix, 1934) pp
423–49, and, 577–606.
(11) Jacob, E. F, "The Fifteenth Century, 1399–1485", (Oxford 1961), p17.
(12) C. C. R. 1399–1402, p 321.
(13) Feltoe, C. L. and Minns, E. H. (ed), "Vetus Liber Archidiaconi Eliensis",
(Cambridge Antiquarian Society, Octavo Publications, no. 48, 1919),
reproduced in E. H. D. vol iv 1327–1485 (ed) Myers, A. R. p 703, doc no. 418.
(14) Kirby, J, "Henry IV of England", (1970), p 127.
(15) Neve, le, J. "Fasti Ecclesiae Anglicanae", ed, Hardy, T. D, (Oxford, 1854), vol
ii, p. 484, and vol iii, p, 205.
(16) C. P. R. 1399–1401, pp 470 and 506.
(17) Ryme, T. (ed), "Feodera, Conventiones, Literae", (1704–35), vol viii, p. 291;
C. P. R. 1401–1405, p. 212; C. P. L. v, p. 537; Le Neve, iii, p. 124.
(18) Exchequer, K. R, "Ecclesiastical Documents, bundle 8, no. 24; C. P. R. 1401–
1405, pp. 61 and 89; C. P. L. v, p. 537; Le Neve, ii, p. 152 and iii, p. 209.
(19) Wylie, J. H, "History of England under Henry IV", (4 vols, London 1884–98);
Exchequer of Receipt: Warrants for issues, box 17, no. 345.
(20) Stubbs, W, "Registrum Sacrum Anglicanum", p 84, (Oxford, 1897).
(21) Barron, C, "Richard Whittington: the man behind the myth "in" Studies in
London History Presented to P. E. Jones", (London 1969), pp. 197–248.
(22) Keen, M, H, "England in the Later Middle Ages", (Metheun, London 1973),
pp 332–3.
(23) Tout, T. F, "Chapters in Medieval Administrative History", vol v, p 107,
(Manchester 1920–33).
(24) Jacob, E. F, "The Fifteenth Century", (Oxford, 1961), pp 426–32.
(25) Tout, T, F. "Chapters in the Administrative History of England", (Manchester,
1920–33), vol v, pp 50–4, 205–11.
(26) Scrope, Reg, fo. 5v "*in quadam camera domini Thome Langley*", Eltham
Manor, 27th December, 1401.
(27) C. P. R. 1399–1401, pp 351–70; cf. Chancery: Warrants for the Great Seal, file
603.
(28) Jacob, E. F, . "The Fifteenth Century" 1399–1485 (Oxford, 1961), pp. 28–9.
(29) Hill, F, Sir, "Medieval Lincoln", (Cambridge, 1948), p 168.
(30) P. P. C. 1, pp 207–8.
(31) Chancery Warrants, file 620.
(32) C. P. R. 1401–1405, p 126.
(33) Walsingham, T, "Historia Anglicana", (Rolls Series, 1863–4), vol, ii, p 257.
(34) Warrants for Issues, 18/599.
(35) Neve, Le. "The Fabric Rolls of York Minster", vol iii, (ss. 1858), pp 193–5.
(36) Foedera, vol viii, p 330.
(37) Chancery Warrants, files 620–1; Warrants for Issues, 18/604.
(38) Rot. Parl. Iii, p 530; see also Baldwin, J. F. "The King's Council in England in
the Middle Ages", (Oxford 1913), pp 153–9.
(39) Myers, A. R. (ed), "English Historical Documents" vol iv, p 456–459, doc no.
268.
(40) C. P. S. 12.

(41) Foedera, viii, pp 364–5; Walsingham, ii, p 263.
(42) C. P. R. 1401–1405, P 408; Rot Scot ii, pp 167 & 169.
(43) Chancery Warrants, file 623; Wylie, iv, p 292.
(44) C. P. S. 13.
(45) Godwin, F, "De Praesulisbus Angliae Commentarius", (ed), Richardson, W, (Cambridge, 1743), p 186; C. P. R. 1401–1405, p 422.
(46) Royal Letters, Henry IV, (Rolls Series, 1860), pp 415–16.
(47) Storey, R. L, "English Officers of State, 1399–1485", (Bulletin of the Institue of Historical Research, 1958, p 85).
(48) C. P. S. 19.
(49) Legge, M. D, (ed), "Anglo-Norman Letters and Petitions", (Anglo-Norman Text Society, 1941), p 109; Parliammentary Proxies, file 42, no. 2090.
(50) Sharman, I. C. "Thomas Langley, a Political Bishop", unpublished lecture paper, (England 1998).
(51) Stubbs, "Constitutional History of England", vol iii, p 50.
(52) C. P. R. 1405–1408, p 66.
(53) P. P. C. 1, pp 264–5.
(54) Stow, J, "The Chronicles of England", (1592).
(55) "Annales Ricardi II et Henrici IV", (Rolls Series), pp 403–5.
(56) Chancery Warrants, 626/4359; Warrants for the Privy Seal, file no 3, no 138.
(57) Jacob, E. F, "The Fifteenth Century, 1399–1485", (Oxford, 1961) p 62.
(58) Chancery Warrants, 626/4391; Warrants for Issue, 20/286; Warrants for the Privy Seal, file 3, no. 138.
(59) C. P. R. 1405–1408, p 22.
(60) Storey, R. L, "Thomas Langley and the Bishopric of Durham, 1406–1437", (London, 1961). p 18.
(61) Thompson, A. H, "The English Clergy and their Organisation in the Later Middle Ages", (Oxford, 1947).
(62) C. P. R. 1405–1408, pp 35–38; C. P. S. 22; C. C. R. 1402–1405, pp 525–9.
(63) C. C. R. 1402–1405, pp 525.
(64) Rot. Parl, iii, pp 458, 568, 572.
(65) Rot. Parl, iii, p 573; Jacob, E, F. "The Fifteenth Century, 1399–1485, p 83, (Oxford 1961).
(66) Jacob, E. F, "The Fifteenth Century 1399–1495", pp 83–85, (Oxford 1961).
(67) Keen, M, "England in the Later Middle Ages", (Methuen, London, 1973), p 317.
(68) C. P. R. 1405–1408, p 186; C. C. R. 1405–1409, pp 123–6.
(69) Reg. nos, 1, 10 and 12; Storey, R. L, "Thomas Langley and the Bishopric of Durham, 1406–1437", (London, 1961).
(70) C. C. R. 1419–1422, p 77; C. P. S. 33.
(71) C. C. R. 1405–1409, P 250; Foedra viii, p 464.
(72) Stubbs, "Constitutional History of England", vol iii, p 61.
(73) Storey, R. L, "Thomas Langley and the Bishopric of Durham, 1406–1437", (London, 1961), p 21.
(74) Warrants for Issues, 23/264.

A feast to celebrate the alliance of John of Gaunt and King João of Portugal

Richard II

Henry IV

Henry V

Tapestry taken from a window in
Manchester Cathedral, *by Joan Felstead*

The battle of Agincourt; a mid-fifteenth century English illustration

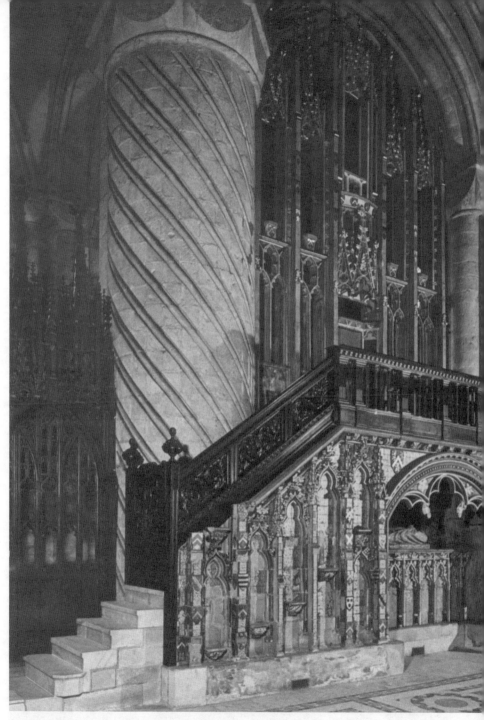

The Throne of the Bishops of Durham

The tomb of Thomas Langley, Durham Cathedral

PART THREE

DIPLOMACY and THE PRINCE OF WALES

> "... for ther is nothing which
> mai be betre aboute a king,
> Than conseil, which is the substance
> of all a kinges governance." **(1)**

The Diplomatic Situation, 1407

During his early years Henry, as Earl of Derby, had travelled extensively both in Europe and the Middle East. This, coupled with the dynastic marriages that Gaunt had secured for his children, gave the Lancastrians access to a number of the ruling houses in Europe as well as close personal ties with the rulers of a number of kingdoms. Apart from the condemnation of France, Henry's usurpation had received tacit support from a wide spectrum. The rebellions of the early years of the reign had meant that the crown had been no more than an interested spectator of events in Europe. Any diplomatic embassies were concerned with the usurpation; England was on the back-foot as the French set the policy agenda. Henry's problems with Wales and Scotland enabled the French to direct their aid to both these countries, keeping Henry occupied and, thereby allowing the French to wage war in Gascony and against the Calais garrison. Langley and the Beauforts realised that they could use the great schism to their advantage by bartering their voting power and influence at the *Papal Curia* for support of a policy designed to undermine and destabilise the French monarchy.

John of Gaunt had arranged two political alliances through marriage for two of his children. Philippa had married Joao of Portugal and Catherine married Enrique III of Castile. Henry IV's second marriage was to Joan of Brittany and his daughter Blanche was married to Lewis of Bavaria, King Rupert's eldest son. Philippa was married to the king of Norway. Henry had endeavoured to broker a marriage between Richard II's widow, Isabella, and one of his sons, but the French would not countenance this. To do so would have been contrary to their view of Henry as a usurper. Flanders, whilst needing English wool exports for its weavers also had France as its nearest

97

neighbour. The periodic internal political instability allowed France to pursue a similar policy as it did regarding Wales and Scotland.

Langley was appointed to the King's Council on the same day as he resigned the great seal, 30th January 1407 (2). He remained in London until the end of the Trinity term arranging loans from the London merchants to pay for the defence of Calais and Gascony. Storey has made the salient point that England and Germany supported the Urbanist Popes of Rome, whilst France, Scotland and Spain supported the Avignonese Popes. At the outset of Henry's reign, Germany was also split, with both Wenceslas of Bohemia and Rupert of the Palatine claiming to be the King of the Romans. The consequences for Langley were that his Bishopric owed allegiance to both regimes. Part of the diocese of Durham lay in Scotland, the cell of Coldingham and other churches being situated in the diocese of St. Andrews. Rome had granted Skirlaw Episcopal jurisdiction in Berwick-upon-Tweed which lay in the diocese of St. Andrews, but this jurisdiction was not recognised in Scotland. Langley had a dual interest in the great schism as well as the political relationship with France and her allies. A foot in both camps, both as a secular magnate as well as an ecclesiastic was a unique position and one that he was able to exploit. He was formally enthroned in Durham on the 4th September, sixteen months after the Papal Bull had been issued.

The French had reconfirmed the thirty year truce of 1396 in 1400. What they carefully avoided acknowledging was Henry as King, thereby negating the truce. The French monarchy was also beset with periodic bouts of unrest as the main barons fought for control of the periodically insane Charles VI. This rivalry between Orleans and Burgundy meant that England was able to maintain its foothold in France. The assassination on 23rd November 1407 of Louis of Orleans in Paris, when he was walking to the Hostel de St. Pol by followers of John the Fearless, brought about conditions similar to those already experienced during the reign of Richard II.

Shortly before this, James, heir to Robert III of Scotland, was captured whilst on his way to France. Robert died not long after his son's capture and Albany was named as governor. Albany's son, Murdoch of Fife, was also Henry's prisoner. To end a good year for Henry, Northumberland and Bardolf decided to again rebel. The winter of 1407–8 was called the winter of *"The Great Frost and Ice"*. It was the severest weather for over 100 years lasting from December to March and England and most of Europe was covered in a blanket of snow. The Earls had returned to Scotland to gather the disaffected Percy retainers for an invasion. Whilst Henry and Langley were travelling from London Sir Thomas Rokeby, the Sheriff of Yorkshire, defeated the rebels near Tadcaster at Bramham Moor on February 19th. Henry stayed at

Langley's manor at Wheel Hall (3); Langley stayed nearby at another of his residences, the manor house of Howden. Northumberland and Bardolf were both killed, and their bodies were quartered and beheaded. A number of churchmen had joined the rebels: the Abbot of Halesowen was hung, the Prior of Hexham was tried for treason (to be later pardoned), and Bishop Bifort of Bangor was imprisoned in Windsor. The only member of the council with the King was again Langley. Other members of the council joined the King when he moved to Pontefract. Langley remained in Yorkshire during May, mainly at Northallerton which lay at the centre of the lands owned by the rebels. From here he moved to Durham before returning to London in October. His pacification of Yorkshire caused him to absent himself from the Convocation of York which had been convened to discuss the Schism and the invitation to the Council to be held at Pisa (4).

The Prince of Wales had been making good progress in Wales retaking all the castles that Glyn Dwr had captured. By the end of 1409, Harlech had fallen and Glyn Dwr passed into folklore. The Lancastrian's "luck" had changed, Henry could now play a more prominent part in European politics, and it was no coincidence that Langley was moved from his post as Chancellor to what was in effect the position of Foreign Secretary. The policy aims towards France were simple: play one faction off against the other to create as much internal unrest as possible.

His close personal contacts with the London merchants would have had a bearing on his appointment. The loans that he was able to extract show that he had their confidence, and the loans were made with the express hope that once conditions on the borders were stabilised, the crown and its ministers would devote all their energies towards the European mainland. In particular, the merchants were looking to see the implementation of policies that would lead to a resumption in trade with Flanders and Gascony. The loans would not have been as forthcoming as they were if the lenders had not received assurances that every effort would be made to achieve this aim; everything had a price, especially support for the government. The same was true in the Middle Ages as it is today. Langley's involvement produced benefits of a financial nature as well as the beginning of a dialogue aimed at re-asserting England's position in Europe. Short-term pain for long-term gain, the doctrine of Keynes, but 450 years before Keynes formed his theories.

The only cloud on the horizon was Lollardy, Chancellor Arundel became the main prosecutor of the followers of Wyclif's doctrine. The overriding aim of all foreign policy was to create a benign relationship with the European heads of state and Rome towards Henry's Kingship, so that his son could ascend the throne as the legitimate heir, recognised by the majority.

Diplomacy

Langley was in his diocese during the summer of 1407, and he attended the opening of the Parliament held at Gloucester on the 24th of October. He was the first-named of the triers of petitions from Gascony **(5)**, a sign that he was concerning himself with issues that affected the merchants; hence the increase in loans from the London merchants. Langley remained in Gloucester where he headed the English delegation that met the French embassy. The two parties met in December. This was part of an ongoing process that had begun the previous year. A marriage between the Prince of Wales and one of the daughters of Charles VI was one of the topics discussed. On December the 7th, a truce in Gascony was agreed to allow more time for further discussions. The truce was to last from the 15th January to the 15th April to enable negotiations to be conducted in a less hostile atmosphere **(6)**. This suspension of hostilities was needed to enable the English to continue their separate discussions with the two warring factions in France, the Armagnacs and the Burgundians. The French desperately needed a truce in Gascony, as the murder two weeks before of Louis of Orleans had thrown the French monarchy into confusion.

The area covered by the truce was considerably larger than that contained in any previous treaties. The English preamble to the commission also contains references to the great schism. It was Langley's view that an agreement with France was essential to English participation in the reunification process. The reason for stating this was to remind the French that England could align itself with Germany if France did not modify its position both to English territorial claims and the Papal situation. Langley was deeply suspicious of the French position regarding the Papacy, his feelings being that the French would look to national self interest **(7)**. Langley spent Christmas in Durham before returning to London in late January 1408. Northumberland's rebellion (see above) took him to Yorkshire where he remained whilst an embassy from France was received at Pontefract. Langley did not personally meet with the ambassadors; he sent his spiritual chancellor, Richard Holme to act on his behalf **(8)**. Langley was aware that the French clergy had threatened to withdraw their obedience from the Pope in Avignon if a reunification had not occurred before the 24th of May. By not meeting the ambassadors, Langley was exerting pressure on the French. The French monarchy could not afford a split with the French clergy as the country's internal problems had left Charles in a precarious position and Langley was reminding them of this fact. By assuming a position of tacit support for the French clergy, coupled with the negotiations with the Burgundians and the

Armagnacs, Langley was isolating the monarchy whilst seeking to move into a position to influence the outcome of events in France. The absence of England's chief negotiator was a better ploy than to attend and harangue the ambassadors.

Both parties agreed to a further extension to the truce to run to the 30th of September, well after the date of the French clergy's ultimatum. It is entirely likely that Langley sent messages of support to the French church, via the clergy that were part of the embassy. Langley the spin doctor had turned his skills to the diplomatic field. The length of the truce, six months, would allow Henry to sound out the Lords regarding mounting an expedition to France to assist one of the two main protagonists, and would give Langley time to prepare the Commons. In this, Langley was working with the Prince of Wales and the Beauforts. Before returning to London Langley visited the Rector of Swinsehead, Thomas, Lord de la Ware, he acted as proctor for the Lord at Westminster. This connection was to lead to the founding of the Collegiate Church of Manchester in May 1421, the church later becoming the Cathedral of Manchester.

Langley was back in London by the end of October. In November, the Archbishop of Bordeaux, Cardinal Uguccione, visited Henry to urge England's participation at the forthcoming general council due to be held in Pisa on the 25th March 1409. He had already visited the French court. His speech convinced the court that England should have a presence and another Convocation was held in York in December. Langley was chosen to represent the northern provinces at Pisa. He was given the power of attorney for fourteen Bishops and one hundred and three Abbots and priors **(9)**. This appointment caused complications in the political negotiations with France. Henry and Langley had met with a delegation from France in November and they had agreed to send an embassy to Paris for a meeting to be held on the 3rd February. The timing of the delegations visit overlapped the visit of Cardinal Uguccione, the French Clergy had carried out their threat to withdraw their obedience to Avignon. The points for discussion at the scheduled meeting contained an agreement that a further truce was to be negotiated and also the possibility of a marriage alliance.

Clearly, Langley's support of the French clergy had paid political dividends. This was the first time that a marriage alliance had been openly noted; the French had steadfastly stood out against this. England's decision to attend Pisa, and to send Langley, ensured that it was the English who continued to set the political agenda. The schism was being used to further England's political objectives.

Henry suffered another bout of illness in January which delayed Langley's departure, an envoy being sent to Paris to explain Langley's delay **(10)**. It was not until the 20th of March that Henry decided to send Langley to Pisa **(11)**. He left at the end of March arriving in Pisa on the 7th of May, two weeks after the English delegation that was led by the Bishop of Salisbury, Robert Hallam. Langley travelled in some style, and he obtained a licence to export £1,000 **(12)**. Such a large sum indicates the entourage that he took with him. One chronicler described him as *viri magnifici* **(13)**, whilst another commented that on his departure to Pisa he was accompanied, *cum magno apparatu* **(14)**. Langley had stopped briefly in Paris. Jean Gerson, *the Proposivio facta coram Anglivis*, stated that he was glad that the churchmen of the two countries were united in their purpose to heal the schism. Langley's interest was purely political, Hallam and Richard Ullerston had recently written a treatise entitled, *"Petitiones quoad reformationem ecclesie militantis"*, which was aimed at the reformation of the church. These two, together with Henry Chichele, Bishop of St. David's, took the lead in the proceedings. The rival Popes were deposed and, on the 26th June, Alexander V was elected. Baldassare Cossa was to succeed him, taking the title John XXIII. The deposed Popes, Gregory XII and Benedict XIII, together with their followers, refused to accept the moral authority of the new Pope. Little is known of Langley's activities at Pisa, but he was given the honour of celebrating mass before the council on June the 13th **(15)**. A clue to Langley's work behind the scenes can be seen by the granting of power to him to collate a number of benefices in his gift, the grant being made on July the 7th. On July the 18th **(16)** he was granted five other faculties. Whilst the awards held no monetary value they provided Langley with positions that he could use to patronise those he wished to promote.

He used his ecclesiastical powers of patronage to repay the debts he owed to the Radcliffe's. George was appointed a member of his diocesan council and John was appointed to the office of treasurer of the Episcopal household. Langley had also granted John a dispensation for his illegitimacy. William Radcliffe was given the prebend of Auckland **(17)**. It seems likely that the award were made as a recognition of Langley's role in the election of Alexander. The Pisan council ended on the 7th August and he was back in London by the17th of October when Alexander was formally recognised by Henry. He returned to Durham until February the 12th 1410, when he attended the first parliament of the year. He remained in London until June the 19th, staying at Durham House.

Whilst he had been away, the Prince of Wales's party had succeeded in having Thomas Beaufort appointed as Chancellor. The Prince was appointed Captain of Calais and Warden of the cinque ports and Constable of Dover.

Clearly, the Prince saw his future linked to English fortunes in France. The struggle for control of the King's council had begun. On the 2nd of May the members of the King's council were named as; the Prince, Langley, the Bishops of Winchester (Henry Beaufort), Bath and Wells and the Earls of Arundel and Westmorland (married to Joan Beaufort), and Lord Burnell, a close friend of the Prince. On the 9th of May, the Prince informed parliament that Langley and Westmorland had asked to be excused from attendance. He cited the duties in the north as the reason, and Chichele and Warwick were appointed to replace them **(18)**.

The reason for Langley's absence can be found in one of the first petitions before the parliament. The petition referred to the need to achieve *"bone et substantial gouvernace"* **(19)**; this was a clear reference to the feeling in the Commons that those with responsibilities for guarding England's borders were not fulfilling this role. The Commons were in no mood to grant further increases in taxation to fund the defence of the borders, and the general feeling was that the major benefactors of the confiscation of the border lands of the rebels should financially assist in the cost of the defences. The fact that Langley spent his time in his Palatinate conducting a thorough visitation indicates that Langley has some sympathy with these views. He was always finely attuned to the underlying mood of the Commons. Langley's attendance during the year was sporadic; he was present in June and from the 20th to the 26th of October. The council moved in November to Leicester where Henry was staying. He returned to Durham until March the 9th, 1411, when he was present at a meeting of the Great Council **(20)**. After this, he again returned to Durham until September the 20th when he was again back in London. During this time he did not draw his councillor's salary; he was one of the least regular attendees of the council during this period.

There has been a considerable amount written about the role of the Prince and the Beaufort's in the King's council. Langley's absence has been interpreted as a sign that he was not enamoured of the Prince's move to control the council **(21)**. His time was spent touring his Bishopric, the internal strife in France coupled with Albany's regency in Scotland having created a calmer climate in the border country. Langely was able to administer his Palatinate free from the constant raiding that had riven the area since 1399. Another factor was the political conditions in France where civil war had broken out, and by setting his Palatinate in order, Langley was ensuring that he would be able to spend more time in London free from any distractions. He was close to the Beauforts and the rest of the council, and had he or the King been concerned that the new council would embark on a new direction in policy, Langley would not have left London.

The Prince's pacification of Wales meant that a new role had to be found for him. His taking a more prominent role in the governance of the country was a sensible move. Henry and the Prince wished to ensure that the Prince was universally accepted as the legitimate heir. By bringing him into the centre of governance, Henry was in effect allowing him to learn the art of administration. There was a greater pluralism prevalent in the crown's relationship with the Commons, mainly due to the crown's shortage of money. Positioning the Prince at the centre of government was a sensible move, considering the King's health, allowing him to become acquainted on a daily basis with the mechanics of the commons was part of the grooming process. Much has also been made regarding the Prince's relationship with his father at this time. Had Henry been overly concerned with his son and his adherents, he would hardly have allowed his closest councillor, Langley, to absent himself. Langley had been with the King all through the severe bout of ill-health that afflicted him in January 1409 **(22)**, and he was also with him at Leicester in 1410. Had he had any misgivings, Langley would have been aware of them. Henry had arrested six knights in October one of whom was the steward of the Prince's household, but no charges were specified.

On June the 6th, 1411, Pope John XXIII created fourteen cardinals including Hallam and Langley **(23)**. He had created them to bolster his position against the two rival parties. Henry declined the honours **(24)** on behalf of Langley and Hallam, the two being too valuable as councillors to allow them to take up permanent residence in Rome. Also, with the church still not united Henry had to maintain a reserved position regarding aligning himself too closely to one Pope. Conditions in France still necessitated the need to be able to court the French clergy as well as to maintain the support of Germany. Storey has passed the opinion that Henry wrote to the Pope refusing the honours without consulting either of the recipients **(25)**. Given the closeness and service that the two had given, I find it difficult to believe that Henry would have taken such a decision without consulting them. Given Langley's deep loyalty to the House of Lancaster, it is likely that he would have preferred to remain in England. In the case of Hallum, his treatise on the reform of the church, written two years before, showed his concerns with the threat of Lollardy to the fabric of the church, something he had stressed at Pisa. He, too, would not have welcomed a permanent position at Rome. Henry would not have risked offending these two staunch allies by not observing the courtesy of consulting them. As a footnote, Langley was never addressed as Cardinal during his lifetime, it was only after his death that people referred to him as Cardinal. There is no record of him ever having worn the red hat.

During this year there had been a number of diplomatic manoeuvres taking place between England and the two rival parties in France. John the Fearless had offered his daughter Anne in marriage to the Prince; this offer was made directly to the King, indicating who really held the reins of power. Langley's recent dealings with the French would have meant that Henry would have consulted him. Another indication of Langley's intentions is that on the 1st of September he appointed a vicar-general, citing the reason as his having to attend the King in Westminster who had committed much business to him **(26)**. This proves that whilst Langley was in the north he was still being kept informed of events by the King.

This business was the expeditionary force of 1,000 men led by the Earl of Arundel that had been despatched by the Prince to aid the Burgundians. The expeditionary forces had a number of successes, and they entered Paris accompanied by 3,000 Parisians on the 22nd of October. The Armagnacs countered this by sending a new embassy, in February 1412, Langley headed the delegation that met them in his London house. They offered to fully restore all of Aquitaine to Henry and to put at his disposal their sons and daughters to marry Englishmen, as well as offering the castles and treasure in the Duchy. The terms were finally agreed at Bourges and were ratified at Westminster by representatives of the Armagnac Duke's and by Henry's four sons **(27)**. Langley had played a prominent part in the drafting. A leaked copy of the document found its way into the hands of John the Fearless who read it before the court of Charles VI on the 6th of April. This brought about an intensification of the civil until Charles called on both parties to renounce their allegiances to England. Charles unfurled the Oriflame, France's symbol of Nationalism, the ethos surrounding the banner worked; on the 22nd of July all the protagonists renounced. A shaky reunification was under way, the loss of both partners being not as big a blow as it may at first appear.

England could now portray itself as the aggrieved party, because to the English public this represented a rebuff by two factions who had reneged on agreements made in good faith. Langley was to use this as part of the arguments when he looked to finance the invasion three years later. Langley again showed himself to be able to manipulate adverse events to the benefit of the crown. Each party had good reasons for leaking the document, Henry because he supported the Armagnacs, the Prince to force the French monarchy to offer better terms than they previously had, and the Burgundians because they felt that they were being out-manoeuvred. The force that had been gathered to assist the Armagnacs still sailed under the command of Thomas, Duke of Clarence. They enjoyed a good success capturing a number of towns before the French offered to buy them off with 150,000 crowns,

100,000 of which had to be paid before the 30th November. The French missed the deadline and the sum was increased to 210,00 crowns. One lesson that was learnt from the expedition was that whilst those who took part gained personally in financial terms, English territorial interests did not benefit.

Langley was in London by the 9th of November, 1411, for the first sitting of the new parliament. The King was still ill and remained at Windsor allowing the Chancellor, Sir Thomas Beaufort, to open the proceedings. Langley was again named as a councillor, the only change coming on the 5th of January when Archbishop Arundel was named as the new Chancellor. A further incident that has excited a large volume of literature concerns the replacement of those councillors perceived to be the Prince's men by councillors favourable to Henry. I doubt that the Prince and the Beauforts ever seriously expected Henry to abdicate. The Lancastrian ethos was to perpetuate the dynasty. This required a smooth transition of power and an abdication would have resurrected the old divisions amongst the Lords. It is more probable that the friction between the two was due to the differences of opinion on the situation in France.

Henry favoured the Armagnacs who could offer the security of Gascony which would bring greater revenues to the country through the wine trade. The Prince favoured the Burgundians who could offer security for Calais through which English wool could be exported to Flanders. A further advantage in supporting the Burgundians was that England would be able to exert pressure on Burgundy (through Flemish dependency on English wool) to respect England's claim to Aquitaine. Despite the uneasy truce in France, both protagonists continued to make overtures to the English crown. The most positive effect of the French alliance was that it united Henry and his son against the French as a nation.

Langley and the Prince of Wales

Henry of Monmouth had from an early age his own set of advisors and courtiers. He was thirteen years old when he was invested as Prince of Wales. By the age of twenty three he had pacified the Principality. He had accomplished this in the face of adversity, French aid to Glyn Dwr and the Percy rebellions having proved a baptism of fire. He was sixteen years old when he fought at the battle of Shrewsbury. Most of the correspondence from Henry to his son was sent through Langley's office, and the Prince's constant shortage of money to finance the Welsh campaign had brought the two into close contact. Henry's career is notable for his loyalty to those who supported him. He will have been well aware of Langley's devotion to the House of Lancaster from his early days in his grandfather's household. As Gaunt's executor, Langley was responsible for administering Gaunt's bequests to his grandson. The Prince took an active part in all aspects of governance, and someone with Langley's experience would be highly valued by the Prince. Langley's ruthlessness in suppressing the rebellions of the early years mirrored the Prince's attitude to the Welsh rebels.

The Prince had served as a regular member of the King's Council since December 1406. He was particularly close to his step-family the Beauforts, all of whom were close to Langley, particularly Henry who attended at Langley's ordination. Langley in effect acted as a conduit between father and son. This became apparent in the last years of the reign. Henry's dismissal of his son from the council in November was a matter of the King's pride being slighted by the way that the French envoys stated that they were empowered to negotiate with the King and the Prince. Clearly, the French were trying to highlight the divisions in policy between father and son. By removing the Prince, Henry was taking the prudent step of closing this avenue. Burgundy's disavowal of the agreements reached the year before were perceived in the Commons as a rebuff to the Prince and the policies he was pursuing, which were diametrically opposed to those of his father. On his return to England, Thomas was created Duke of Clarence, a further sign that the Prince had been out manoeuvred by his father. The clearest sign that Langley was especially close to the Prince came at the end of June, 1412. Langley had returned to London from Durham on May the 10th for the reconvened parliament. The Prince had been forced to issue a letter stating his loyalty to his father whilst he was in Coventry, the letter being issued to refute the rumours being spread that the Prince was gathering his armed retainers about him to challenge the authority of the King **(28)**.

Within two weeks Henry, *"with much people of Lords and gentles, in numbers such as has not been in those days"* **(29)**, arrived in London, where he stayed at Durham House. The Prince was clearly concerned with the pernicious rumours that were being circulated. The king's health was again failing, and he had nothing to gain and everything to lose by using force. The fact that he chose to stay at Langley's house, somewhere he had often stayed in the past, exemplifies the position of respect and trust Langley held not only at court but in the minds of father and son. This also indicates that the Prince was in regular contact with Langley. His depth of experience was respected by both, and he was the ideal person to bring about a reconciliation between father and son. All the other members of the council were in the capital. Both father and son had their supporters amongst the councillors, but it appears that only Langley was perceived as being above the two cliques. Both cliques had their own personal agendas, Langley having an eye to the future, particularly with events in France, and being also aware of the King's failing health.

There was a good deal of anger in the country regarding the handling of policy towards France. There had been correspondence between the King and Sigismund, Emperor Elect of the Romans. Langley would have urged restraint. Sigismund was concerned that England was backing both sides which was hampering the negotiations to heal the schism. The reconciliation took place on July the 8th at Westminster. Henry had been at the Priory of St. John in Clerkenwell from where he moved to the Bishop's Palace at St. Paul's, and became practically a neighbour of his son. John Stow writing a hundred years later, but basing his account on the Earl of Ormonde's observations, stated that the King was *"greenouslie diseased"*. The Prince demanded that those who had slandered his name should be punished. Henry replied that the matter could wait. This was enough to placate the Prince and the two were reconciled. It would have been evident to the Prince that Henry was fatally ill, but he could afford to put matters on hold. There are some very colourful stories of the reconciliation from the chroniclers, most seeming to be flights of fancy in the language that they use to describe the meeting between father and son. Henry was rarely seen in public, his illness having reduced him to the state that he was carried in a litter into the meeting with his son, Langley being by his side on a daily basis. It is far more probable that whilst the Prince was with Langley, the Bishop had voiced his thoughts on the impending demise of the King.

Henry tended to stay in residences that were adjacent to the Thames to allow him to travel by Royal barge between Westminster and the Royal Palaces. He moved to Rotherhide in the summer, whilst Langley travelled to Middleton, the place of his birth where the rebuilding of the parish church of St. Leonard's had been completed. The Bishop of Coventry and Lichfield, John Bourghill, granted a licence to Langley to consecrate the church on the 22nd August 1412 **(30)**. The consecration took place during September, this being the first time that he had visited the place of his birth since his enthronement as Bishop of Durham. There is only one other record of his being in the vicinity and that is between the 8th and 10th of August 1421 when he was in Manchester. His departure for Thetford and Cambridge in his early teens meant that he did not develop any deep-seated attachment to his place of birth. It is unclear how long Langley stayed in Middleton, but he was back in London by October the 13th. This was the day after the chroniclers wrote that *"Upon the twelfth day of October, were three flouds in the*

Thames, the one following up on the other and no ebbing betweene: which thing no man then living could remember the like to be seen". Durham House was close by the Thames and the area around his house would have been like a swamp for days. The filth and the smell would have been appalling. He visited Richard Whittington on the 21st of October at Merton as the crown's finances were again under pressure. The troops in Wales had not been paid and the Calais garrison's finances were in a perilous state. Richard Whittington lent the crown £1,000.

1413

Henry IV spent Christmas at Eltham where he summoned the Prince to join him. He was concerned that his sons were showing signs of friction to each other. From January onwards Henry's health deteriorated rapidly, and the chroniclers reported some fanciful tales concerning the Prince's conduct during his father's slide into death. All cannot be taken seriously and I cannot give credence to any of them, being fourth-hand accounts written many years after the event. Henry kept close to the Thames, staying at Lambeth twice, and at Greenwich. He visited Parliament twice in February before collapsing. He died in the Jerusalem Chamber in Westminster Abbey on the 20th March, St. Cuthbert's day. The Saint patronised by his father, the Saint venerated at Durham where he was buried, and the Saint commemorated some years later by Langley in the window at York Minster. He was forty-six years old, and the constant strains and tensions that accompanied his reign had taken their toll. He had ruled for 13 years 5 months and 21 days. He was buried in Canterbury Cathedral. Langley and his confessor, John Tille, had been with him constantly since the 3rd of February.

Langley was named as one of the king's executors, a duty that he had performed for Henry's father. The king died heavily in debt; the executors had to ask parliament to grant the sum of 25,000 marks so that they could settle his debts. Archbishop Arundel was to die nine months later. Of the triumvirate who did more than anyone to establish the Lancastrian dynasty on the throne, only Langley was left alive. Henry's death would have been a personal loss to Langley, the two having been friends for thirty-two years. Each had benefited from the association, each owed the other their position, and each had sustained the other through the most trying of times. Above all they had remained faithful to each other, and considering the strains that their relationship had to undergo, it speaks volumes for the pair that they never quarrelled. Langley would have felt a genuine sadness at his close friend's death. Their greatest achievement for the house of Lancaster was that they were able to pass on a reasonably peaceful kingdom to a legitimate heir. One who was universally recognised as the anointed heir, a legitimate King, with no enemies of strength to threaten the perpetuation of the Lancastrian dynasty. They had achieved what they had set out to do, the price being the premature death of Henry of Derby born in Bolingbroke.

The greatest long term benefit for the country was to be that the two had ushered in a more pluralistic government and a more accountable monarchy. Whilst it cannot be argued that this was born out of necessity, it is worth noting that Henry had, through Langley's advice and guidance, accommodated these changes with a public good grace. A less pragmatic ruler would have dug his heals in; the debt to these two should not be under-estimated. His place at the fulcrum of Henry V's government shows that this was recognised. It would not be unreasonable to say that had it not been for the efforts of the pair, the bloodshed that followed Richard II's deposition would have been worse than it was. Henry left an England in a greater state of peace than it was at the start of his reign.

Notes and References

(1) Gower, J. (ed) Macauly, G, C. "The Complete Works of John Gower" m(4 vols., Oxford, 1899–1902), vol. iii, p 344.

(2) Warrants for Issues, 23/264.

(3) Rot Parl. iii, pp 608–9; Storey, R. L, "Thomas Langley and the Bishopric of Durham 1407–1437", (London 1961), p 23.

(4) Reg. nos. 91 and 95.

(5) Wylie, J. H, "History of England under Henry IV", (4 vols, London, 1884–98), vol. iv, p 297.

(6) Foedra, viii, pp 484–5, 499, 504–9.

(7) Foedra, viii, p 504, "Au fin que mieulx puissons entendre a l'apaisement du Schisme qi est en L'Esglise".

(8) Foedra, viii, pp 513–19.

(9) Mansi, J. D. (ed), Sacrorum Conciliorum Collectio, xxvii, cols 348–50, (Florence and Venice, 1759–98).

(10) Warrants for Issues, 24/236 and 298; Foedra, viii, p 571.

(11) Chancery Warrants, 1362/44.

(12) C. C. R. 1409–1413, p 444.

(13) St. Albans Chronicle, p 81.

(14) Eulogium, iii, p 414.

(15) "Thome Trotati Manuale Concilii Pisan", fo. 64 v, (Vatican Library).

(16) C. L. P. vi, pp 151–2, 154–5; Reg nos. 139, 213–21.

(17) Reg. no. 220 and 272.

(18) Rot. Parl. iii, pp 632 and 634.

(19) Rotuli Parliamentorum, iii, pp 474 and 624.

(20) P. P. C. ii, pp 6–7.
(21) Storey, R. L, "Thomas Langley and the Bishopric of Durham, 1406–1437", (London 1961), pp 27–28.
(22) Nicholas, N. H. (ed), "Testamenta Vetusta", vol. i, pp 17–18 (1826); C. C. R. 1405–1409, p 498.
(23) Cristofori, F. "Storia dei Cardinali di Santa Roman Chiesa", p 268, (Rome, 1888); Ciaconi. "Vita et Res Gesta Pontificum et S. R. E. Cardinalium", vol. iii, col. 803, (1677).
(24) British Museum: Harley M S. 431, fo, 1.
(25) Storey, R. L, "Thomas Langley and the Bishopric of Durham", 1406–1437, (London, 1961), p 29.
(26) Reg. no. 226.
(27) Galbraith, V. H. (ed), "The St. Albans Chronicle 1406–1420", (London 1937)
(28) Galbraith, V, H. (ed), "St. Albans Chronicle, 1406–1420", (London 1937), pp 65–7.
(29) Galbraith, V, H. (ed), "The St. Albans Chronicle, 1406–1420, (London 1937), p 67.
(30) Reg no. 276.

HENRY V

I have no spur
To prick the sides of my intent, but only
Vaulting ambition (1).

Prologue, Pre-Agincourt

The principal problem for the historian studying the reign of Henry V is not the lack of information but the fact that there is almost too much material available. Ever since Shakespeare embroidered a section of Henry's life as a paean of praise written at a time when the nationalism of the Tudor reign was at its peak, historians have been blinded by the victory of Agincourt. The drama of the Bard's prose conveyed a mood of a victory given to a King who was the epitome of Kingship, St. George in a living being. His death at an early age has merely added to the mystique surrounding his rule. The imagery was again used in 1943 when Lawrence Olivier directed and starred in the film adaptation of Shakespeare's play. This mystique the ethos of Kingship, was created by Langley who employed all his considerable political talents to perpetuate this myth.

Four further books are ready for publication. They have been written as a factual story; it is my attempt to dramatise the events in a way Shakespeare would have done had he been able. The fact that he had to blur the more questionable events in Henry's reign was due to the cult-following Hal had amongst the Tudors. A consequence of this has been that the focus for studies on this period have almost entirely been on Henry with little work being done on the civil service behind the King.

This is a generalisation; certainly the work of G. L. Harriss, Christopher Allmand (who has written the definitive biography of the King), Maurice Keen and the late K. B. McFarlane, are honourable exceptions. Much of what follows has been gleaned from their books and papers. Whilst all the aforementioned have commented on Langley's role in affairs none have written exclusively about him. This section is dedicated to them, being my way of thanking them for the help their work has been. The last word has to go to the late K. B. McFarlane, who said of Henry that he was he was perhaps "the greatest King ever to sit on the throne of England". The conditions that created this "greatness" were brought about and maintained by Langley without whom, particularly during his Chancellorship and also thanks to his Ambassadorial visits to France, was able to bring about the perception in the country that France was the enemy. He "spun" the propaganda to the extent that in the end the Commons and the populace of England were totally united in their support of their King. Just as the reign of Henry V has been portrayed as a golden age in England's history, so to it was the golden period of Langley's life.

Henry's rule is often referred to as the highest example of Kingship. If this be true, and it is a not unreasonable view, then the period could also be described as the pinnacle of Langley's political career. He raised to a new height the arts of governance and diplomacy. Under him, the civil service took up the position that it has maintained to this day, the department developed into an indispensable tool of governance. The age of the career civil servant whose profession enabled those who entered into the service to wield a power that became indispensable to any ruler, whether they be a monarchy or an elected government. Service became an honourable career with rich rewards, consensual government becoming independent from the factions that had been based on the patronage of the Lords. It became a tool to be used solely by the elected Commons and the King, a more sophisticated form of government, virtually an art form, a refining of the way the country came to be administered.

When one studies this period it is easy to become drawn into abstracts; by this I mean that the student of the period reads of the results of the various meetings and embassies without taking cognisance of the fact that those involved actually spoke to each other. We, unfortunately, do not have a full transcript of what was said. Nor do we have any report of the body language that was adopted. We have descriptions of the splendour and size of the envoys and their escorts, what we lack is the detail of the nuances of language. The minutia of the cut and thrust of debate.

For example were friendships made? Did private discussions take place between the opposing diplomats away from the debating chamber? The detail that would be of the greatest use would be a record of precisely what each of the diplomats said to each other regarding the relevant positions that they were taking on behalf of their masters. If you like, the gossip that one can only glean from memoirs. What we are left with are bias comments from chroniclers often written many years after the events, and frequently second or third hand. (see the following section under the sub-heading *the Tennis Balls, A Public Relations Coup?*). We do not know how long each session lasted. We know that the ambassadors were entertained by tournaments, much the same as taking high ranking foreign officials to the cup final. They did not sit next to each other in silence, we are only able to analyse what may have been said by scrutinising the events that ensued from the negotiations. There were no news briefings, no agreed communiqués. Such is the art of the historian, to put flesh on the bones, to breath life into the characters that we are writing about. Did the French find Langley's Lancashire accent difficult to understand? How did they actually view Langley? Did they find him cold and evasive or friendly and open? On a personal level was he liked or disliked? We shall never know. We can only deduce.

We are told that there was a disagreement as to which language to debate in with the English ambassadors stating that they did not speak French; Latin was the chosen language. I find it difficult to imagine that neither Langley or Courtney could speak French, was this merely stated to irritate the French? What did those who escorted do whilst the discussions were taking place? Did they go sightseeing?

The great expansion in education brought about by the increased wealth of the merchant classes ushered in a more pluralistic society. Into the two-tier class system, the Lords and others, was inserted a new class, a middle class. The system of patronage shifted from land to commercialism, and trade became an honourable endeavour until it came to rival service in the armed forces or the church. The control of education began to shift from the church to the mercantile classes. People of all classes had new horizons to look to, and the strength of community came into being. The beneficiaries of this were the Commons and democracy; a type of medieval socialism was born.

Many decades would pass before the old order was supplanted, but the seeds and shoots were sown and grew in the second decade of the fifteenth century.

The basis of religious belief was questioned and although it was ruthlessly suppressed it did not die out completely. What follows is an extract from a lecture given by the author in November, 1998, in the town of Langley's birth, Middleton, situated in what was once Lancashire but is now Greater Manchester:-

"The centralisation of the machinery of government gathered pace. The custom of the lawcourts, chancery and privy seal, was to live together in Inns or hostels kept by a senior clerk and situated in the area now known as Chancery Lane, where the Inns of Chancery used to be and the Inns of Court still are. In the Inns, as in the academic halls of Oxford and Cambridge, the juniors were apprenticed to the professionals. This gave a good deal of power by way of patronage to the professional administrators. The Chancery functioned from Westminster Hall with the status of a separate court. The Chancery clerks were another closed corporation, headed by a Master of the Rolls and eleven other clerks or cursitors. Chancery was a world of its own, and its clerks were not yet civilians. They had some grounding in Roman procedures and in matters of civil law; they were advised by doctors of civil law. During the reign of Henry V there were to be only two Chancellors, Henry Beaufort and Langley.

The Council had already acted with a good deal of autonomy during the illness that afflicted Henry IV during his later years. An inner core had met on a daily basis in the Star Chamber, and this office was and did act as a complete government. Attendance was flexible but the indispensable core in 1413–15 consisted of the Chancellor Beaufort, the Treasurer Arundel, the keeper of the Privy Seal, John Prophet, and two ministers without Portfolio, Dr. Henry Chichele and Langley. Henry V's almost continual absence abroad meant that they acted semi-independently but were cognisant of the King's will.

Policy of Expansion

The prime consideration in Henry's decision to commence hostilities with France lay in his perceived need to legitimise his Kingship. As has been seen in the later part of this century when there is criticism at home regarding the governance of the country, mobilisation for war acts as a unifying catalyst. To an extent, his father's illness and death did jar at his consciousness in that the popular belief that the illness was God's retribution for his having usurped the throne did play on his mind. His view that a successful campaign would assuage this feeling was one of the motivating factors in his pursuit of hostilities. The actual campaign is well documented. What has not been explored is Langley's role in the process that led to the slaughter of Agincourt and the effective bankruptcy of France which ensued. One of the first issues that the crown had to consider was the strength of France. In particular, which of her neighbours would come to her aid? Flanders was far too dependent on the supply of English wool, Germany being more concerned with the schism and being in the process of soliciting English support. An embassy was sent to the King of Castile to remind him of the alliance made between Henry III and Alphonso, and their heirs. At home they clearly had the support of the Lords whose raison d'être was that they existed to wage war. This upper caste of the kingdom had inbred in them the belief that they and only they could wage war and raise levies on behalf of the King; commerce and trade could be left to the merchants. The management of their estates and land holdings was left to their staff. They existed for one purpose only: to engage in armed conflict for profit.

The critical issue for Henry and his ministers was the management of Parliament whose members would naturally seek to maximise the benefits by extracting as many concessions as they could reasonably expect. To this end he was reliant on what we would nowadays call his "fixers", the principal of whom was Langley. The King had to portray himself as the injured party who was making reasonable claims against France. The fulcrum upon which the King's ambitions lay was Langley, who above all others was privy to the King's private thoughts and had the necessary diplomatic skills that would be needed.

At this juncture I would like to pose a question that I feel is salient in assessing Langley's role in the reign of Henry V. Who is the more responsible for the loss of life and the carnage that accompanies warfare? It is the actual soldier who commits the act of killing or the person who provides the wherewithal through the financing of the machinery of warfare? Who is the most culpable? Is it the King aided and abetted by the Lords and Barons, or is it the Government Ministers who organise the country and channel its gross domestic profit towards meeting the cost of conflict, thereby providing the tools of killing?

For over a hundred years England and France had been at loggerheads over the English claim to territories they viewed as theirs by historic right. The English claim to the Lands in France was based on the Treaty of Brétigny which had been concluded in 1360. England sought three things: restoration of the lands that were ceded in the aforementioned Treaty, the payment of the outstanding money due from the ransom of King John II, and the possible marriage of Henry to Katherine the daughter of Charles VI. In August 1413, John, Duke of Burgundy, was expelled from Paris which left a weak central government in the hands of the Armagnacs. The usual form of military activity was the chavaunche, the aim of which was to spread as much havoc as possible thus demoralising the enemy and the populace.

The Holy oil of St. Thomas had been allegedly given to Thomas Becket by the Virgin Mary who had appeared to Becket as he was at prayer in Canterbury Cathedral. Just where this legend was created is open to debate. It is clear however that in his father's reign, the councillors around the King, and particularly the churchmen, gave an additional sacredness to the legend to attempt to legitimise the usurpation. The implication was that anyone duly anointed by this oil was blessed not only by St. Thomas but also by the Virgin Mary (2). The chronicle of Adam of Usk sardonically says *"That same rotting did the anointing at his coronation protend; for there ensued such a growth of lice, especially on his head, that he neither grew hair, nor could he have his head uncovered for months"*. In other words there was a good deal of scepticism surrounding the sanctity supposedly associated with the oil. In spite of the cynicism of the chroniclers, to the common man the anointment with the sacred oil struck a deep chord of religious resonance, and the symbolism of the unction was respected and believed. The fact that great play was made of the legend exemplifies this. It will not surprise you to know that the French had a similar unction which they claimed was nine hundred years older. Nevertheless a good deal of propaganda was given to its use at Henry V's coronation held on the 9th of April 1413, Passion Sunday. He now ruled over two million people. Coupled with the "spin" on the sanctity of the oil was a legend that the Virgin had told Becket when he was given the oil that the Kings who were anointed with the unction would recover Normandy and Aquitaine. Both Richard II and Henry IV had been anointed by the oil, but this legend was not proclaimed then. Langley being the spin-doctor, it is clear that the decision to promulgate this legend was taken prior to Henry's coronation.

Of all the members of the council Langley had been closest to Henry IV during his last days. He above all had been privy to the dying King's last thoughts and wishes. Immediately after his father's death Henry would have been closeted with the council, principally so that they could agree the policies that were to be pursued and the methods needed to achieve their aims. The legend of the holy oil was employed to signify that Henry was the chosen blessed instrument of god, whose sanction for the conquest of England's territories in France was contained in the oil. Even God and religion were pressed into service by Langley, the *de facto* Foreign Secretary of the council Yet again Langley was putting the House of Lancaster before the Church.

Within three days, Henry had received the oaths of allegiance from the nobility, something unprecedented but also vital. Langley will have noted with some satisfaction that the nobility had quickly associated itself with the new King. There was a general feeling of expectation in the air having a properly anointed King, the fact that he was the son of a usurper being ignored by all but the French''

The King's Council

The inner core of personnel at the centre of government, the back room staff, numbered circa 200. The key individual in regards of the preparation for war was Nicholas Merbury, the master of the ordnance. It was remarked by the chroniclers that the expedition that sailed in 1415 was extremely well equipped. Sir William Hankford was appointed the Chief Justice, and Henry Beaufort was given the office of Chancellor. Both he and Langley after him had Simon Gaunstede as Master of the Rolls at the head of their staff, with eleven clerks under which were a number of junior clerks known as cursitors and apprentices. They worked exclusively in Latin, which they developed into groupings with a set formula. Both were advised by Ralph Greenhurst, a doctor of civil law who was Henry's notary in the chancery office. The Earl of Warwick was the hereditary chamberlain of the exchequer, and he appointed William Kynwolmerch as under-treasurer. Henry Somer continued as head of this department. This department underwent a great expansion during Henry's reign. The area that recruited additional staff was the department of foreign audit, this reflecting the expansion of mercantile trade.

The City of London was to lend over £32,000 towards the war effort. This was only superseded by the church who, through a levy lent, £44,243. The office of Privy Seal increasingly dealt with foreign correspondence. Langley and Henry Beaufort controlled this department, particularly in the early years of the reign when it was constantly engaged in diplomacy. The chancellor of Florence, Coluccio Saluati, opined that a good letter of diplomacy was worth a thousand troop of horse. Robert Frye acted as secretary to the council which met daily, usually in the Star Chamber in Westminster. The lists of the King's servants and ministers is extensive, the largest common-denominator being that the significant majority had served in either the Duchy of Lancaster household or with the Prince in Wales. It is important to remember that Henry was still the Duke of Lancaster when he came to the throne. They were a close-knit group who acted as executors for each other. The chancellor of the Duchy of Lancaster, John Springthorpe, left Langley a belt in his will. Langley, Henry Chichele and Hugh Mortimer were to become the supervisors of Henry's will. (See Allmand, chp 16, for a full list of the household).

Langley was in the capital until August when he went to the convocation of York. It was during this time that a two-pronged diplomatic initiative was commenced. He was again noted as a trier of petitions in the first parliament (3). He returned briefly to his diocese during September and October before returning to London on the 11th of November.

France and Preparations for War

English policy towards France centred on the terms outlined in *A Policy of Expansion.* One thing is clear during the flurry of embassies that passed between the countries, that whilst the envoys were, on the face of it, sincere in their negotiations, England was preparing for war. This brings into question the probity of the ambassadors. It is possible that Henry was openly preparing for war as a way of exerting additional pressure on the French. This theory tends to ignore the fact that the expectation of the Lords was that war *was* to be waged, something that they regarded as their raison d'être. The majority of the heads of the main lordships were occupied by young men who had not tasted warfare, and they were eager to earn their spurs. War as an expression of national identity. To have settled matters through diplomatic channels would have disappointed the Lords and could have weakened their backing for Henry. It is also highly likely that the council's assessment was that an agreement with the French would never be reached. In Henry Beaufort's opening address to parliament, the medieval equivalent of today's Queen's Speech, he stressed that *"bone governance"* would be Henry's aim, the maintenance of the laws, assistance to foreign allies and resistance to enemies. As today, every facet of governance was covered. Note that the plural "allies" was used, as was the other plural "enemies", this enabling the ambassadors to treat with both parties in France as a matter of stated policy.

The juxta-position of this was not lost on the French. When John, Duke of Burgundy was exiled from Paris, discussions were instigated to seal an alliance with the Burgundians. The negotiators were named as Henry Chichele and the Earl of Warwick, Richard Beauchamp. They were also instructed to treat with the French to secure a truce. This was agreed at Leulinghem on the 23rd September 1413 and was renewed in January 1414. It was extended twice during the middle of the year (4). Whilst this was going on, Langley was treating with envoys of Charles VI for the marriage of Henry to Katherine. The meetings took place in Durham House, and at the end of January, Henry agreed to marry no one other than Katherine, this agreement to run until the 1st of May. Langley ensured that the views of the English negotiators became public. It was announced that the discussions were favourable, this was Langley's way of applying pressure for further concessions from the Burgundians.

Negotiations had also been taking place with Brittany which concluded with a truce that was to last for ten years. Henry needed Brittany's neutrality to enable his ships to ply their trade free from the threat the sailors of Brittany could provide. A further embassy was treating with the Emperor Elect Sigismund, and they were seeking to enter into a league of alliance. At the same time, Langley met with ambassadors from the Duke of Burgundy in Leicester in mid-May. They discussed the possibility of Henry marrying the Duke's daughter, this despite the promise to Charles VI. As a background to this, envoys had been sent to the court of Aragon to discuss the possibility of Henry marrying the Aragonese Princess. Every diplomatic strategy was being used to maintain the pressure on the French government. All these diplomatic manoeuvrings were designed to detach and isolate France from her allies.

On the 31st of May, Henry formally announced the names of his ambassadors to visit France: they were Langley, Bishop Courtney, and the Earl of Salisbury **(5)**. They left London on the 10th of July and arrived in Paris on the 8th of August. They were entertained by the Duc de Berri, the embassy comprising five hundred men, a sign that Henry wished to impress the citizens of Paris. Charles, who was enduring one of his periodic bouts of insanity, and his council were absent from Paris and the talks never really achieved anything. The demands were increased, with suzerainty of Normandy, Touraine, Maine, Anjou and Aquitaine, and the payment of the outstanding balance of John's ransom being raised. This was linked to the marriage negotiations which would include a further large sum as a dowry. This suited Langley who was able to report to the King on the 3rd of October that the embassy had been unable to have any serious discourse due to Charles's absence **(6)**. The French were not to be trusted, Charles illness was never mentioned to the Commons.

From the French perspective they were equally mistrustful. In June, an embassy was also received from Burgundy its purpose being to discuss Henry's marriage to his daughter Katherine. Discussions also took place as to the amount of aid that the Burgundians would give if Henry invaded France, the decision to invade was now publicly known. The agreement to marry only Katherine, that had expired in May, was renewed on the 18th of June. Parliament met on the 3rd of November, and grants for war were applied for and were given. A caveat to the grant was that all avenues of negotiation had first to have been exhausted **(7)**. Langley had anticipated this, and he received a further commission from Henry dated on the same day when the Exchequer was authorised to make payments to Langley and Courtney to enable them to prepare a further embassy to France.

The mood of the Lords and the Commons can be judged by the number of subsidies that were granted to chancellors Beaufort and Langley during Henry's reign. When the war effort was at its height during the years 1414–1419, subsidies of eight and one third were granted, and these and other subsidies were collected quickly **(8)**. No restrictions were attached to the grants, a clear indication that the Commons were already assured that the money would be spent on the invasion. Hints were given that once English lands in France had been regained, the burden of taxation would be reduced. This was aimed at the merchants who were to make substantial loans to the crown.

Beaufort, in his opening address, had stated that Henry had firmly set his mind to recovering what was lawfully his and that his subjects must fight for justice, even if it meant that they must give their lives on behalf of the national cause. The aim was a country united behind its King, monarch and subjects as one with a common purpose. Langley and his fellow councillors were careful to stress that the King was only pursuing his legal rights to territories that were the crown's by historic rights, a judicial point that was being made to put Henry in a favourable light. The musters were issued, which meant that word spread across the country that war was imminent.

To maintain control over the discussions of so many embassies, whilst at the same time ensuring that they all followed a pre-determined policy objective, was difficult. The overall strategy was the council's. Henry, Beaufort, Langley and Courtney (the distinguished lawyer and former chancellor of Oxford), were the ones who co-ordinated the process. The outcome of each embassy had to be presented to the public through the Commons, the propaganda war being as important as the actual embassies themselves. The council publicly stated that Henry's claims to both his historic land and the French throne should be made a matter of public record; public opinion was being massaged. All the manoeuvrings culminated in one final embassy to Paris, headed by Langley, Courtney, and Thomas Beaufort; its clerks were Philip Morgan and Richard Home, the king's secretary. The formal commission was given to them on the 5th of December **(9)**. It left London on the 14th of December, but high seas delayed it at Southampton and they finally crossed from Dover, arriving in Paris sometime before the 24th of January. The ambassadors were accompanied by six hundred men.

Realising the seriousness of the situation Charles VI entertained them with lavish hospitality **(10)**. The negotiations proper did not open until 12th of March, when Langley and Courtney met with the Bishop of Noyet, Pierre Fresnal, Charles, the Count of Eu, Berri's chancellor, Boisratier, and Gulliame Martel, Lord of Bacqueville **(11)**.

In the interval between January and March, Langley and Courtney had been busying themselves comparing the rules of the order of the Celestines and the Benedictines at the request of Henry who was seriously considering founding a house for the Celestines at Sheen. There is a scurrilous story written by the French astrologer Fusoris which claimed that whilst Langley poured over the rules that governed the two orders, Courtney lounged in the garden of the house of the Celestines *"eating almonds"*. Fusoris claimed that Courtney owed him some money for some books on astrology that he had supplied. Given Courtney's orthodoxy I cannot give any credence to this account, it being far more likely that both Bishops were engaged on the investigation into the rules of the two orders. Henry did eventually install the Carthusians, one of the most austere orders, at Sheen.

The marriage was the chief topic of discussion. The English were willing to reduce the size of the dower to 1,000,000 crowns, on condition that Charles provided the trousseau, and also provided the Princess with jewels and clothes. The French pronounced themselves unwilling to concede to Henry's demands, but they did state that they were prepared to cede part of Aquitaine and were willing to pay a dower of 800,000 crowns, whereas they had initially offered 600,000 crowns. The most unacceptable part of the French offer concerned Aquitaine which they stated Henry had offered *"to leave his adversary with the greater portion of what he was entitled to in law"*.

This was a not unreasonable statement from the French point of view. The chief sticking point was that Henry also laid claim to the throne of France, his claim being based on a right of succession from his great-great-grandmother, the daughter of Philip IV, wife of Edward II. It was an extremely tenuous claim made chiefly to appeal to English public opinion, primogeniture governing his right of succession in France; and a good international lawyer would have demolished the proposition in a morning. This facet of the negotiations was designed to further antagonise the French. It was to lead to the split between Charles and his last surviving son Langley would have been in constant contact with Henry. The French too, through their diplomats at Henry's court, would have been aware of the mobilisation taking place across the country. The negotiations broke up when Courtney and Langley announced that they did not have sufficient authority from the King to accept, or reject, the concessions offered by the French. One does not send ambassadors as experienced as Langley and Courtney without giving them bargaining powers, a negotiating bottom-line. To the French it would appear that the only power that the ambassadors had was the power to only agree should Henry's demands be met in full.

Intransigence is hardly a basis for any negotiations, and the French would have been well aware that the embassy was merely window-dressing for the Commons. Langley and Courtney would have been well aware of the views which the French would form over this. It speaks much for their commitment to the cause that they agreed to head the embassy when they were so obviously hamstrung. I believe that this exemplifies the seriousness with which the inner circle of Henry's court treated the diplomacy taking place. Consider this from a neutral's point of view. Observed with the benefit of hindsight, the English position was bullish to the point of insulting. How could anyone treat with a party to a dispute that refused to negotiate on any terms other than those laid down by themselves? To be even-handed, the French had meddled in English internal politics during the period 1399–1406/7 when they had given to aid Glyn Dwr and also to the Scots. The climate between the countries had been frosty since 1350, and not for nothing did this period become known as The Hundred Years War. The last act of the ambassadors was to agree to the further extension of the truce that was due to expire on the 1st of May, and it was extended to the 8th of June.

The Tennis Balls, a Public Relations Coup?

On their return to England the ambassadors would have immediately reported in confidence to Henry and the inner council. They had achieved their purpose, no terms had been agreed and the concessions offered by the French had been unacceptable. Henry also needed to buy some time whilst he mobilised the country. Another critical factor was the timing of the diplomatic initiatives, these channels needing to be curtailed in enough time to allow Henry to mount an invasion before the end of the summer months of 1415. Adam of Usk is alone in stating that the ambassadors were greeted with derision on their return as they had achieved nought. Given the mood of the country, only the pacifists, clearly a silent minority, would have claimed this, and I can put no credence to Adam's claim. The ambassadors had to announce a report of the negotiations that left no doubt in anyone's mind that there would be no further point in continuing with the diplomatic approach.

Tellingly, Langley had been preparing draft letters to be sent to King Charles, his Secretary, and the Duc de Berri **(12)**. These were being written whilst the council deliberated over the ambassador's report. Clearly, Langley and the King were confident that the council members would concur with Langley's view that the time for meaningful diplomacy had passed; that is, if it ever existed in the first place. In the letters Langley, besides reiterating England's disappointment over the inconclusive negotiations, blamed the continuation of the Schism on the enmity that the French had caused. Yet again Langley had the broader picture in mind: The French Church would be pleased with this wording; they were still opposed to Charles's view, as would the Emperor whose principal concern was to remain the re-unification of the Papacy.

Part of England's strategy had been designed to goad the French into indiscretions. The story of the tennis balls could well have arisen out of French frustration if you consider the chronology of the literature that surrounds this event. In particular, was this the most famous pieces of P.R. ever foisted on the public of Medieval England? Shakespeare based his dramatic account of the French ambassadors delivering the casket containing tennis balls on a story written by John Streeche, approximately ten years after the event **(13)**. Streeche was a canon of Kenilworth who in his record of the times reports the arrogance of the French. It seems likely that he heard the story from someone who was present when the ambassadors reported publicly on their return from France.

Henry would have asked for Langley's views on the French demeanour and how they had viewed the court of the English king. Given the obvious exasperation that the French were feeling, it is not implausible that someone at the court of Charles VI voiced the opinion that Henry was inexperienced as a ruler and that he would do better to gain experience before embarking on a war with a ruler who had greater experience than he. It is also probable that a comment was passed that Henry would do better to look to his creature-comforts, by implication that he had too much of a juvenile disposition to present any threat to the might of France. Langley would then have reported that the view of the French was that Henry was a young inexperienced King who was inclined to indolence. The mistake in this view was that the French had overlooked the fact that Henry had already pacified Wales and at sixteen fought at the battle of Shrewsbury. One can imagine Langley reporting that the French viewed Henry as an inexperienced child when it came to matters of Kingship. Thanks to Chinese whispers and Shakespeare's gift for the dramatic, the legend of the tennis balls brought in by the French ambassadors found its way into the nation's conscience. The government's line was that the enemy thought England's King an amateur and that the only course open to Henry and his subjects was to correct this perception by mounting an invasion. Further, as has already been pointed out, the negotiating stance of

Langley and Courtney was hardly taken as a means of solving the dispute by diplomatic means, but it is doubtful that their intransigent attitude in Paris ever became public knowledge.

The Commons had to be left in no doubt that warfare was unavoidable. The fact that a later French embassy was not given a public hearing served to underline the point that Henry and the Council were still concerned that public opinion could waver should they discover the duplicity of the ambassadors in Paris. The control of news was as fundamental in the build-up to the invasion as it was to become in the twentieth century. Tellingly, the French historians make no mention of what would have been such a fundamental statement, had it been made. The chronicle of Walsingham also fails to mention the event. A ballad attributed to Lydgate in 1421 deals with the incident, but no first-hand account details what would have been a significant insult.

If the slur had been voiced and the balls delivered, Henry would very properly have broken off any further diplomatic negotiations; he did not. The writer of the Brut also embroidered the story, claiming that the tennis balls were placed in hard gun-stones and were used against the walls of Harfleur. The crux of the matter is that once the layers of propaganda are peeled back, what we are left with is that Langley, with the compliance of the King and Courtney, had hinted that the French were not taking England's claims or the threat of invasion seriously, and he compounded this by implying that in the eyes of Charles and his courtiers, Henry was a child when it came to the practice of Kingly values and negotiations. Courtney, as an experienced lawyer and theologian, had been chosen to lead the embassy with Langley so that he could counter any points of international law, a training that Langley did not possess. Langley was the diplomat with the experience of parliament that Courtney did not have, and they made a formidable pair. Any P. R. that emanated from the proceedings would have been part of Langley's remit, and Courtney would have reported on the legalities appertaining to Henry's claim and the points raised by the French negotiators. Finally, Langley was frequently in London during 1421-2, the year that Lydgate's work was in circulation. Langley was a keen collector of books judging from the number he left in his will and he would have certainly been familiar with the work. Like anyone who is mentioned in a book, the human weakness of vanity would have seen him perusing the pages which dealt with the events that he was involved with. There is no record of his having offered any criticism regarding Lydgate's work. As chancellor of England, had he voiced any critique it would have been recorded.

Were the negotiations being conducted seriously, with the aim of a peaceful resolution to the situation? If one traces the various ambassadorial manoeuvrings that were running in parallel the only conclusion one can reach is that a good deal of hypocrisy was being practised by Henry and his negotiators, chiefly by Langley. There is no record, other than the Commons statement that all avenues of diplomacy should be exhausted, of any dissenting voices being raised by any members of the council. The duplicity that was being practised by the negotiators indicates that they were in agreement with the King's policies. Langley could, if he had been opposed to Henry's invasions plans, have excused himself from his participation in matters. He could have pleaded that the responsibilities of his diocese required his presence in the north. If he had privately asked the King to be excused, Henry would have agreed. His willing participation in the events leading to the invasion show that he was in agreement with the policies. Do not forget that he had experienced the horrors of warfare when he attended the battle of Shrewsbury, and he was not blind to the carnage and misery that accompanied battle. Nor was he blind to the blood-letting that the vanquished suffered. How he reconciled this, as the third highest churchman in England, is difficult to understand.

The "spin" of a properly anointed Christian King recovering what was his in God's eyes, was the church's balm. The schism in the Papacy meant that Rome was unable to exert any influence. Arbitration did not play any part in the proceedings. To the medieval common man the tacit sanction of the church was fundamental to the endeavour of waging war, the image of the cross and the crusade having been burned deep in society. To die in the knowledge that one was making the ultimate sacrifice, sanctioned and sanctified by the English church, was fundamental. The propaganda that the country was subjected to was one-sided, the majority of it being promulgated from the pulpit, the battle for the soul of England being fought by a compliant church. The citing of the treaty of Brétigny (1360) brought with it the reminders of the two great battles that culminated in the signing of that treaty, Crécy (1346) and Poitiers (1356), something that was ingrained in the national psyche. The old nationalism quickly rose to the surface, and all strata of the English peoples did not take too much persuading to mobilise for war. The diplomacy that Langley was engaged in was a facade, a veil, a cloak of propriety, behind which Henry was manipulating the country. It was medieval P. R., "spin doctoring". It was as important in 1414–15, as it was in 1914, 1939, and as it is today; Langley was, throughout his life attuned to the zeitgeist.

Whilst Langley had been engaged in diplomatic exchanges, Henry had been dealing with a revolt of the Lollards, the leader of which, Sir John Oldcastle, had escaped from the tower. The Lollards hatched a bizarre plot to capture the King, but the revolt was only supported by 100 men and was quickly suppressed. Oldcastle finally met his death in 1417. The movement against the Lollards was led by Henry Chichele, archbishop of Canterbury, Robert Hallam and others. Although Langley is not noted in the literature of the times as being a leading figure in the churches suppression of this movement, it should be noted that there is very little mention of outbreaks of Lollardy in his diocese. The main point for consideration is that the outbreaks of Lollardy served to nudge Henry into underlining the orthodox churches blessing for the war.

Langley remained in London until the second week in May. During the month of April the great council met and appointed Bedford to the Lieutenancy of the realm. Langley, the Bishop of Winchester, the Archbishop of Canterbury and five other lords were named as the councillors to whom Bedford should seek advice whilst the King was abroad **(14).** Langley briefly visited his diocese before returning to London by the second week of June. During his absence from the capital the preparations for war were well advanced. The French sent another embassy which consisted of the archbishop of Bourges, the bishop of Lisieux, the count of Vendome, and Charles, Lord of Ivry. They were accompanied by a large retinue which reached London after Henry had left the capital on the 15th June. Langley accompanied him to Winchester where the French ambassadors caught up with the royal party. Henry, his brothers, Langley and Courtney met them at the bishop's residence at Wolvesey Palace so that they could not glean any intelligence regarding Henry's preparations. The discussions lasted from the 2nd to the 6th of July.

After addressing the King the ambassadors went into closed discussions with Langley and Courtney. As a background to this, men, arms and equipment were flooding into Southampton, Portsmouth and the New Forest. The discussions must have been strained, Langley knew that the invasion was now irreversible. The concessions offered by the French were considerable. The dowry of Katherine was increased to 850,000 crowns, although no firm date was given for bringing Katherine to England. The main demand by England for the return of the lands theirs by historical right was, in part, conceded. The claim to the throne of France was dismissed out of hand. As has previously been mentioned, the claim to the throne was spurious at best, and Boisratier retorted that he, Henry, had no right to the throne of England let alone the throne of France. A formal rejection of the terms offered by the

French was handed over and the embassy was informed that their departure would be delayed so that they could not take any intelligence regarding the size of the English army back to Charles VI. Ever mindful of the need for propaganda, copies of the Treaty of Bourges were made and sent to the general council of the church that was meeting at Constance; Sigismund and other European heads of state were also sent copies. The aim of this was to portray Henry as the wronged party who was now forced to resort to force of arms to recover what was legally and historically his. It is doubtful whether the document cut any ice with its recipients the point of the document being to legitimise Henry's claim in the eyes of the English people.

The stressing of the legality of the cause was fundamental to Henry, above all needing to prove to the public that as his cause was just, those taking part in the enterprise could be assured that God would uphold the integrity of the undertaking. I have dwelt at length on this episode in Langley's career for a number of reasons, not least because the diplomatic exchanges are well documented. I have also tried to be even-handed in my assessment of events. Had the positions been reversed, England would have taken up the same negotiating position as the French did. In the last exchange between the negotiators, Boisratier had touched a raw nerve when he stated that Henry had no proper right to the English throne. Henry's religious orthodoxy, bordering on the zealousness of the recent convert, was in part driven by the thought that his father's premature death was a visitation from God, a punishment for the usurpation and murder of Richard II. It seems to me that Boisratier had an eye to a wider public when he made his statement before the King and his courtiers. I believe that he had already come to the conclusion that the invasion of his country was inevitable. The French were trying to catch up in the propaganda war.

Does Langley come out of it with any credit? The answer is inevitably yes and no. It has to be borne in mind that he was a Political Bishop, not a Bishop Politic. As a member of the inner circle of the Great Council his duty was firstly to the King and secondly to the country represented by the Commons. His office as the third-highest ranking churchman in the land was clearly secondary; in his mind he may even have divorced one from the other, thus assuaging his conscience. Had he been a dispassionate observer of events he would have found it difficult to support all of England's claims. The other salient point is that whilst he was busily engaged in the diplomatic exchanges these were being undertaken against the background of the mobilisation for war that had been gathering pace. In reading this section I would ask you to put aside the fact that Langley was a member of the clergy. He was acting as a minister loyal to the crown, his Lancastrian affinity foremost in his mind.

Throughout history, government ministers have pursued policies that they privately did not agree with, and you only have to read any of the plethora of diaries published during the last twenty years by politicians of all parties to verify this. There is no record later in his life of Langley voicing any regret over the actions he took. I would offer the conclusion which has been frequently stated already in this book, that Langley's loyalty to the House of Lancaster took precedence over even his loyalty to God. This explains why he was so indispensable to the crown, and it also explains why he was to remain at the centre of government throughout the reign of Henry V. He was assiduous in his duties as Bishop of Durham, Storey rightly stresses this point. What this indicates is that he possessed a complex mind and that he masked his innermost personal feelings well. He was undoubtedly orthodox in, and faithful to, his religion. The mind of the clergy and the politician in the fifteenth century had to confront many issues that today are clearly divorced from the offices of the church. In medieval times it was not always possible to do so.

Witness archbishop Scrope's dilemma earlier: Langley took the opposite path, but who is to say which of the two was right? I do feel that Langley followed his conscience and that he was in agreement with the policies of the Lancastrian Kings he served. To this end his loyalty is to be commended and admired. Many of his fellow clergymen adopted the same stance as Langley: he was not unique, but he differs from others of the cloth in that his political career took precedence over his religion. Finally, it should be born in mind that in this age of technology with its access to instant news the opposite was the case in the middle ages; the majority of the population did not hear about events for many months and even years after they occurred: Also, the hold of the Church on the population's soul was virtually unassailable. Likewise, it was not possible for the majority of people to have first-hand accounts of the daily workings of government, nor was it possible for them to fully voice their concerns. The actual number of people who knew what precisely transpired in the negotiations during 1413–15 would be limited to the Lords, some of the Commons, (certainly not all members), and some of the civil servants based in London. I would offer the opinion that no more than 2,000 people out of a population of 2,000,000, less than one percent of the population, were fully aware of the whole picture. Contrast that with today, the age of the sound bite, and the internet.

Langley's role in events was clearly recognised by Henry, who, on the 24th of July, executed and sealed his will. The majority of the Duchy of Lancaster lands were granted to a group of feoffees, Langley being one of this number as well as his appointment as an executor. There is also an insight into

Langley's orthodoxy in religious matters: Henry bequeathed him a missal and a breviary, the most personal and intimate of gifts that a monarch could leave to one of his subjects **(15)**. It also indicates the personal closeness of Henry and Langley, a very public statement of the affection and standing Langley had in the eyes of the King.

From here the council accompanied the King to Porchester Castle and it was here that the Earl of March, whom Henry had freed from imprisonment the day before his coronation, told the King of the plot by Richard earl of Cambridge, Thomas Grey and Henry Lord Scrope, nephew of the ill-fated archbishop. Earl Richard was married to Maud Clifford, his second wife, and his brother-in-law, John Clifford, was married to Hotspur's daughter, Elizabeth. Part of the plan concerned the use of Hotspur's son Henry, who was being taken north to be exchanged for the sum of £10,000 and Murdoch the son of the Duke of Albany. Murdoch was taken from his guards as he was being taken through Yorkshire. The ring-leaders were rounded up and tried, the majority losing their lives. The Scots were defeated by Robert Umfraville, keeper of Roxburgh Castle.

The Southampton plot was the last attempt by the disaffected to depose Henry, they realised that once he landed on French soil they would find little backing in a country so firmly behind their King and his foreign policy. There have been many theories put forward as to the motivation of the plotters, one plausible view being that the conspirators had received financial help from France. The reason for including the event in this book is because immediately that Henry sailed, Langley returned north to ensure that the flames of rebellion had been extinguished. The head of Grey was sent to Newcastle-upon-Tyne to be publicly displayed. The plot had shown that the old enmities were still percolating below the surface.

The actual campaign that led to the battle of Agincourt is one of the most copiously written about events in English history. The campaign and the battle have no bearing on this book other than the effects that the campaign had on the political landscape in England. For anyone wishing to study the campaign a bibliography can be found at the end of this book. The point has previously been made that I am of the opinion that Langley, even though he was not actually in France during the campaign, had a culpability connected with the events. The best commentary ever written on the battle is ''The Face of Battle'' by John Keegan (Harmondsworth 1978). In his section on Agincourt he brilliantly dissects the battle and most importantly he sets in context just what the conditions of battle would have been for the medieval soldier. Medieval set-piece battles were coming to an end; the advent of artillery combined with the fact that the French had learnt, by bitter experience, that risking all on one set-piece confrontation was a high risk strategy were telling factors; the spilt blood of the French had taught them this.

There was no glory to Agincourt, this great misconception having its roots in the literature of romance and chivalry that was then in the process of undergoing a renaissance. The reality was that the battle was fought by a thoroughly dispirited and desperate group of men led by a King for whom failure would have spelt political catastrophe at home. The battle conditions were appalling, heavy rain having turned the field of battle into a morass of mud; a look at the television pictures of the Glastonbury Festival bears comparison. The indiscipline and over-confidence of the French led to an English victory, a victory that they should not have gained. A number of the French court came to detest the ambassadors that had brought this about almost as much as they hated the King and his army. Langley cannot be credited with any praise for his role in the events that culminated in a quagmire in Picardy on a cold September day.

Post-Agincourt

Langley had remained in his diocese until the November of 1415, a check against the Scots should they attempt to take advantage of the absence of the king and the majority of the fighting men of the country. After the pressure of the last years, Langley deserved a sabbatical.

Interregnum: A Division of Labour

Langley was now fifty-two years old, and he had served the grandfather, son, and grandson of the House of Lancaster. It has been remarked by writers of this period that Langley was dependable and indispensable, and to what degree is best exemplified by what follows. It is salient to assess and analyse the amount of time that Langley shared between his twin professions, as a servant of the crown and the third-highest churchman in England, in effect, his division of labour. In compiling this analysis I am deeply indebted to Dr. Storey who included in appendix A of his book **(16)** an itinerary of Langley's movements from his appointment as Bishop of Durham to his death. The following analysis is not intended to be definitive. I have initially divided the number of days that Langley was the incumbent of the see of Durham into two sections. One deals with the number of days that he spent in his diocese or at residences that were connected with his see, the other section deals with the number of days that he spent either in London or in other parts of the country when it is known that he was engaged on duties connected with his position as a member of the King's council. I have dealt with the time spent travelling by allocating this time to the work that Langley was engaged in prior to his departure to any given place.

I would also make the point that whilst Langley was in London, for example, he did not deal exclusively with governmental business, and vice-versa when he was in his diocese. His London residence was Durham House and he would have dealt with ecclesiastical matters on a daily basis; his vicars-general would have regularly reported to him. The following table is intended to be indicative of the number of days that he allotted to his dual roles. Given the length of time that he spent in the service of government, greater than any other cleric of his age, this analysis is virtually unique. In total, from the date of his consecration on the 8th of August 1406 to his death on the 20th of November 1437, we are dealing with 11,375 days. It should be borne in mind that from 1430 when he was approximately sixty-seven years old, he had virtually retired from active service as a Minister of the crown. Remarkably, the number of days spent in the service of the crown, 5,705 days, is virtually matched by his time spent on diocesan duties, 5,670 days. I have allocated the time he spent at the council of Pisa, April to October 1409, to the ministerial total as it appears to me he spent his time there more as a politician than a cleric.

YEAR	CHURCH	POLITICS
1406		135
1407	104	261
1408	246	119
1409	39	326
1410	24	125
1411	20	163
1412	17	189
1413	13	226
1414	33	332
1415	114	251
1416	115	250
1417	181	184
1418	75	290
1419	—	365
1420	84	281
1421	107	259

YEAR	CHURCH	POLITICS
1422	52	313
1423	91	274
1424	206	159
1425	219	146
1426	134	231
1427	137	228
1428	302	63
1429	204	161
1430	341	24
1431	332	33
1432	272	93
1433	250	115
1434	289	76
1435	328	37
1436	365	—
1437	293	—
TOTAL	5,670	5,705

If the years 1430 to his death are removed from the calculations, then the number of days he spent on diocesan duties is *3,200 (37.50 %)* against *5,327 (62.50%)* in the service of the crown. Contrast this with the last seven years of his life when he spent *2,470 (86.9%)* days in his diocesan duties against *378 (13.1%)* days in crown service. Clearly it was only in the later years of his life did his spiritual life overtake his governmental career.

The number of miles that someone of his rank travelled is remarkable when one considers the inadequacy of the roads. As a rough guide, Langley travelled from the north to London, or vice-versa, eighty-one times from 1406–1437, an approximate mileage of 20,574. If one allows a percentage of 40% of this total for his perambulations between the capital and the various places that the council was meeting, or the journeys around his diocese, then this figure increases to 28,803 miles.

To qualify this, let us take Langley's movements from London during the year 1417. From Bishop Auckland he went via Howden to Huntingdon, then on to London, Mortlake, back to London, Reading, London again, Tichfield (which is near Portsmouth), Southwick, Lewes, Hastings, London, Guildford, Winchester, and finally back to London. This amount of travelling is typical in any given year, if, in his diocese he undertook the same number of journeys around the north. I have also added the length of the journeys he made abroad to produce a figure of 31,447 miles; this equates to 1,014 miles a year, a staggering accumulation, particularly as he did very little travelling in the last three years of his life. Because of this, I have calculated his average yearly mileage from 1406 to 1434. On average he made the journey between the north and London two-and-a-half times a year. Langley always travelled with a considerable retinue, both as Chancellor and Bishop; he had a staff of over 200 connected to his diocese. I would estimate that they would cover approximately 18 miles a day, obviously dependent upon the weather. The English army covered 16 miles a day before the battle of Agincourt and Langley's progress would have been comparable. On this basis he would have spent somewhere in the region of 56 days of each year on the road. Particularly during his tenures as Chancellor, a number of his household servants would have travelled in advance of the main party. This would have been to ensure that the places chosen for the nightly stop-overs were prepared. His retinue would number not less than fifty persons and frequently more.

The speed of his progress could be greatly increased if events dictated. He travelled from London to Nottingham in 1403 in three days, an average of 40 miles per day. This serves to underline the caution I have attached to claiming these figures as definitive. This is why I must underline that these are an approximation, although I do feel that they are fairly accurate. Again, I would recommend anyone who is interested in this facet of his life to consult the itinerary in Dr. Storey's book. It is also worth remarking that in the years of the increased diplomatic negotiations, 1413–1415, a total of *558* days (*76.9%*) were spent in the service of Henry V against *172* days (*23.1%*) in his diocesan duties, virtually a ratio of 3:1.

As I have stressed, these calculations are not completely definitive. What they do serve to underline is my contention that throughout the greater part of his life, from the age of 43 to 67, his time was predominantly spent as a civil servant first and a cleric second. If you also add to this his service to Gaunt and Henry IV, prior to his consecration, (he was 18 when he entered Gaunt's service, and 43 when he became a Bishop), the overwhelming amount of his time was spent in the service of the House of Lancaster. During the years 1381 to 1406 when he was firstly a clerk in Gaunt's household, then Keeper of the King's Signet and then Privy Seal, something like 90% of his time was spent as a civil servant. These stark figures and percentages serve to explain the eminence that he was held in by the Lancastrians and they also show the standing he enjoyed in the eyes of the Commons and on the wider European stage. His entire adult life was spent in service to one master or the other. This points to a life of austerity and total dedication, unmatched by his contemporaries and peers, and until Thomas More, unmatched on a percentage basis. He gave 56 years of unbroken service to Gaunt and his sons, and if one were to argue that his time at Thetford and Cambridge was by dint of the educational training that he was receiving, then the years spent in service increases to around 62 years.

He outlasted all those, both lay and spiritual whose careers commenced in the 1380's, and many more who came into service after this decade. To achieve this with never a fall from grace puts into context the remarkable abilities of the man, his humble origins only adding a lustre to his life and career. I hope that you will forgive me for reiterating my remarks in the introduction that his life and career have been overlooked. I trust that this commentary on his perambulations has given an insight to the dedication of the civil servant in the Middle Ages.

Euphoria and Finance

The battle of Agincourt was fought on Friday the 25th October, news of the victory not reaching London until the following Tuesday the 29th. Langley was on his way to London when he heard the news, and he arrived in the capital by the 8th of November. Henry arrived at Eltham on the 23rd of November accompanied by the most valuable of the prisoners. The victory parade went via St. Paul's to Westminster, and the chronicles carry colourful descriptions of the pageantry that spread across London. Agincourt, whilst being a significant set-piece victory, did not carry the financial benefits one might expect. Certainly a number of the French nobility were either captured or killed, but in terms of territorial gains the campaign did not yield the dividends that the financial expenditure warranted. The delay at Harfleur had proved costly, and in terms of expansion all Henry had gained from the campaign was a foothold on the coast of France.

The Duc of Burgundy had not been present at Agincourt and France was still able to put a considerable army into the field if it were needed. All the major cities between Harfleur and Paris were well defended and could only be taken by a prolonged campaign of siege warfare. A bridgehead had been formed, but Parliament and the merchants would have to be approached to fund a further campaign to build on the achievements of 1415; the euphoric climate in the country would have to be utilized. The chief beneficiary of the campaign was the ethos of Henry's Kingship, the emphasis on God's assistance in the victory being foremost in the propaganda that was issued by the court. In the minds of Henry and Langley also would have been the fact that they could now portray Henry as the legitimate King, blessed through victory by God, and the usurpation was pushed into the deepest recesses of the shadows.

Langley had three jobs in the coming new year: he had to obtain further loans from the London Merchants, deal with the diplomacy which came after Agincourt, and had to arrange for the ransoming of the prisoners. He returned briefly to the north before attending the opening of the February Parliament. Beaufort opened the parliament with the words *"He* (the King) *hath opened for you a way"*, clearly indicating that the war was to be pursued. Langley was able to conclude the negotiations with the Scots, and Albany's son Murdoch was exchanged for Henry Percy. He was immediately restored to his father's lands and was also appointed the warden of the east March and the Scottish borders **(17).** Was this through the behest of the chief English negotiator, Langley, being an act of atonement for his hand in the death of Percy's father? A conciliatory gesture.

The constable of France, Charles d'Albert, had been killed at Agincourt and Bernard d'Armagnac was appointed to replace him; he was bitterly opposed to Burgundy, and this continuation of the split at the French court suited the English. Diplomatically England's policy was to continue treating with both sides whilst at the same time pursuing further alliances with other European heads of state to isolate the French monarchy. England's first task was to strengthen Harfleur, the only tangible gain from the campaign of 1415. The skirmishing around Harfleur was prolonged and intense, it culminating in the battle of Valmont, a battle Dorset was lucky to win. Again, the victory was cited as proof of God's continued support.

Chancellor Beaufort and Langley were to use this as a way of extracting further finance from a compliant Commons and the London Merchants. Beaufort's opening address to the commons stressed the righteousness of Henry's cause by emphasising that the victory had been given to a King who had placed his trust in God; Langley was again named as a member of the council.

During the first days of May, the Emperor Elect Sigismund accompanied by an entourage numbering 1,000 and including the French ambassador, the archbishop of Rheims, arrived in England. He had previously been at the court of Charles VI where he endeavoured to broker a settlement between the two countries. He found the French divided and not amenable to his overtures which they felt were too biased towards England. He was lodged at Westminster in considerable state. His first proposal was that Harfleur should pass into his control whilst peace negotiations commenced; neither Charles or Henry were in favour of this suggestion. By June the French had sent the archbishop of Bourges to continue with the negotiations. Langley reported to

Henry that the French were trying to delay matters to allow their mainland forces to continue the siege of Harfleur.

During Sigimund's stay he was made a Knight of the Garter and was given a gold SS Lancastrian collar, further propaganda. William, count of Holland and the brother-in-law of John of Burgundy, came to London at the end of May; he was also the father-in-law of John the second in line to the French throne. He joined in the discussions with the French but soon concurred with Langley's view. The crown issued letters to the sheriffs announcing that the discussions had broken off due to the lack of intent of the French ambassadors. Again Langley was ensuring that the propaganda machine continued to emphasise that the French still could not be trusted.

Henry was busy with the preparation of the mainly naval force which was to take supplies to Harfleur. He left his brother John Duke of Bedford in charge while he continued his discussions with Sigismund who was now lodged at Leeds Castle. Langley broke off the negotiations with the French and briefly returned to his diocese before joining the King and Sigismund at Sandwich on the 4th of September. From here they moved, via Rye, to Canterbury where they were told of the sea victory of Bedford and his fleet against the mainly Genoese-manned French ships. The battle had been fought on the feast day of the Virgin's Assumption, and English propaganda again cited this as further proof that God was steadfast in his support for the King whose cause was just. On the day of the battle Henry and Sigismund sealed the treaty that Langley and the Emperor's advisers had drafted. It was a Treaty of Perpetual Alliance, its most significant clause stating that both would recognise the other's rights to pursue their claims to lands in France. The lavish hospitality and its cost were rewarded, another coup for Langley who had been able to portray the French in the unfavourable light that persuaded Sigismund to align himself with Henry

When the Emperor returned to Constance, the French Cardinals were mortified to see the way that Sigismund publicly aligned himself with the English delegation, wearing the SS Lancastrian collar at all times, this being further isolation for the French, and the Anglo-Imperial alliance was working. The truces with Burgundy had been regularly renewed and on the 1st of October Sigismund signed a guarantee of safe conduct for the Duke. Langley crossed to Calais with the royal party where, on the 3rd of October, they met with the Burgundians. The Duke recognised Henry's right to the throne of France, however the document is considered to have been drafted by the English **(18)**. This is underlined by an ambiguous clause in the document whereby Burgundy pledged to support Henry save and except against the King of France or his son. In other words Burgundy had inserted a get-out clause. The discussions that had led to this agreement had been conducted in secrecy. Various interpretations can be put to this clause. If it appeared that Henry in the future captured enough of France to be deemed in control of the country, did this then mean that Burgundy would recognise Henry as King? I believe that this clause was viewed by Langley as being double edged in that should John side with Charles VI then Henry could again point to the duplicity of the French, which could then be used in further propaganda. This seems the most likely explanation for this curious clause. John sent no aid to Henry when called upon to do so in 1417.

Langley returned to the north after the November parliament had appointed him, on the 8th of December, to a commission to negotiate the release of their King with the Scots. His true purpose in returning north was to visit Pontefract where the Duc de Bourbon and the Sier de Gaucecourt were held.

1417

One of the strands of policy that Henry and Langley were tentatively pursuing was the coercion of the leading French nobles who had been captured in 1415. This policy was being investigated by Langley alone, and there is no record of Henry having discussed this initiative with any other members of the council. The aim was to appeal to the nobility to act as emissaries to Charles VI; Henry and Langley hoped to detach Charles from his ministers and courtiers. Langley hoped to pursued the captives that the only way to censure a lasting peace between the two nations was for Charles to recognise Henry as his heir. Part of the argument concerned the two rival factions, the Burgundians and the Armagnacs. Langley was putting forward the view that whilst these two continued to allow the enmity between them to divide the country, coupled with the inability of a weak crown unable to exert any sustainable control from the centre, France would remain riven with virtual civil war. This was not an unreasonable point of view, the majority of the captives having no love for the Burgundians who had failed to come to their aid in 1415. This policy contained one major weakness: it ignored the claims of the two remaining French Princes, John and Charles; Louis, reputedly an alcoholic, had died on the 18th December 1415 aged nineteen. Little wonder that the French court was so inept, with a drunken heir and a periodically insane King.

Secret Diplomacy

The driving force behind this policy was finance, as a long campaign of siege warfare would be expensive and difficult to sustain. Henry was about to have, thanks to Langley, agreements with two of the leading groups in France which could be used in two ways. Either they would be honoured or Langley's propaganda machine could use them to illustrate to the country and Sigismund the duplicity of the French. Langley first sought the written obligations of Bourbon, the duke of Orleans, Boucicaut the Marshall of France, and Gaucecourt, guaranteeing that they would return; he was also given a bond by the captives **(19)**. One thing concerned the Frenchmen: they requested that their change of allegiance be kept secret so that they would not suffer in France. Langley explained this to Henry in a report dated the 18th January at Pontefract **(20)**: *"This same Monday at nyght, with Goddes grace, I shal mete my lord of Westmerland as York, and abide al Tyseday to solicite the chevance that ye have commanded us. And from thennes atte first I go to Durenward, with youre gracious leve, to sumwhat ordeyn for my litell and symple governance ... remembered the said Duc of Bourbon that he write to yow with his awen hand how he contynuth his willie and entent in the matire secret"*.

The captives had signed an agreement that said that if they were unable to pursued Charles to recognise Henry as heir, then they would support Henry as King of France; little wonder they asked for secrecy! On the 25th of January, Henry wrote to his envoy with Sigismund, John Tiptoft, *("so that all Christendom should know of the injuries that the duplicity of the French had inflicted on him"* **(21)** *"and Tiptoft, ye should understand that the lands had been named by him (Bourbon) also, much as is comprehended within the Great Peace, in the form as they therein be comprehended; and Harfleur with as much of Normandy that lieth next to it as I will agree me; ...* that Bourbon had agreed to terms which were, *"reasonable and great ... But Tiptoft ye shall pray my Brother that I wol not leve my voyage for any Tretee that they make, with Godds Grace; for sekirly, with his Mercy, I shall not fail"*.

This letter indicates that the King already had the signed agreement to hand. The other members of the council were unaware of this document or the forthcoming initiative. Only Gaucecourt made the journey to France, and he reported that the Armagnacs were more entrenched than ever.

Langley spent the first four months of the year in the north, the Chancellor, Bishop Beaufort having indicated to his step-nephew that he wished to go on a pilgrimage to Jerusalem. Langley was attending to matters in his diocese before returning to London where he was to spend the greater part of the next four years. During this time the Convocation held at York between the 5th and 12th of January had voted through a whole tenth, and Langley had acted as a member of the council and not as a churchman at this convocation. Coupled with a similar vote taken at the Canterbury Convocation in

November the previous year, Henry received £136,000 from the church in England. Langley was back in London by the end of March where he attended a Council meeting that was assessing the state of readiness of the forthcoming expedition to France; his talents in extracting loans was needed! Also an embassy was to meet with the Armagnacs at Alencon. A letter from the council, probably drafted by Langley, began by rehearsing all the diplomatic manoeuvrings before insisting that any peace had to be lasting and on England's terms; intransigence was now openly stated due to the success of Agincourt, and public opinion was such that this entrenched position found acceptance.

Langley was continually in the company of the King at Mortlake, Reading and finally Southampton. Beaufort would not have decided to go on pilgrimage on a whim, this would have been discussed with the King. He had only got as far as Ulm when Henry sent word that he was to attend the council at Constance which was reaching its final stages. The position of Chancellor was the fulcrum upon which the ability to pursue the campaign in France rested. On the 23rd of July whilst he was at Southwick near Portsmouth the King appointed Langley to the Chancellorship for the second time, and Bedford was appointed Lieutenant of England. Henry finally sailed for France at the head of an army that numbered around 10,000 men, transported by 1,500 ships.

Langley's next spell at the Chancery was to be totally different to his previous tenure. Henry V was fully conversant with the mechanics of governance, and despite spending the next three years in France he still judiciously sent copious letters under the privy seal to both Langley and Bedford regarding all manner of issues. Henry's successes in France assuaged the Commons concerns regarding the cost of war, and although there were still criticisms regarding the cost, they did not prove detrimental to the campaigns. The diplomatic issues were now handled directly by Henry in France, freeing Langley to deal with the twin tasks of Chancellor and Bishop. The correspondence from the King to Langley is copious and shows that Henry was kept well informed about political matters whilst he was abroad. Over 75% of the existing correspondence from Henry was to Langley.

The Second Chancellorship

It is clear from the terms of reference that Henry gave to Bedford and Langley that it was his intention to keep a tight grip on the reins of power whilst he was abroad. Bedford was told that he was the military keeper of the realm and he could summon parliaments and consult with the Lords and

Commons. He was also allowed to grant elections for capitular bodies, although significantly Henry alone retained the right to appointments in the church. He could accept fealty but the acceptance of homage was reserved for the king only. He did not have the authority of the King in parliament and he had no discretion to grant petitions. The most telling restriction was that in all things connected with the governance of the country, Bedford had to have the assent of the council "and not otherwise" (21). Bedford's military duties frequently kept him away from the council, but Langley presided and was also the most regular attendee. On one occasion only he and the deputy-treasurer William Kynowlmersh (22) were present. There were fifteen meetings of the council between 1418 and 1421, Langley attending them all, the next most regular attendee being the Archbishop of Canterbury who attended on five occasions.

So complete was Henry's position in the country that it is reasonable to say that he was able to direct the entire populace and the finances available to the crown towards his pursuit of his foreign policy aims. The nationalism that broke out after Agincourt, coupled with the advent of new trading opportunities that the merchant class felt were imminent, enabled Langley to channel the nation's wealth towards its foreign objectives. With every fresh success that Henry enjoyed in France, so the Lancastrian dynasty became embodied in a spirit of nationhood that had not been experienced in living memory. Taxation to sustain a weak monarchy was never as easy to impose as a tax yield gathered to sustain and enhance a successful monarch. The greater powers that the Commons had enjoyed under Henry IV receded as England became the premier military power in Europe. The capture of swathes of territory in Normandy enabled Henry to exercise a power of patronage that had not been available to the crown in his father's lifetime. This patronage proved to be double edged during the next two decades; those who became the recipients of the crown's largesse bequeathed to their families inheritances that were to drain the resources of their English lands. Nationalistic fervour over-rode any measured analysis. Henry had delivered what the two previous Kings had not: additional territories that were, in the English psyche, the nation's by historic right.

Henry was conducting a campaign of siege warfare the consequences of which were the high cost of rebuilding the towns and cities devastated by the English army. Any additional revenue that the crown could extract from the conquered lands had to be spent on refortification. The devastation that the Normandy countryside suffered effect had a significant on the economy of the Duchy. The cheavanche was an accepted part of warfare. Its premise was that by devastating the land, the towns and cities would capitulate, and this worked in part, but the major centres, Rouen, Falaise and Caen, were well fortified. Consequently, the conquered territories could not support the army and supplies had to be constantly sent from England. Requests for re-supply occupied a large part of Langley's time. He was now also acting as a quarter-master general.

The expense of rebuilding was compounded by the drop in revenues from the agrarian receipts. This was caused by the inclement weather that the Normandy agriculturists had to endure during the years 1418–21. Taxation levels on a variety of goods were higher in France than they were in England. Luxury goods such as salt, gold and cloth bore the brunt of the increases. This was a sensible policy in that the taxation increases affected the wealthy more than the poor.

Despite this, the Commons were wary of granting taxes without stipulating the use to which any new tax could be applied. Only in the first parliament after the Battle of Agincourt was no restriction placed on the way the additional subsidies were to be spent. In all, eighty percent of the subsidies granted by parliament between 1414 and 1419 were spent directly on sustaining the war in France. The principal source of finance was still the private loan. In 1421 Henry received a loan of £17,666 from Beaufort to bolster his income of £55,700 from various sources ranging from custom's duties to shire revenues; 50% of this income came from wool.

Langley was by far the busiest of the crown's ministers. Besides the normal duties of the Chancery, the propaganda regarding the war in France, supplies, and muster rolls were organised by Langley. Naval stores, the staffing of the royal offices in Calais, Guinne and Ireland also fell under his remit. Judicial matters were dealt with by various commissions who reported to Langley. The maintenance of the seas was one of the prime concerns and Langley ordered the seizure of a number of ships, principally Breton and Dutch ships which were taken as compensation for the losses that the English Merchants were suffering due to acts of piracy. Borrowing by the crown during the years 1413–22 reached a peak that was to decline by 17% during the next reign. Langley was Chancellor, *de facto* Prime Minister, Master of the Rolls, and Quarter-Master General.

During the seven years of his occupation of the office of Chancellor, he spent 499 days in his diocese and 2,189 days on crown business. This equates to 22.83% of his time allocated to his spiritual duties against 77.17% of his time spent on temporal duties. As an average, this represents 312 days a year on crown duty, 86.20% of the year. An impressive figure when one considers that the see of Durham was one of the largest in the country with palatinate powers that involved the office-holder in work that was outside that of a purely spiritual nature. The mechanics of the see of Durham are not the concern of this book but I would ask you to take cognisance of these duties when considering the workload that Langley had.

The repayment of loans was usually guaranteed by the crown pledging future revenues against specific loans. For example, a London merchant could be assigned the income from the port and customs duties of Hull. At the appointed date the lender would redeem his wooden tally to the relevant official. This system worked so long as the crown's revenues were not exceeded by the number of tallies due. If the revenues were not available then the creditor would seek to have the debt enrolled by the chancery and redirected to an area where money *was* available. A snap-shot of the crowns finances can be taken by comparing the amount of assigned loans against the actual cash available to satisfy the promissory notes (**23**). During Henry IV's reign the actual cash available as a percentage basis is 29.6% against assignments of 51.1 %. During the years 1413 to 1422 the percentage of cash available to repay loans rose to 54.8% against a lower level of assignments at 31.7%, this affording a good insight into the prudence with which Langley conducted the business of Chancery. This stability helped to induce a climate of benevolence from the financiers to the crown; the knock-on effect was that it became easier for the crown to raise loans which in time enabled Henry to expand the crown's revenues through conquest.

There is evidence from two years, 1415 and 1421, that Henry asked for a statement of the expected income from both fiscal policy and the Royal estates: the yearly spending revue. This type of request shows Henry in the light of a ruler who was fully conversant with all aspects of governance. To someone of Langley's experience to work with a King who understood all aspects of the nation's finances would be a relief. The suppliers to a campaign and the men who were to fight expected payment in advance, which meant that a war-chest had to be built up. The sum of £60,000, rising to £80,000 per year, was collected by Langley from the lay and clerical subsidies (**24**).

In the parliament of 1417 the tax on exports was substantially increased, and so Langley then offered to forego these additional moneys if the foreign merchants would be generous with the loans that they had been induced to lend to the crown. I doubt if parliament realised that this was Langley's purpose when they granted the increase. Langley and Beaufort had on previous occasions threatened the foreign bankers with imprisonment if they refused to lend towards the Agincourt campaign. One cannot but admire the political adroitness of the Chancellor, and little wonder is it that Langley remained as Henry's Chancellor throughout his reign.

Also in 1417 a high number of loans were raised, 286 in all, totalling £31,595. This money was badly needed, the total expenditure for the years 1416/17 amounting to £256,885, 15 shillings and 10 pence; this was set against an income of £216,868,9 shillings and 10 pence, a deficit of £40,000, and hence the need for loans. The largest loans came from Beaufort £14,000, Whittington £1,333,6 shillings and 8 pence, £1,860 from the City of London, and 1,000 marks from the City of Bristol. Further loans were raised which by the 29th of September totalled £34,146,17 shillings and 7 pence; there was a good deal of arm-twisting needed to extract these large sums. The ransoms due from the prisoners captured at Agincourt were used as either pledges or they were sold at a discount rate; the mortgage system of its day. During this period there was a shortage of bullion for minting. The main source, Bohemia, was being ravaged by the religious wars that were to grip the country for the rest of the century. This problem affected *all* the Western European countries.

Despite this fiscal prudence, on his death the debts owed by Henry together with the outstanding debts of his father totalled 40,000 marks **(25)**. The revenues of the Duchy of Lancaster also increased to over £15,800 per year; this was mainly achieved by the reduction of the annuities that the Duchy paid. The yield from the crown leases increased by an average of 5% per year. The income from ancient revenues and crown dues increased from £10,260 to £15,210 by 1421 **(26)**.

A large part of the royal finances that had come from the export tax on wool came to be replaced by returns from the export of cloth as the trade routes to Flanders improved. Customs houses were established in all the major ports. Despite the fact that wool exports fell to an average of 10,000 sacks a year, the average gross yield was £49,000 per annum, this comparing with an average of £47,000 during the later part of Henry IV's reign **(27)**. Henry was granted the wool subsidies for life in 1415. Langley also reduced the annuities paid from the crown's receipts to £12,000 per year, approximately half the amount paid out by the previous regime. This tightening of Henry's expenditure was welcomed by the Commons and certainly aided Langley when he needed to raise additional money to finance the war in France. A profligate King, no matter his successes abroad, would not have found the Commons so amenable.

Langley endeavoured to make the crown's dependencies self-sufficient, but this was not wholly successful. The Gascon garrison was permanently in arrears and in 1422 the Calais garrison revolted. Langley carried out an enquiry into the gifts that had been made by Richard II and Henry IV from the revenues accruing to the Gascon lordship. A number of these were cancelled in an effort to curtail the continual drain on the crown's resources. The notable exception to this was the income from Wales which increased from £1,000 in 1400 to an average of £3,100 between 1409–20 **(28)**. The income from wardships and the temporalities of churches within the royal gift increased from £10,260 for the years 1406–7 to £15,210 for the years 1420–21. This was achieved in two ways: the cost of granting marriage licences for wards of court increased, and benefices were kept open for longer periods than had previously been the case.

I am indebted to Professor Jacob's book *"The Fifteenth Century, 1399–1485" (Oxford 1961)*, for the calculations of the grants made to the crown by the Commons and the Clergy during Langley's Chancellorship.

The laity were subjected to the following grants as voted through the Commons:

> On the 16th of November 1417: two 1/15 and 1/10: 1/15 and 1/10 due on the 2nd of February 1418; the other 1/15 and 1/10 was due on the 2nd of February 1419. On the 16th of October 1419: One and a third 1/15 and 1/10 on the 2nd of February 1420; the third by the 11th of November 1420. The third, devoted as before to repayment of lenders, to be levied for their benefit before Martinmas.
> (Ordinance for money to be kept within the realm. *Rot. Parl. iv. 118*).

Seven and three-quarter tenths and fifteenths in little more than six years. The subsidies voted by the northern convocations were forthcoming due to Langley's standing within the northern provinces. Generally, the southern convocation's grants mirrored those of the northern provinces thanks to Bishops Chichele and Beaufort.

The overall impression that comes from Henry V's reign is that the crown, through Langley, undertook a much needed root and branch review of all aspects of the crown's income and expenditure. A greater professionalism was brought to bear to all spheres of the Chancery. The fact that Langley occupied his post throughout the reign of a King who was exceptionally *au fait* with the mechanics of governance shows his qualities. A word frequently used to describe Henry is meticulous. This equally applies to Langley. Langley's assiduousness clearly dovetailed with Henry's personal inspection of all the Chancery accounts that was a feature of his reign. The attention to the minutiae of finance does not indicate a parsimonious regime, as the cost of the war in France was high. King and Minister recognised that the patience of the King's subjects was not infinite when it came to matters of taxation. Henry regarded the accumulation of finance as part of his overall strategy towards France, a means to an end.

With the gradual pacification of Normandy, communication became easier and the average time for letters to be delivered was ten days **(29)**. Issues were listed with the council's suggestions in the margin, with Henry then indicating next to the suggestions his wishes. The system worked well and rarely, if at all, did Henry rebuke Langley for making suggestions that were contrary to his wishes.

Property and Residences

On the 30th of April 1419, Langley purchased the manor of Knole near Sevenoaks in Kent. He paid £133,6 shillings and 8 pence **(30)** for the 800 acres, roughly 16.5 pence per acre. Today the same land would cost circa £350,000 per acre, equivalent to 28 million pounds. There is no record of him ever having stayed at Knole. This house was eventually given to Henry VIII by an obsequious Archbishop Cranmer who had purchased the house some time earlier. In 1430 he purchased a single messuage for the sum of £100 to extend his gardens at Old Ford **(31)**, his house three miles north-east of London.

Langley appears to have spent a fair amount of money on valuable items of plate as well as personal items for his own comfort. His collection of books whilst not being extensive was selective, and four books alone are valued at £80. In his will his twelve personal servants received a horse each. His annual income from the Treasury was approximately £4,000, more than half of which was used to meet his private expenditure **(32)**. The annual income of the Bishopric was £13,333,6 shillings and 8 pence. It appears that Langley viewed his income as belonging to the diocesan office, to be expended on buildings within the diocese. The overall impression that I have formed is that whilst he undoubtedly lived in some splendour he did not accumulate any personal wealth. The surplus that accrued from the diocesan receipts was spent on a major rebuilding programme.

On his death he left bequests of money totalling £600 as well as some significant pieces of gilt and silver. One further indication of Langley's wealth can be found in his Durham treasurer's account for the year 1428–9. The clerk of the kitchen took delivery of sixty lambs, one hundred and forty sheep, three large and three other beeves and thirty-two quarters of malt; these items cost £45,8 shillings and 4 pence. His requirements in London would have been at least double this.

In the north he had castles at Durham and Norham, his Episcopal palace, and a further residence at Bishop Auckland which seems to be where he mostly stayed when in his diocese. Within his diocese he also had residences at Darlington and Stockton. In Yorkshire there was a palace at Northallerton, a castle at Crake, a manor house at Howden and the manor of Wheel Hall. In the capital, besides Old Ford, he had his official residence of Durham House, between the Strand and the Thames. The expense of the upkeep and staffing of all these residences would have taken the biggest part of his yearly income.

Assessment

The resumption of the Hundred Years War brought with it the burden of extraordinary expenditure that spanned the full period of Langley's tenure of office. The main consequence for the governance of England was that a new discipline of efficiency had to be brought to bear on the department of Chancery. Without the measures of austerity and efficiency that Langley introduced, Henry would not have been able to promote and sustain his campaign against the French. There can be no doubt that Henry took as much interest and devoted as much of his energies to the governance of his realm as he did to his campaigning. A less adroit or capable person than Langley would have buckled under the strains that the continual need for finance and supplies placed on his department. The gains that accompanied the aftermath of Agincourt could not have been achieved if the war effort had stalled through lack of money. Equally, whilst the nation basked in Henry's triumphs against England's traditional enemy, the country needed financial stability. Since 1377 when Richard II had fatefully taken control of his own affairs the crown had been consistently living beyond its means. Henry IV had tried in vain to keep expenditure under control. However, the rebellions of the early years of his reign meant that the crown was in debt throughout his reign. Merely to stabilise and bring into credit the crown's finances would have been a major achievement. Henry died in debt. However, set against his achievements, this debt would have been far greater had the finances of England not been so effectively handled.

A further danger that accompanied any prolonged campaign abroad was that the populace grew weary of being subjected to a regime that was constantly demanding additional revenues. The wane in enthusiasm for the French "situation" that marked the reign of Henry's son exemplifies this. I would go so far as to say that the only other person who could have carried out the job of Chancellor was Beaufort. Had Langley not been available, then Beaufort would not have been able to play the effective part that he did at the Council of Constance. The main feature of Langley's tenure was the speed with which royal revenues were collected. His tenure was a model of efficiency and ushered in the dawning of a far more professional attitude amongst the staff of the Chancery. The seeds of the early-modern department of Chancery were sown by Langley, and his dedication was never again surpassed.

Do not underestimate the difficulties that Henry imposed by his almost over-zealous passion for every detail of government. Had Henry lived, then the benefits that should have accrued from the gains he made in France may have been realised. Conjecture maybe, but this cannot hide the fact that had this occurred, the Nation's debt to Langley would have been even greater than it was. It is worth remembering that Langley was the only Chancellor between 1417 and 1422, a long tenure. There is no record of Langley ever incurring the King's displeasure. If Henry was the exemplar of Medieval Kingship, then equally Langley was the epitome of an efficient and dedicated Chancellor. The fact that he was so unobtrusive adds a lustre to his career. The esteem that the government and its ministers were held in was at an extremely low ebb when Henry ascended the throne.

Between them, Henry and Langley delivered the *"bone governance"* that Beaufort had promised would be the hallmark of Henry's reign in his first speech to the Commons. Without Langley, Henry would never have been able to sustain his Kingship and more importantly, the Lancastrian dynasty would have floundered as it was to do so in the later stages of his son's reign. The charisma that has surrounded Henry V has tended to cast a shadow over the careers of a number of significant people, Beaufort, Bedford and Chichele excepted. Before these three great servants I would place Langley, the fulcrum upon which Henry's government rested. None of Henry's success could have been accomplished without him. There is one single statistic that underlines this: during the years 1415 to 1420, eighty percent of the money voted to the king through parliament was actually collected.

Langley's fidelity shows that he was in agreement with the continental policies that Henry was pursuing. The King's growing intransigence towards the terms offered periodically by the French are indicative that after Agincourt Henry had set his sights on the throne and nothing less. Whilst there was some justification for the original territorial claims, there was no sound basis for his desire for the Valois throne. Certainly by the year 1420 a certain disenchantment began to affect the country in regard to the continuation of the French wars. This was chiefly due to the perception of the consequences of the Treaty of Troyes, the details of which will be discussed in the next section. It is doubtful whether the country would have continued to support Henry's continued expenditure in France. Those who read the political runes were concerned that the Treaty of Troyes had locked Henry into the position of having to conquer those lands not already in his control when the Treaty was signed.

Langley was not a particularly innovative Chancellor, the methods he employed for the raising of revenue being the methods that were well established. Nor was he one for either the grand gesture or for confrontational politics; the country would not have stood for either, facts that he was well aware of. Langley's standing was based on the admiration that his peers had for his unflappable professionalism coupled with the knowledge that he enjoyed the King's utmost confidence and respect. This was no mean achievement considering how hard a task master Henry was.

From 1418 when the Keeper of the Privy Seal was transferred to France, Langley was running the entire machinery of government. Frequently the rolls show that a decision is recorded as having been made *"by the advice of the Council"* (33). The only Councillor in attendance was Langley. Certainly Henry made his wishes known on nearly every aspect of business that the Council dealt with. Also his long experience of government meant that he would be the one to explain the details of a variety of issues that the Council had to deal with. To sum him up in two words, he was Henry's Managing Director.

Langley regularly reported privately to Henry, as did Bedford, one the check on the other, but Henry never entirely lost his mistrustfulness. Bedford was often instructed to act with the Chancellor over certain matters. There is one example of the autonomy that Langley enjoyed over Bedford. In 1419 it was strongly rumoured that the King of Castile was about to attack the south coast. Henry instructed Langley to organise the defensive measures in conjunction with Bedford *"and other suche as semeth to youre discretion"* (34). Clearly the King had every confidence in Langley's abilities to organise military matters in addition to Chancery and Diplomacy. Langley was also negotiating in London with the Flemish and Genoese envoys over aid and trade agreements.

A further aspect of governance that fell on Langley's shoulders were petitions to the King. Henry had little time to fully consider the large number that were put to him. Petitions sent to France were re-routed to Langley with annotations from the King in the margin. More often than not Langley was instructed to *"doo unto hem both right and equite, and in especial thay ye see that the porer partye suffre no wrong"* (35). This wording concerns one particular case but forms a good composite of the instructions that accompanied the petitions to the King. The term *"by your good avys"* (36) is the most frequent term used. To protect the rights of his soldiers whilst they were in France, Henry suspended the taking of assizes. As a consequence, those seeking redress went directly to Langley. He dealt with over 200 such cases during his seven years in office; in total some 400 or so petitions were handled by him, an average of fifty-seven per year. Each one was different from the last and requiring careful study. These petitions were extremely varied, everything from the right to inherit lands, often disputed by disenfranchised family members, to applications for pensions. All points of law were covered, theft, robbery, land-holding rights, i. e. the terms of tenure of one party, points of *jurance prudance*, objections regarding the levying of customs dues, taxes etc. There is no recorded criticism of his judgements in any of these cases.

So what were his motives? During his tenure he very rarely left London, and it was only in 1421 when Henry returned to England that he returned north for any length of time. If we assume that he worked a fourteen-hour day, and, given the breadth and diversity of his various offices this is a reasonable assumption, then he put in 30,646 man hours, 4,377 hours a year. The best description would be that he was a workaholic. Work was everything and everything was work. The comfort that he lived in was richly deserved. We can but admire the depth and breadth of his experience in all aspects of government. I have previously referred to him as the first truly professional civil servant. Given the diversity of instances cited in this section I believe that he earned this sobriquet. The generous gifts that he bestowed in his will to his servants show how he valued the service that they gave him. A master with so many responsibilities would indeed have been a hard taskmaster. The advantage of being in Langley's household was that he never fell from grace, thereby providing a permanent job for the faithful retainer. The respect that he was held in meant that positions in his service would be the most sought after amongst those who saw their careers lying with the civil service. Tutelage by Langley would be the most highly prized of all positions, and from here one could be assured of employment in any household or government department. There is no record of his ever having accepted an inducement to take someone into his household. His patronage was based on ability, which is one of the reasons for the efficiency of his department.

As a postscript to this section I would like to discuss the nature of advice that Langley would have given to the king. Hindsight is always easy. However, the lack of any meaningful diplomatic initiatives after Agincourt point to a King who in some ways chose to ignore the option of accepting the enlarged territorial concessions that the French were willing to concede. Henry was driven, in my opinion, by the spectre of his father's premature death, a visitation from God for the usurpation and murder of Richard II and also for the beheading of Scrope. He would have been comfortable discussing these matters with Langley who, whilst being intimately involved in these events, was also his father's closest confidant (see my earlier comments on his role as Keeper of the Ducal, and, later Privy Seal). There can be no doubt that in his mind he truly believed that God was on his side and that his cause was just. Originally it was, the hereditary territorial rights that he claimed being properly the crown of England's.

In all the propaganda that emanated from the diplomatic missions, this fact is constantly stressed. In this, thinkers such as Langley would have been satisfied that they were upholding the anointed King's rights and privileges. The same could not be said for the claim to the French throne. Langley, perhaps above all others, would have been privy to the kings innermost thoughts and reasoning. Testimony to this is seen in that when he was in Paris in 1414, Langley interviewed the Celestines with a view to Henry endowing a foundation for them at Sheen. This type of endowment was a highly personal one and would have been the subject of deep theological discussions between the two men. Henry would have laid part of his soul bare to Langley during these very private talks. Remember also that he left Langley a missal and a breviary in his will, one of the most personal of gifts, signifying the spiritual bond between the pair. Someone of Langley's intelligence would have found, on a purely legal basis, difficulties in sustaining the arguments surrounding Henry's position.

The victory of Agincourt owed a good deal to luck. The delay caused by the difficulties encountered in capturing Harfleur had meant that Henry would have had to return to England with only a small tangible gain, which had to be set against the expense and the expectations that accompanied his departure. The chevaunche that he embarked on that led to Agincourt was an act of bravado designed to deflect any public criticism at home. Do not forget that Henry sued for terms before the battle offering to make reparation for the damage he had done since he landed. The French should have let him go and had they been more unified, they would have done so; he would have experienced considerable difficulties in coercing the Commons into support-ing a further expedition. Had he not triumphed Langley would have received, by association, the brunt of the Commons anger. His career would probably have been irretrievably damaged. Do not also forget that Henry ordered the massacre of a number of the prisoners, something completely contrary to the laws of chivalry. Commentators have opined that this was done out of expediency. I see it as the actions of a King gripped by blind panic when the goal of victory was in the balance. Henry had no heir, legitimate or otherwise, and his death would have seen the country plunged into another civil war as the Beauforts and Henry's brothers fought against those who had been disaffected since Henry's ascension; the Southampton plot had been a warning.

Demons drove Henry, something that Langley above all would understand. Henry would have listened to his chief councillor's advice. By virtue of his long service to the King's Grandfather and Father he was the most senior of all the councillors available to Henry. The misconception attached to Henry's reign is that he was an autocratic monarch who alone dictated foreign policy. The point has already been made that there is little point in having councillors if one does not consult them. To not do so would have seen the King isolated in the Commons. He could not bludgeon his policies through, the crown did not rest that securely on his head. The Lollards were, at the beginning of his reign, a movement to be reckoned with. There is no record of Henry's discussions with Langley, we have to work by deduction to elucidate the substance of discussions from the events as they unfolded.

Langley would have been accustomed to the trappings of power that came with his high office. The time he spent away from his diocese show that believed that he should be in London, the adrenaline of power. He had experienced the ignominy that accompanied a fall from grace, both with Gaunt and Henry Bolingbroke. He was in a securer position in that he could always pursue his career in the church. Many other intellectuals assisted Henry in his grand design, but did they also agree with Henry's contentions? I believe that the over-riding consideration that bound all these men together, Henry and Langley the most, was the continuation in power of the House of Lancaster. This was not a question of blind allegiance to a dynasty, it was a case of loyalty to one's country, with a country and its people united behind its ruler who was exercising his divine Kingship. Langley's support for the House of Lancaster is beyond question, and I further believe that the unrest that he had lived through during the past twenty-three years since Bolingbroke was exiled imbued in him a loathing for anyone who threatened the stability of the country. Scrope, the Percy Family, and a number of others who rebelled, are a testimony to this. The fact that events in France ran out of control after Langley's semi-retirement from public service was no coincidence. His retirement was not the prime reason, but never the less it was a factor.

Politics, 1417–1421

The Treaty of Troyes was to have a profound effect on English politics for the rest of the century. Langley only had a minor role in the negotiations that led to the signing, however, but, given the status that England attached to the document during the minority of the next reign, a brief outline of the events that led to the Treaty being signed is necessary as it was to cause Langley some considerable difficulties. As a preamble, we shall start with conditions and perceptions in England.

The majority of business conducted by the Commons during this period concerned the campaigns in France. In each of his addresses Langley stressed that the King was carrying out a war that had *God's blessing*. It then followed that all the King's subjects out of loyalty to the crown were duty bound to assist the King in bringing to a successful conclusion a war that was being waged on behalf of God and for the benefit of the kingdom. His addresses were more of a sermon than a statement of political intent. Only once was Henry present to hear his Chancellor's opening speech. At the opening of the parliament in November 1417, Langley apologised for the King's absence saying that he had gone to win his right in France. His opening words were *"Be valiant and show yourselves men, and you shall obtain glory"*. The address of 1418 saw him coercing the Commons by explaining that if the subsidies being requested were not forthcoming then the campaign would have to be abandoned; in 1419 he explained that, with the country's help, he was winning the war that had been forced upon him *"Let us not be weary in well-doing"*. Then in 1421, the first time that Henry was present, he emphasised that England's successes had been achieved because they were really the work of God **(37)**. This type of statement may seem incredible to anyone reading this as we approach the new millennium, but in the Middle Ages people truly believed this. The theme of linking religion, God's blessing, and war, was not new. The rhetoric that was used to induce the crusaders to the Middle East was mirrored in the second decade of the fifteenth century.

During Langley's period at the Chancery parliament became more business-like. It was not a talking shop; neither the King nor the chancellor being the type to indulge its members. There were eleven parliaments during Henry's nine-and-a-half year reign, each sitting averaging four weeks **(38)**. The king was in attendance at only five of these parliaments. Every new success in France was portrayed as being achieved with the aid of God and was a testimony to his divine blessing. For anyone opposed to the war this was virtually impossible to argue against, and to do so would have aroused suspicions of Lollardy. Caen fell in the August of 1417, and Rouen at the beginning of 1419, the road to Paris lay open. During this time Henry's commanders had subdued most of Western Normandy.

All was not harmonious with the soldiers in France, a letter written by a one of those involved in the siege of Cherbourg in 1418 spoke of the conditions that the English army had to endure; " ... *the long time we have been here, and of the expenses that we have had at every siege that we have come to, and have had no wages since that we came out of England, so that we have spent all we had"* **(39).** A rat cost thirty pence, a mouse sixpence.

At home, Oldcastle was captured in the December of 1417 and brought before parliament on the 14th of the same month. He was condemned as a traitor, and as such suffered death by hanging after which he was roasted whilst he hung. He hardly helped himself by declaring before the Commons that he believed that Richard II was still alive in Scotland and that he detested all priests. He was escorted by eighty armed men to his place of execution which was attended by a large crowd at St. Giles Fields, which is now the junction of Tottenham Court Road and New Oxford Street. Bedford presided over his trial with Langley seated next to him throughout the proceedings. The execution cost fifty-six shillings **(40)**, and Langley would have felt that this was money well spent. Henry profited from his persecution of Lollardy with the church perceiving him as a protector of the orthodoxy of Christian teaching. The perception of the clerics was that he was the supreme head and guardian of the church in England, something that Langley was not slow to exploit when he needed to raise money from the church.

Towards the end of the decade the Commons were again re-asserting their authority in the way that grants through parliament were to be allocated. Any loans that were raised on the third that was granted for the year 1420 were to be spent in England. The theme of law and order was specifically mentioned by Langley in all his addresses. Rioting in Lancashire, Cheshire and Staffordshire was reported to parliament in 1421. It was time that England's King spent more time at home. We shall return to the parliaments of 1420 and 21 after the next section. The mood of the Commons markedly changed after the Treaty of Troyes was signed.

The Treaty of Troyes

The Commons had been growing uneasy regarding the increased demands for additional taxation to sustain the war effort. As Chancellor, Langley had to advise the King that a truce with the French would be politic. Henry took his advice, he could not afford to alienate his chief minister. Conversely, Langley would have been privately assuring the waverers that he would broach the suggestion. The merchants had been patient but they now wanted to reap the commercial benefits, a return on their investment being overdue. It was due to his standing in the Commons that no great amount of public dissension was voiced; they trusted him, and he in turn repaid their faith. A further factor was that the French had been successful in recruiting a number of mercenary forces, and resistance was stiffening.

The timing was opportune John the Fearless had been murdered by the sixteen-year-old Dauphin Charles's men on the bridge at Montereau on the 10th of September 1419. He had occupied Paris on the 14th of July 1418 ousting the Armagnacs from control; the Armagnacs controlled the lands to the south-west of Paris. The problem for both groups was that they could not oust the English without unifying their forces. The murder drove the Burgundians into seeking a further alliance with England. Henry's terms were that they would support his claim to the French throne. Charles would be left in place, Henry would marry Katherine and would forego any dowry in return for Charles recognising him as his heir, and he was to ascend the throne on Charles's death. Given the hatred that the Burgundians had for the Dauphin, their agreement was easy to solicit. The alliance was sealed on Christmas day, 1419. An additional clause was added whereby one of Henry's brothers would marry the sister of Philipe the new Duke of Burgundy. A century later, the Carthusian prior of Dijon was to remark that *"the English entered France through the hole in the skull of the Duke of Burgundy."*

The alliance held, and by the time that Henry entered Troyes on the 23rd of March 1420 the war had been won, Charles and his Queen Isabel were waiting for him. As incredible as it may seem, Isabel was even prepared to deny that Charles, who was enjoying a period of sanity, was the father of the Dauphin. Henry had agreed to pay the sum of £40,000 a year towards Katherine's dowry, the cost to be born by the English exchequer (**41**). For us this is an important point: Henry would not have agreed to this without first consulting Langley. Clearly Langley had been kept informed of negotiations throughout. Henry and Catherine were married on the 2nd of June in the Cathedral of Troyes. Langley travelled to Southampton arriving by the 23rd of April. Bedford had been summoned together with 2,000 archers and 800 men-at-arms, and in Henry's absence the Duke of Gloucester was appointed regent.

The Perception in England

At the beginning it is worth making the point that before the Treaty was ratified the Commons understandably took the view that from now on the financing of the war should come from the revenues to be gathered from France. They wanted a clear distinction between Henry's rule in France and his Kingship in England (**42**).

The negotiations had started whilst Rouen was being besieged. The Dauphin had sent a party of negotiators to Alencon, and the English position was that a marriage between Katherine and Henry would be the starting point for a cessation of the war. England also wanted the terms of the Treaty of Brétigny honoured, and then any claims to the French throne would be put in abeyance. An alliance between the two against Burgundy was mooted with the aim of capturing Flanders. Meanwhile, Burgundian envoys had been in England, the English delegation consisting of Langley, Chichele, Philip Morgan and Warwick. Again no agreement was reached. The Burgundians also opened negotiations with the Dauphin. Henry was not to return to England until the following year. He was too busy subduing the cities that were still held by the forces loyal to the Dauphin, and it was left to Langley to prepare the Commons. He would only have been able to do this if he had been kept fully informed of events in France.

The Commons had been growing restive about the King's continual absence abroad, as he had not been in the country for three and a half years. He returned at the beginning of February 1421. The pageantry that greeted the returning conqueror and his new Queen was even greater than in 1415. Katherine was crowned Queen on Sunday the 23rd of February by Archbishop Chichele in Westminster Abbey and Langley was in attendance. He had organised the expenditure needed for the banquet that followed at Westminster Hall.

With the King back in England, Langley took the opportunity to visit the north. He had been back in his diocese barely a month before the King had sent for him (43). Scottish ambassadors had arrived at Howden to discuss the release of their King and, whilst Henry was here he received the news that his brother, Clarence, had been killed at Bauge in Anjou. The Chancellor was the highest-ranking prelate with the King; he would be the first person Henry would have turned to. His natural inclination would have been to return to France, but Langley would have advised against this. He had been in the country barely three months, and the Commons would have cited his departure as proof that events in France were taking precedence over affairs in England. Much has been made of the fact that Henry did not tell his entourage until the day after he received the news. I believe that the true reason was that he and Langley were assessing the implications before informing everyone. The murmurings in the country could not be ignored, such a major set-back being viewed with alarm. It would appear to many in the country that the English forces could only triumph when Henry was leading them. From here Langley returned to London with the King and Katherine who was now heavily pregnant.

The Last Parliaments of the Reign

The parliament had been summoned for the 12th of May. Prior to this, Langley, on the 6th of May, presented Henry with a balance sheet which showed just how precarious the financial position was. The anticipated receipts were £55,743,19 shillings and 10 pence; this was made up by anticipated customs receipts of £40,676,19 shilling and 9 pence and a figure of £15,066, 11 shillings and 1 pence. Expenses were anticipated at £52,235,16 shillings, this leaving a credit balance of £3,507,13 shillings and 11 pence. From this Henry had to meet all his household expenses as well as the cost of a number of building projects that the crown was committed to. The country could not afford to continue its support for Henry's continental ambitions. Within these figures there was no allowance for the debts attached to the garrisons at Harfleur and Calais. Henry's perambulations had raised £34,131, most of which came from the usual lenders, Beaufort and Whittington being the providers of the largest amounts (**44**). Prudently, no subsidy to support the campaign in France was to be sought; Langley had read the political runes. Loans would again have to be raised to support Henry's continental ambitions. The tour of the country that had been undertaken was a flag-waving exercise with the intent of eliciting loans. It having been carefully planned to take in the main devotional shrines.

In his opening address to the May parliament Langley made no mention of the Treaty of Troyes. It was ratified without debate, the presence of the King cowing those who had voiced concerns previously. The rest of the parliament concerned itself with currency reform and the election of shire officers. Langley was to obtain a further subsidy in the December parliament. The birth of an heir at Windsor of the 6th of December certainly made his task easier.

Clarence's death had lent an urgency to the Scottish problem, the force that had defeated him at Bauge having been largely composed of Scottish mercenaries. Langley brokered a deal with the earl of Douglas whereby a force of 200 knights and the same number of mounted archers would serve under the King in France. In return, James would be restored to the Scottish throne provided that hostages were given to ensure his loyalty, and the daughter of Beaufort, Joan, was to be his bride.

Langley had also been continuing the negotiations with the French prisoners. Bourbon had accepted the Treaty of Troyes, his ransom having been agreed at 100,000 crowns together with the ceding of six *"notable places"* in his lands, the cost of the upkeep to be born by him. He was unable to raise the ransom money but Henry had obtained a further ally regarding the Treaty of

Troyes. Langley had also been engaged in discussion with the Genoese and they had agreed to offer no aid to the Dauphinist forces.

Langley accompanied Henry to Dover, where, on the 10th of June, he embarked for France, and he was never to see his King alive again. Langley returned to London where he remained until the end of July. From here he made only the second journey to the place of his birth, his express purpose being to check on the progress of the collegiate church at Manchester. He stayed for four days before returning to his diocese via Skipton. During his journey he continued to deal with the business of chancery: issuing letters concerning the election of priors **(45)**, appointing commissioners to Cumberland and Westmorland **(46)**, coroners for Yorkshire and Cambridge were ordered to be elected and port officers were appointed for Newcastle **(47)**.

He attended the northern convocation held at York on the 22nd of September where he induced the clergy to grant a subsidy to the King. He was back in London by the 9th of October. He remained in the capital during the following year, visiting Southampton from the 6th of April to the 2nd of May to supervise the revictualing of the army in France; he was briefly back in London before returning north. During this time the war in France had become a campaign of attrition with gains and reversals. He was on his way back to the capital when a messenger brought him news of the king's death. The King's health had been deteriorating for some months, something Langley would have been made aware of. He died in the arms of his confessor, Thomas Netter, in the early hours of Monday the 31st of August at Vincennes. He was thirty-four years and 348 days old and he had ruled England for nine years, only four of which had been spent in England. He was only the second King to die outside the country, Richard 1st, the Lionheart, being the first.

Assessment

Langley had served him throughout his reign, the last five years as his chancellor; 1,059 days were as Foreign Secretary/Diplomat, 72% of his time and 1,690 days service, 93% of his time were as Chancellor. Without a shadow of doubt he had been Henry's closest minister. What had they achieved?

The country had a more united look about it, the foundations for this having been laid in the previous reign. The Lancastrian dynasty had no serious rivals and during the reign the machinery of governance had risen to a level of professionalism that had not been seen before. Without Langley Henry would not have been able to pursue his grand design. There was an intolerance about Henry, but this had never been directed at Langley. The amount of his time spent in service shows him to have been a willing servant. The crowning event, Agincourt, had created a false euphoria, the events of the next reign proving this. Langley had profited from his service, power and wealth having been given but never abused. I find it strange that a man of his experience and undoubted intelligence had not seen the difficulties that Henry's crusade for the throne of France would cause the country. All that they had to show for their efforts was a reconquered Normandy that presented a narrow inroad to Paris. Beyond that, two-thirds of France remained out of reach. The drain on the financial resources could have created a climate of dissatisfaction; the fact that it was only in the last years of the reign that a disenchantment had set in, was thanks to Langley's unstinting service as Chancellor. The pair had left the infant heir a fragile position in France, a poisoned chalice. I also find it strange that after Henry's death Langley did not suggest a rapprochement to England's position in France. The country would have been better served by cutting its losses and settling for what it had started out to reclaim, its lands as agreed by the Treaty of Brétigny.

There is one clause in the Treaty of Troyes that I have not commented on so far, and this is because I feel that it should be discussed in this section. This clause stated that "... *by God's help when it shall happen to us to come to the crown of France, the duchy of Normandy and all other places conquered by us in the realm of France shall be under the commandment, obedience and monarchy of the crowns of France*" **(48)**.

Notwithstanding the Commons strictures that the thrones of England and France should be treated as separate bodies, this clause firmly locked in the English lords who had been awarded estates in Normandy, all these awards having the condition attached to them that these lands had to be disposed of to Englishmen on the death of the estate holder. The effect of these two clauses was that should the King of England's position as King of France be threatened, then any of the major Lords who had a duality of landed interests would naturally bring pressure on the Commons to vote through subsidies to assist the war effort on the other side of the channel. England's aspirations in France were inextricably, and I believe deliberately, locked together. Should the Dauphin seek to reassert his position, something he was to do, then the Commons would be left with no option but to support the English forces against any attempt at reconquest. This was to prove disastrous for the Lancastrian ruling clique and was one of the prime reasons for the disenchantment that led to the War of the Roses. The majority of the landholders in France were Lancastrian in sympathy.

As I have previously stated, Langley had to steer the ratification of the Treaty through the Commons, he being far too experienced not to recognise the future problems that these clauses would create. Henry had deliberately structured the Treaty to ensure the continued involvement of England both financially and politically in affairs in France. Those who had drafted the Treaty, and this includes Langley who would, as Chancellor, have been particularly interested in the implications for the English Chancery, did England a disservice in allowing the clause to remain in the final draft. Obviously, when the Treaty was ratified Henry was in good health and his premature death was not contemplated. However, his hazardous pursuit of his ambitions in France had to be taken cognisance of, and the possibility that he would die in battle was a very real one.

Whilst Langley had steered England's Chancery through the minefield of debt that threatened to engulf the country in supporting Henry's pursuit of the French throne, he was to hand to his successor the proverbial poisoned chalice. All his life he had striven to preserve the Lancastrian grip on the throne, but this one piece of calculated judgement was to prove the undoing of his entire life's work. It was little wonder that he was to gradually withdraw from political life in the next five years. The culpability was not his alone, the envoys who had negotiated the Treaty share some of the responsibility.

The point that I am making here is that Langley was the most powerful man in the Commons, he was *the de facto* Prime Minister, and it was through his efforts that the document received the assent of parliament. Prior to his Chancellorship he had acted as England's first Foreign Secretary, he was conversant with the thinking of the French crown, and it is inconceivable that he did not foresee the ramifications of the Treaty. There is one further point: the Treaty was signed by three of the four protagonists, England, Charles VI and Burgundy. The document was presented as being the Treaty upon which the war would be settled, but clearly, with the Dauphin able to command a significant army, this was not the case. Any euphoria was misplaced. I feel that given the unrest and disenchantment in the country, Langley may have believed that this would assuage the doubters.

Finally the document had been signed by England's anointed King. The function of the Commons was to ratify the Treaty: would they have dared to refuse their consent? This would have been very unlikely, but given the concerns expressed by the Great Council that assembled after Henry's death in regard to the status of Gloucester's Regency, it appears that an undercurrent of dissatisfaction *was* simmering.

As will be seen in the next section, Langley continued to serve the crown and clearly he saw it as his duty to ensure the perpetuation of the House of Lancaster's grip on the throne. He had now outlived the grandfather, son and grandson, and he was about to serve the great-grandson of his first patron. He was to act as an executor to Henry, the third such time he had carried out this task for the first family of the Lancastrian regime. He was now fifty-nine years old.

Epilogue

Henry's will had been drafted in 1421 with a codicil having been added on the 26th August 1422. Gloucester was appointed guardian, and the child's education was entrusted to Thomas Beaufort whose duty was also to appoint the servants who were to care for the Prince. Langley was named as one of the executors, and Henry had requested that the royal dignity be preserved. Langley was to retain possession of the will until 1426 indicating that the bulk of the work of the executors was undertaken by him. Langley travelled to Dover, where on the 31st of October, the fleet escorting the coffin landed.

The body was brought by stages to London and on Saturday the 7th of November it was interred in Westminster Abbey. As a final point Langley had also been appointed as one of Henry's feoffes for his estates in the Duchy of Lancaster; he was also appointed as one of the trustees of the lands that had been given to the new nunnery at Syon. This is telling, and taken with the bequests of the breviary and the missal, it points to a spiritual bond, as well as professional ties between the two men.

Notes and References

(1) Macbeth, Act 1, scene 7, 25–27.
(2) Sandquist, T. A. and Powicke, M. R. (eds), "Essays in medieval history presented to Bertie Wilkinson; The Holy oil of St. Thomas of Canterbury", (Toronto 1969); Sharman, I. C. "Thomas Langley, a Political Bishop", unpublished lecture paper, (England 1998).
(3) Rot. Parl. iv, pp3–4; Chancery, Charter Rolls, non, 180–2; P. P. C. ii, pp 131–5.
(4) Douet d'Arcq, L. (ed), "Chronique d'Enguerron de Monstrelet", six vols., (Paris 1857–62), vol. ii, p 391.
(5) Waugh, W. T. and Wylie, J. H, "The Reign of Henry the Fifth", (Cambridge 1914–29), vol. ix, pp 102–4 and 131–2.
(6) Baye, de, N, "Journal of the Society de L'Histoire de France", (Paris 1885–1888), vol. ii, p 190; Exchequer L. T. R: Foreign Accounts, no 47, rot. C;

Accounts, Various, 321/20, 26 and 620; "Chronique du Religieux de Saint Denys", (Coll. des Documents Indentis), (1829–52), vol. v, p 376; Ursins, J, Juvenal des, "Histoire de Charles VI", (ed), Godefroy, D, (Paris 1653), p 281; Foedra, ix, pp 131–2.

(7)   Rot. Parl. iv, pp 34–5; P. P. C. ii, 150–1.
(8)   Harriss, G, L. (ed), "Henry V, The Practice of Kingship", (Oxford 1985), "The Management of Parliament", pp145–6.
(9)   Issue Roll, 619, m 4; Foedra ix, pp 183–8.
(10) "The Chronicle of St. Denys", v, p 408.
(11) Jacob, E, F., "The Fifteenth Century 1399–1485", (Oxford 1961), p 141.
(12) P. P. C. ii, pp 153–4.
(13) Myers, A. R. (ed), E. H. D. vol. iv, 1327–1485, (Eyre and Spottiswoode, London 1969), the passage from Streeche is reproduced on p 208, doc. no. 101.
(14) P. P. C. ii, pp 153–8.
(15) Foedra, ix, pp 289–93; C. P. R. 1413–1416, pp 356–7.
(16) Storey, R, L., "Thomas Langley and the Bishopric of Durham, 1406–1437", (London 1961), appendix A, pp 226–244.
(17) Walsingham, T., "Historia Anglicana", (ed) Riley, H, T., (Rolls Series, London 1863–4), vol. ii, pp 300; Rymer, Thomas, "Foedra, Conventions et Litterae", (London 1709), vol. ix, pp 244 and 458.
(17) Allmand, C., "Henry V", (Methuen, London 1992), p 110–11.
(18) Foedra, ix, pp 423–7.
(19) Ancient Correspondence, vol. lvii, no. 79.
(20) Gesta, p 16.
(21) Foedra, iv, iii, 9. Jacob, E, F., "The Fifteenth Century, 1399–1485", (Oxford 1961), p 430. C. P. R. 1416–1422, pp 112–13, 234–373.
(22) Jacob, E, F., "The Fifteenth Century, 1399–1485", (Oxford 1961), p 431; P. P. C. ii, 245–6.
(23) Steel, A., "The Receipt of the Exchequer", (London 1954).
(24) Harriss, G, L. (ed), "Henry V, The Practice of Kingship", (Oxford 1985), p 165.
(25) C. C. R. 1413–19, pp 17 and 180; Rot. Parl. iv, 172–3.
(26) Harriss, G, L., "Henry V, The Practice of Kingship", (Oxford 1985), p 173.
(27) Wilson, Carus, E, M. and Coleman, O., "England's export Trade, 1275–1547", (Oxford 1963), pp 56–7; Harriss, G, L., "Henry V, The Practice of Kingship", (Oxford 1985), p 173; Ramsey, Sir, J, H., "Lancaster and York", (Oxford 1892), i, pp 151 and 313.
(28) Allmand, C., "Henry V", (London 1992), p 389.
(29) C. P. R. 1416–1422, pp 132–414; Chancery Warrants, 1364/5.
(30) C. C. R. 1419–1422, pp 111 and 192; Fleet of Fines, file 290, no. 283.
(31) Common Pleas: Fleet of Fines, files 88 no. 6, and 89, no. 45; C. C. R. 1413–1419, p 513; 1419–1422, pp 250, 255, 257 and 258.
(32) Storey, R, L., "Thomas Langley and the Bishopric of Durham, 1406–1437", (London 1961), pp 96–7.
(33) C. P. S. 32 and 33 as but two examples.
(34) Ancient Correspondence, xliii, no. 162.
(35) Proceedings in Chancery, vol. 1, p xvi, (Record Commission, 1827–32).
(36) Chancery Warrants, 667/905, 1364/66 and 71 also 1365/9.
(37) Rotuli Parliamentorum, vol. iv, p 71 onwards.

Thomas Langley

(38) Harriss, G, L. (ed), "Henry V, The Practice of Kingship", (Oxford 1985), p 145.

(39) Newhall, R. A. "The English Conquest of Normandy", 1416–24, (New York, 1924).

(40) P. R. O. e, 364/52, m. i. d.

(41) Jacob, E, F., "The Fifteenth Century, 1399–1485", (Oxford 1961). For a detailed analysis of parliament.

(42) Myers, A, R. (ed), E. H. D. vol. iv, doc, no. 113, p 225–26.

(43) Reg. fo. 275.

(44) Jacob, E, F., "The Fifteenth Century, 1399–1485", (Oxford 1961), pp 194/5.

(45) C. P. R. 393 and 395.

(46) C. P. R. 451 and 461.

(47) Exchequer L. T. R: Original Roll, 186, m. 63; C. C. R. 1419–1422 p 250; C. P. R. 394.

(48) Myers, A, R. (ed), E. H. D. vol. iv, pp 225–7, docs. no. 113, i, ii, and iii, (London 1969).

PART FOUR

HENRY VI;
LANGLEY and the MINORITY

"The griefs of those who stood in high degree
And fell at last with no expedient
To bring them out of their adversity.
For sure it is, if Fortune wills to flee,
No man may stay her course or keep his hold;
Let no one trust a blind prosperity.
Be warned by these examples, true and old." **(1)**

The Early Years of the Minority

Preamble

Henry V's premature death left the Lancastrians with two distinct problems:
how to rule England and France, and the fact that the circle of courtiers
around the infant King was composed of those who were either Lancastrian
by birth, marriage, or though patronage. Tact had to be exercised, otherwise
control by an oligarchy could lead to dissatisfaction amongst those who felt
excluded. There were enough Lords and Government Ministers alive who
had lived through the turmoil of the later years of the reign of Richard II.
Henry V had bequeathed to the nation an unsustainable position in France.
Also, during the last years of the reign there had been increasing numbers of
reports of outbreaks of disorder. The campaigning in France had totally
dominated politics during the last decade; this was the European issue of
its day.

The tensions in society were rising to the surface again, the murmur of
Lollardy percolating below the surface. Henry's premature death was seized
upon by the Dauphinists as proof that God was not on England's side. The
church in England spun the propaganda by saying that the King had
sacrificed his life doing God's work and he was portrayed as a crusader
who had made the ultimate sacrifice on behalf of the nation. The infant King

was at Windsor, whilst his mother, Katherine, was escorting her husband's body back to England. The ruling clique had the personage of monarchy in its control, for Katherine had not been Queen long enough, she having no power base from which to exert any control over events. This was an important factor as history had shown and was to show again within the next fifty years. Also, the vast majority of the Lords Temporal were in France and the conduct of affairs was principally in the hands of the Archbishop of Canterbury the experienced Henry Chichele, Henry Beaufort and politically Langley,who was the countries chief minister. He held the purse strings and was keeper of the Great Seal without which no enforceable orders could be sent out.

The infant was not only heir to the throne of England but also to that of France, and so those who were to be charged with his upbringing and safety had to appear to have been drawn from as broad a sphere as possible. The feeling was bubbling below the surface that yet again the curse of the House of Lancaster had been visited on the head of the family. Gaunt, the father of a usurper was rumoured to have died of venereal disease, Henry IV had died at a comparatively early age, and his son had died in the prime of his life. To counter–balance this, the infant prince was undoubtedly the son of an anointed King which is why no voices were raised against his ascension to the throne.

A number of the major Lordships were held by young inexperienced men who did not have the political power–base to cause the Lancastrians any serious problems. There is also a further factor that has to be weighed. Amongst the Lancastrians Langley's experience was almost revered; he was the elder statesman of the Lancastrians, the father of their political house. Even amongst those who were opposed to the French campaigns, and this was a larger group than many realised, Langley was respected for his loyalty to the crown. He was almost viewed in the Commons as *"A"* political, the perception being that he was the most professional of all the crown ministers, one who assiduously carried out the policies of the monarch. The French initiative was clearly seen as being the prime policy of Henry V, Langley having suffered no damage to his reputation. The increasing responsibilities that he had shouldered, particularly the hearing of petitions, had enhanced his reputation. As I have discussed in the previous section, Henry's almost permanent absence in France resulted in more and more petitioners going directly to Langley to have their suits resolved. The soundness of his judgements was never questioned. There is one thing more: Langley was a prelate with no heirs and significantly no members of his family at court. Any patronage his friends and family had enjoyed, and this was limited, had been given from the Duchy of Lancaster lands and titles. He was not the leader of a clique, certainly he was overtly Lancastrian, but his was not a blood relationship. There were no family skeletons in his cupboard.

Finally, the army and its leaders were in France and no armed insurrection could be mounted. Provided that a proper transition of power took place, and for this the Commons had to be fully involved, their assent to matters being crucial, then no rebellion would take place. The messenger who brought news of the King's death would have informed Langley that Chichele was in Windsor with the infant, and so on his journey south he had enough time to assess matters and gather his thoughts.

Whilst Henry's death had taken most of the country by surprise, the ruling clique had been aware of the King's failing health for some time, giving witness to the speed and smoothness with which the transition had been accomplished. Contrary to beliefs the problems of the minority had been the subject of discussion for some time. There were three critical issues: the care of the infant King, and the governance of England and France. These last two had to be seen as being distinctly separate, the Commons having already made their views known. Langley's prime concern was the continuation of *"bon governance"* business as usual.

1422, The Problems Confronting the Council

When news of Henry's death reached England seven days after it had happened, Langley was at Crake in Yorkshire. It took a further three days for the news to reach him and a further three days for him to travel to London, thirteen days in all (2). Langley was the pivot of the government; he had the Great Seal and his was the most senior rank. No decisions could be taken by Chichele, Henry Beaufort Bishop of Winchester or by Gloucester, who were with the infant King, until Langley arrived. The Commons had to be summoned and the passage of transition plotted, and there was also the matter of preparing the capital to receive the corpse of the King.

On the 28th of September, Langley symbolically resigned the Great Seal to the infant King at Windsor (3). Simon Gaunstede, the keeper of the Chancery Rolls, took charge of the seal. The Lords who were with the infant King sent out the summons for a parliament to be held on the 9th of November. Later minutes of a meeting of the Lords Temporal and Spiritual held on the 1st of October noted *"maior et sanior pars omnium dominorum et procerum regni"* (4); they obviously had taken the view that they should continue to act as the Great Council. The summons had been sent out and sealed in the Star Chamber of the Palace of Westminster by Gaunstede under Langley's direction. Prior to the parliament, on the 5th of November all the senior Lords met in London to discuss the terms of reference under which Gloucester would conduct the forthcoming parliament. They were in effect, taking part in the age–old tradition of agreeing their "slate" in the proverbial smoke–filled room; after all it *was* winter. This council contained seven members of the clergy of whom only Langley and Chichele had any practical experience of government, and fifteen Lords, the King's extended family amongst them. Given that the King's brothers had a vested interest, it is highly probable that Langley as *de facto* Chancellor would have chaired the meeting. He had a foot in both the church and the government camps and was trusted by both sides.

Henry V's interment took place on the 7th of November, after which Langley read aloud the will and its codicils to Archbishop Chichele, Bishop Beaufort, Gloucester and Exeter. The actual will and its codicils has been lost, and the chroniclers are equally divided as to precisely what the Lords who had been present at his death attested as being his last words. In the end it was agreed to put to the Commons the proposition that Bedford should act as regent in France should the Duke of Burgundy decline the post, which he did. Gloucester was named as protector and defender of the realm and the church, and principal councillor to the King. Precedents were consulted as to the powers granted to former regents. In this, Langley would have been anxious to avoid any constitutional impropriety, the ascension of Henry VI needing to be beyond present or future challenge as the perpetuation of the Lancastrian Dynasty was all–important.

The last parliament of the reign was opened by Archbishop Chichele on the 9th of November, there being no Chancellor yet appointed which is why Langley did not open the proceedings. The powers of the council were to include all appointments, to shire and port positions as well as to control over the wardships and marriages in the hands of the crown. Most importantly for the future, the council took into its powers the right to grant the King's feudal patronage, and, prudently a quorum of four was set. On the 16th of November Langley was appointed as Chancellor, his third time in office **(5)**.

The terms under which not only Bedford and Gloucester but all the councillors and ministers held their posts had to be carefully thought out. It was a question of balance, parliament would expect some degree of control, this had to be offered; to not do so would have risked sparking civil war. It was here that the drafting skills and experience of Langley would come to the fore. One can visualise the horse–trading that went on before the agreed document was placed before the Commons for formal ratification. The members of the council head to swear an oath "*assumptus ad concilium regis et admissus*" **(6)**. There authority was defined as acting in a collective way with the responsibilities *"the whiche duryng the tendre age aforseide of the Kyng, Governe and Reule undre hym, and by his auctoritee"*. This clearly stated that Royal authority was vested in the council; their position had to be unchallenged. Above all there had to be assurances that no one councillor would act independently. In all eighteen councillors were named, in reality for the first twelve months of the reign Langley with John Stafford, the Keeper of the Treasury, and William Alnwick, the Keeper of the Privy Seal ran the administration. On the 25th of January the Commons received a form of representation on the Council when Thomas Chaucer, the son of the poet, who had been Speaker five times, and William Allington, were given positions.

Gloucester was far from happy with the strictures that were imposed on his position. Significantly the Commons insisted that when Bedford was in England he should take over as regent in England. As they were the direct heirs of Henry VI they were in an difficult position. This division of responsibilities meant that no cohesive policy could be followed in France, given the terms in the Treaty of Troyes this was to have the effect of hamstringing Bedford in pursuing the implementation of the Treaty.

The first parliament of the reign commenced on the 5th of December, it reaffirmed that the new council could not proceed unless either Bedford or Gloucester was present. Any appointments that the Treasurer made had to be ratified by Langley. The instruction was given that Langley was only to divulge to the Council the state of the King's treasury; his salary was set at £200 for every attendance at council. Langley was in attendance on a daily basis, whilst he still retained a good deal of autonomy he had to report every major decision to the council whose consent he had to obtain. He sent 2,000 marks to the Calais garrison with a further £2,000 being sent on the 15th of January. They also received an assignment of 13 shillings and 4 pence on each sack of wool coming from the Calais Staple together with the revenues of the towns in the area. Langley was making a start on the stipulation voiced at the debate on the Treaty of Troyes that France had to finance itself. Again his political nous averted a potential catastrophe. Further efforts were made the following year to direct funds towards making Calais self–sufficient. In a way this was Langley clearing up business that had been interrupted by the death of Henry V.

Gloucester was to cause the country and Langley further problems in the next parliament. At the beginning of 1423 he had married Jacqueline Countess of Hainault who was still not divorced from John of Brabant, the Duke of Burgundy had been named as their heir. The parliament of 1423 recognised them as wed, clearly they were not. Gloucester, thanks to the vast resources at his personal disposal mounted an expedition to recover his wife's lands. The Commons may have seen that in the recognition the marriage they would be ridding themselves of Gloucester and with Bedford fully occupied in France they would have control of the infant Henry VI. A further point is that Gloucester's actions placed a great strain on the Anglo–Burgundian alliance that Bedford needed to maintain.

During 1423 Langley took time to visit his diocese during Easter as well as in August when he took the opportunity to meet a delegation from the Scots at York. Philip Morgan and the earl of Northumberland attended the discussions, it was eventually agreed that James should marry an English-woman of rank and that he would provide a ransom of 60,000 marks to be paid in instalments of 10,000 marks a year. The agreement was finalised on the 10th of September being later ratified in parliament on the 21st of November 1423; it was then incorporated and sealed in London on the 4th of December after which parliament formally ratified it on the 24th of January 1424 **(7)**. His last address as Chancellor to the parliament that commenced on the 20th of October 1423 began with the words *"Fear God, honour the King"* **(8)**, this sitting lasted until the 28th of February 1424.

Langley together with Bishop Kemp had been nominated to lead an English embassy to Scotland. James and his bride Joan Beaufort were taken with them to Durham where in March the discussions were due to be held. The English delegation contained the earls of Westmorland and Northumber-land together with the Keeper of the Privy Seal, Sir Richard Neville; the Lords Greystoke and Dacre also attended **(9)**. A truce of seven years was agreed on the 28th of March the terms of which included an agreement that both sides would not aid the others enemies. In the August of the following year Langley and Sir John Scrope, who was the new Keeper of the Privy Seal, were in Berwick to discuss the violations to the truce that occurred that year.

Henry Beaufort had been back in England for a year. He took over the leadership of the council, he was also Langley's closest friend amongst the Beauforts. He had been the biggest single lender to Henry V, £35,000 in total, during his step–nephews reign, this would have brought him into close contact with Langley. Also his conduct at the Council of Constance had added to his prestige, on his return he foreclosed on the loans which had been secured on the customs. At this time he was owed £20, 149, and 5 pence being the balance of two loans that he and Langley had negotiated on the 12th of June 1417, the 13th of May 1421 and on the 31st of August 1422. He made a further loan of £17,666 to the new King and in return he was given the right to appoint collectors in each port. He had foreclosed to protect the repayment of his loans. Langley had received the approval of parliament in 1422 to reduce the customs duties payable on wool by native merchants from 50 shillings to 40 shillings. Beaufort had many friends amongst the Flemish mercantile class, the group most affected, Langley was merely responding to the outbreak of anti–Flemish protests that had swept London.

He returned from Durham for the next session of parliament that commenced on the 28th of May and lasted to the 16th of July. At the close he journeyed to Hertford Castle, the place where Henry IV had appointed him Keeper of the Privy Seal; here on the 16th of July 1424 he resigned the Great Seal **(10)**. He had occupied the office of Chancellor for 2,546 days, one of the longest chancellorships of the Middle Ages, only exceeded by Ralph Neville two hundred years before. He was now sixty–one years old; and was to remain a member of the Great Council. He was succeeded by Bishop Beaufort who held the office for less than a year; he was replaced by the Archbishop of York, John Kemp on the 13th of March 1426.

His Last Years in Public Office

Langley returned north where he remained until December, during this time he attended the York convocation. His presence would have re–assured the northern clergy regarding the upbringing of Henry VI. He was still not able to detach himself from political affairs he journeyed to London to report the decisions of the convocation to the council.

He was briefly in London for three months during 1425 where he was in daily attendance at council meetings as well as being named as a trier of petitions before the Commons. From here he embarked on a perambulation around his diocese which included a visit to Holy Island and a tour of the Scottish lands of the diocese.

On the 20th of November news reached him following Gloucester's return after his abortive attempt to secure his wife's lands, trouble had broken out in London between the Duke and Bishop Beaufort.

Langley was at Raby where he was receiving Richard Neville's oath as an executor of the Earl of Westmorland. Neville was the nephew of Bishop Beaufort and it seems probable that he asked Langley to intercede. Despite his age, he was now sixty–three, and the fact that it was now winter, he decided to journey to the capital. On the 29th of October Gloucester had ordered the mayor of London, John Coventry, to "*keep well the city that night and make good watch*". There was a rumour that Bishop Beaufort was going to attempt a coup. An altercation between their followers was averted by the intercession of Chichele and Beaufort's nephew Pedro, the Portuguese duke of Coimbra. Bedford returned from France on the 20th of December, and when he arrived at the capital he lodged with Langley at Durham house. Yet again this exemplifies Langley's standing amongst the Lancastrian hierarchy, the situation being comparable to that in 1406 when the then Prince of Wales had stayed with Langley whilst he mediated with his father, the King.

After a series of meetings, Gloucester agreed to place his complaint to a commission of nine peers to be headed by Chichele, Langley and Morgan of Worcester together with the majority of councillors available. This commission heard submissions from both sides on the 7th of March in Leicester. Eventually, both parties were prevailed upon to publicly swear an oath of allegiance that was witnessed by the infant King and the Commons. The Leicester Parliament became known as "The Parliament of Bats", an apt description. No one was allowed to wear arms during the parliament, men concealed bats about their person, hence the name given to the parliament. Langley briefly returned to his diocese before attending the reconvened parliament at Leicester.

During this parliament Henry VI had been seated next to his uncle, Bedford, who knighted his nephew on the 19th of May. This was highly symbolic, a reminder to the Lords and Commons of the majesty of the King. It was also a prerequisite to coronation. The four–year–old then conferred knighthood on a number of the heirs to the main titles in England. In addition, thirty–six knighthood's were awarded, the recipients being mainly soldiers who had served in France as well as members of the nobility who were generally not Lancastrians. The reason for this is obvious, being to achieve balance, or the perception of such. You can detect the diplomatic hand of Langley in this.

On the 1st of June 1426, Langley asked the council sitting at Leicester if he could be excused from further attendance. He emphasised that he would forever remain loyal to the throne but his age was now great, he being sixty–three. He went on to explain that his health was now impaired due to the long years in royal service and he wished to attend to matters in his diocese so as to ensure that his soul was not impaired. There is no doubt that Langley had chosen the path of royal service as opposed to his spiritual calling, and his request was understandable. There is little information available regarding his "illness", but he had pleaded infirmity once before when asking to be excused from council meetings (11).

The reference to his soul is interesting, and also his admission that he had neglected his diocese. It would be interesting to know how he was viewed by the members of the chapter, but sadly there are no recorded remarks. The distance from the capital of this, the most northern of provinces, meant that he was by necessity absent for prolonged periods. The reference does, I believe, also carry a tone of remorse. Was it only the neglect of his diocese that he felt imperilled his soul? I think that the answer is that there were a number of skeletons in his closet.

The application was refused. Despite the Lords in attendance, it was felt that his experience was needed. At this time Bishop Beaufort was still on pilgrimage abroad. There were tensions between the Beauforts and their legitimate half–brothers and cousins as well as between Gloucester and Bedford. Archbishop Chichele, the only other permanent member of the council with the stature to broker harmony, had his own problems with the new Pope, Martin V. It speaks volumes for him that the Lancastrians felt that they could *not* allow their elder statesman to retire.

So, why did the council feel that Langley's presence was still necessary? The answer could lie in the disposal of the many wardships in the King's hands. It required tact and diplomacy to dispose of these wardships, and Langley was one of the few who was perceived as not having any blood interest in the disposals. Patronage during a minority has to administered delicately. Another factor was the absence at this time of Bishop Beaufort who was still on pilgrimage. Langley was particularly close to the Bishop of Winchester, but it was Beaufort who had, at Langley's request, assisted at his consecration. Bedford was also close to him but his regency of France prevented him, from attending many meetings of the Great Council. It seems probable that those sympathetic to the Bishop prevailed on Langley to remain in London for the rest of the year, with a break to attend the northern convocation at York which lasted from the 12th of August to the 9th of October. He did not return to his diocese until April the following year. What kept him in the capital despite his wish to retire? In assessing this it is worth noting that he was now no longer Chancellor, which meant that he therefore had more time to devote to the business of the council. Also, most of the diplomatic issues were being handled in France, so Langley could devote his time to the Great Council.

Certainly the friction between Gloucester and Beaufort had revealed rifts that he would have felt concern about. He may have felt that a situation could arise that bore comparison to the position that Gaunt was placed in during the late 1370's and the following decade. A letter exists, written during the trouble between Beaufort and Gloucester, where the Bishop had written to Bedford who was at that time in France. It is worth reproducing the letter as it shows the problems that were below the surface (see below).

There were further issues that have a bearing on the refusal of Langley's request. The drain on England's finances by the continuation of the war in

France was becoming serious. By 1433 the debts of the crown had risen to
£164,815, this proving how exceptional Langley's Chancellorship had been.
The debts of the crown were never anything near this figure. This in part was
due to the Commons reluctance to vote through emergency subsidies, a
problem that had never arisen during Langley's time in office.

There was also the problem of the wearing of liveries; a number of earls
were building up what amounted to private armies. There were a number of
complaints brought to parliament regarding various lords indulging in
skirmishing in many parts of the country. Langley's calming presence was
deemed to be the balm to quell the various groups. It was felt that he was
trusted by all parties.

Here is the letter:

> *"Right high and mighty prince, and my right noble one after one (i. e., the
> king) levest lord. I recommend me unto you will all my heart and service.
> And as you desire the welfare of the king our sovereign lord and of his
> realms of England and of France, and your own weal and ours also haste
> you hither; for by my troth if you tarry, we shall put this land in adventure
> with a field (i. e., a battle). Such a brother you have here. God make him a
> good man. For your wisdom knows well that the prosperity of France
> stands in the welfare of England."* **(12)**

When this letter, written after the trouble in London, became known to
Gloucester, it served to exacerbate the situation. Bedford stayed in England
until the 19th of March 1427, and as soon as he left London so did Langley,
more than just coincidence I feel. During the period 1426–7 a number of
significant appointments were made, the majority to those who could be
perceived as of Beaufort's party. Four Sheriffs were appointed: Sir Thomas
Wykeham to Oxfordshire–Berkshire, with, William Allington, Sir Richard
Vernon and Thomas Stonor being appointed later in 1427 when Langley was
again in London **(13)**. Bishop Neville was also provided to the see of
Salisbury; he was also close to Beaufort.

The Commons had voiced concerns regarding the awarding of patronage
during the minority. In the December parliament of 1422, after negotiations
between the Council and the Commons it had been announced that any
disposal of wardships, marriages and properties, should only be undertaken
for the financial interest of the King **(14)** *"Without partiality favour or
fraud"*. Earlier in the year a proclamation had been put before parliament on
the 4th of March. It invited anyone who wished to purchase a wardship or
marriage to appear before the Treasurer on the 23rd of May. Preference was
to be given to the highest bidder.

The Beauforts and Patronage

The Beauforts did well from the pool of patronage. John de Vere, whose father had died in 1417, was placed in the wardship of the Duke of Exeter, Thomas Beaufort. In the September of 1425, de Vere married the daughter of Sir John Howard who was in the service of the dowager–queen, Joan. Thomas Courtney, the earl of Devon, married John Beaufort's daughter Margaret. The property of the late Lord Scrope was placed in the hands of Sir Richard Neville, a nephew of the Beauforts.

Richard, duke of York, was twelve years old and on the 13th of December 1423 his custody was awarded to Westmorland, brother–in–law of the Beauforts. Within a year, he was married to one of the duke's daughters, Cecily. Some of the York estates had been granted to him by his uncle the earl of March who died in Ireland in January 1425, and these were granted to Exeter. One of the Beaufort's sons–in–law, Sir Edward Standing, and received custody of the earldom of March whilst Thomas Chaucer was given the custody of Sir John Drayton's daughter Joan. Thomas, Lord Roos wardship, was in Gloucester's hands.

These are but a few of the wardships and guardianships that the Lancastrians/Beauforts plundered. Without Langley, and others, they would not have been so able to procure these valuable assignments. The point here is that Langley, from his unique position in the council, was able to assist in directing the powers of patronage to the House of Lancaster, and this would explain why he remained in the capital. He would see these awards as adding stability to the dynasty, the extension of the web binding the upper nobility to the monarchy.

The Last Years

Langley continued to divide his time between Durham and London during 1427, and he attended the council meetings in February and March. He was busy attending to matters concerning the wills of Henry IV and Henry V. From the beginning of December he remained in the north until the following June. The council meeting which was convened for the 1st of June 1428 was to deal with the education of the prince, something he would naturally be interested in. Beaufort returned from pilgrimage after Langley had left the capital. Langley asked to be excused from the next sitting of parliament owing to ill health.

He entertained Bishop Beaufort in his manner at Crake when the bishop journeyed north to meet the king of Scots. Langley had been in negotiation with the Scots for a number of years, most recently in regard to returning their King; the visit would have had a dual purpose. Langley and Beaufort met James at Berwick–on–Tweed in February. The Scots were still aiding the Dauphin with troops, although the pretext for the meeting was to discuss Beaufort's proposed crusade against the Hussites. The talks appear to have concluded with no firm agreements, and there are no records of what was discussed. He returned to the capital to attend the Great Council meeting on the 17th of April 1429. He was later again in Scotland engaged in another round of talks, the violations of the truce continuing unabated.

Again, in February 1430, Langley, in the company of the earls of Salisbury, Northumberland, Greystoke and Scrope together with the Bishop of Carlise, Lumley, travelled to Scotland, the talks again breaking up in disarray. The same negotiators tried again in November **(15)**.

Gloucester again attacked Bishop Beaufort before a meeting of the Great Council in 1431. Citing precedence, Gloucester claimed that on Beaufort's acceptance of a Cardinal's hat, he should have resigned his see of Winchester, and further, that he should return all the revenues that he had enjoyed during the period. Beaufort returned to England in 1432, and Beaufort again persuaded the council to dismiss Gloucester's case. Behind all this, Beaufort had agreed to return the crown jewels which he held as a pledge against a number of loans. One can detect Langley's hand in this; of all the members of the Great Council, he was the closest to Beaufort. Also, the Bishop had been abroad, and of all the members there was only Langley whom he could rely on for unbiased advice.

Towards the end of the 1420's it became clear that whilst the crown's income could just match its expenditure, the drain on its resources by the demands for further finance in France meant that the crown liabilities were outstripping its expenditure. Beaufort again came to the assistance of the crown, making substantial loans during the early years of the 1430's.

He was in attendance at Westminster Abbey when, on the 6th of November 1429 for the coronation of Henry VI **(16),** he attended in his capacity as Bishop of Durham. Again the holy oil of Canterbury was used. After this time his attendance at Westminster was sporadic, and he asked to be excused due to infirmity on the 2nd of January 1432. He attended later in the year when Gloucester attempted to deprive his uncle, Bishop Beaufort, of his see. He remained in the capital until the 30th of November.

He had to journey south in April to attend to diocesan matters in the capital. His liberties in his palatinate were the subject of challenge. His governance was autocratic and strict, something his tenants resented. He also had to deal with matters concerning the will of Henry V. His final attendance at Westminster was on the 8th of November 1435 when he surrendered the will to parliament. At the age of seventy–two he made his final journey from the capital to his diocese.

During 1436 he undertook various perambulations around his diocese, attending the northern convocation at York on the 11th of June. From the 16th of October he remained at his residence at Bishop Auckland which was set in parkland by the River Wear. His infirmity lasted for thirteen months. He died on the 20th of November 1437; he was seventy–four years old. He was interred in a marble tomb in the Galilee Chapel in Durham Cathedral, a chapel that he was responsible for building.

Recapitulation

At the beginning of this book I posed the question: why is a political biography about Langley needed? I hope that this tome has answered that question. Unlike the majority of his peers, his promotions were due to ability and not to his position in the pecking order. It should be borne in mind that he was one of the first chief ministers of the crown to come from within the civil service, his main clerical promotion coming after he had attained the Chancery. As a chancellor he was not particularly innovative. However, his effectiveness is clear to see. Henry V would never have been able to promote the war in France had Langley not been chancellor. Similarly Henry IV would not have achieved the measure of stability that he did without Langley's help. The most noteworthy fact is that during his Chancellorship, money due to the exchequer was collected quicker and more efficiently than had previously been the case. His position as the third–highest cleric in England assisted the crown in its taxation of the clergy, and the amount raised, particularly from successive northern convocations, would not have been as forthcoming had Langley not used his influence.

The reason for his career being overlooked is easy to define. The events of 1397/9 have overshadowed many men's careers, the changes being so fundamental that, generally, historians have tended to overlook Langley. Similarly, the Kingship of Henry V, the victory of Agincourt and events in France, have been the main focus for study of the period.

As I stated at the outset, this is a political study, his religious career having already been written. I have only commented on his religion when it has been affected by his political career. The fact that whilst he was in Paris he undertook an investigation into the rules of the order of the Celestines for Henry V are a pointer to his orthodoxy. The king was pious in terms of his religion, and it would appear that Langley was like–minded. As an executor of Henry's will he was intimately involved in the foundation at Syon. He also appears to have been close to Chichele and Beaufort, both from the mainstream of Catholicism. His attendance at the Council of Pisa was as a politician more than as a churchman, although he had the proxies of the clergy from the northern church.

We have no contemporary description of Langley's physical appearance, in the Langley window he is shown as bearded; this type of depiction was a common portrayal of church dignitaries. Storey has rather sniffley commented that he was not a learned man. He bases his comment on a sample of Langley's handwriting in a letter addressed to his receiver–general as well as by looking at his signature. Storey describes his hand as "bastard secretary", a style used by clerks. I cannot agree with these comments. Anyone who had occupied the high offices of state that Langley did, and for so long, was no fool. Just as today, the handwriting of many professionals is often illegible, consider deciphering your doctors writing, so the same is true of Langley. He was a very busy man who literally wrote and signed copious numbers of documents in a day.

A further aspect of his character concerns his attitude to illegitimacy. The most famous family who he legitimised were the Beauforts. He also legitimised two of the Radcliffe family. When he died he had obtained a Papal licence to use a font that he had paid for in the Galilee Chapel for the baptism of children whose parents had been excommunicated. It appears by this action that he took the view that children should not be penalised for the deeds of their parents.

His handling of the Commons was masterful, a mix of tact and firmness. In a changing society when the merchants powers increased, he was able to ally the new mercantile class to the monarchy. His success in raising loans did much to broaden democracy throughout parliament as the new men formed coteries. All his addresses to the Commons stressed the image of the monarchy's unity with God, and this represented a powerful symbolism to Medieval Man.

This begs the question: how effective would he have been had he not been hamstrung, firstly by the rebellions of Henry IV's reign and then by the burden of directing the country's wealth towards the financing of the French campaigns? I believe that he, like Henry V, saw that by launching such a sustained campaign the Lancastrian dynasty would, through the unity of the nation, tighten its grip on the throne. Whilst one can understand the pursuit of this policy, I feel that it was flawed. Clearly Henry Bolingbroke was a usurper, and the perception of his son, Henry of Monmouth, was that he was the legitimate heir to the throne. One needs to remember that rebellions and warfare occupied the greater part of the period of Langley's occupation of the highest offices of state in that the whole financial machine was geared towards raising levies both at home and abroad. Had these issues not been so prominent then Langley, as Chancellor, would have presided in a gold age of prosperity as the resources of the crown could have been used to benefit the community of England.

The resumption of the war with France was the only solution to Henry's feelings of doubt over the right of him and his father's right to occupy the throne of England. The deeply held belief in the country that should England prove victorious then God was indeed satisfied that the throne was occupied by a man who was justly entitled to wear the crown was the credo that permeated the thinking of Henry and to some extent his senior Lords.

The undercurrent of Lollardy was, perhaps, one of the prime reasons behind the pursuit of the war. Henry certainly had a case for the return of the lands as agreed in the treaty of Brétigny. Again a clear demonstration of God's support would provide the English clergy with enough proof to argue that the teachings and beliefs of the Lollards were contrary to God. Should they have God's support then England would not have been given the victories that it enjoyed. This argument was also used regarding the Treaty and the lands that England was claiming. After Agincourt he could have claimed these, and the French would have ceded them. Twenty years after his death, the unsustainable position in France was to prove the downfall of the dynasty.

How Langley squared this pursuit of war with his religious beliefs is an interesting point. A man that has been consecrated and taken the vows that he did, particularly concerning his mortal soul and the members of his diocese, had deeply opposing views to marry together. In the middle ages those who held senior positions in the church and government invariably chose the path of pragmatism. In order to achieve stability and harmony it was necessary to undertake military campaigns to create these conditions. Church and Crown were wedded in that both existed to maintain the status quo and to keep each other in power. In this lies the burden of office, in Langley's later years there are signs that he did feel some remorse for his actions. The Window in York Minster, the rebuilding of St. Leonard's, the foundation of the collegiate at St. Mary's, Manchester, the rebuilding of the Galilee Chapel, all point to a troubled conscience.

The demons that drove Henry, and his father before him, also propelled Langley. The hidden belief that Henry IV's premature death was due to God inflicting his debilitating illness in revenge for the murders. His complicity in the murder of Richard II is beyond doubt, his involvement in the death of

Archbishop Scrope being more so. In both instances, his loyalty to the House of Lancaster took precedence over any religious scruples he may have had. I am convinced of his culpability in the slaughter of Agincourt, the point having been made that he was intimately involved in the diplomatic events that formed the prologue to 1415. His ability to provide the finance for Henry's war machine places him in a culpable light both in terms of the deaths and the political consequences that ensued.

Diplomatically, Langley followed a path that was designed to create the general feeling in the country that the French could not be trusted, war being the only solution. The propaganda that emanated from the crown during the reigns of Henry IV and Henry V was chiefly the work of Langley. How he squared this as a leading member of the church, only his confessor knew. The window in York Minster holds a clue. Clearly, from his remarks to the council when he asked to be excused, a request that was, out of necessity, refused, show that he felt he had to make some kind of peace with God. To me this is an indication that he felt that he had matters to atone for.

His obtaining of the document of legitimisation of the Beauforts produced profound consequences for England. The Tudors owe their descent from this family, as did the heirs of Buckingham, Warwick and most of the senior nobility in England. They would have been legitimised in any event. The point here is that when Langley drafted the petition to the Pope he would have been aware of the fact that a whole new dynasty, attached by blood to the Lancastrian Kings, was being founded. Had Langley not been available to Henry V, the only other person who could have occupied the Chancery would have been Bishop Beaufort. This would have deprived England of a prelate who, no matter the criticisms of his wealth, enhanced the country's position in the church by his decisive intervention at the Council of Constance.

The other major event that he had a hand in is one that has been overlooked. As a young man of thirty-one, he had carried messages of support from Gaunt to Richard II when Gaunt's enemies at court were spreading pernicious gossip concerning Gaunt's ambitions. Had Richard, in one of his mood–swings, decided to place some credence to the murmurings, the Lancastrian dynasty could have foundered. His persuasiveness did much to assuage Richard's concerns.

He was only able to diligently pursue his career from a base of security. The only powers of patronage that he used were vested in his Bishopric. Anyone whom he wished to reward were rewarded from the Durham patrimony. John Radcliffe was the Treasurer of the Episcopal household and his brother George was a member of the diocesan council (17). William

Radcliffe was collated to the prebend of Auckland, and two other members, as well as John, were granted dispensations for their illegitimacy. John Newton, Nicholas Hulme, and Richard Buckley, who were all from the area that Langley came from, were successive receivers–general of Durham. John Thoralby was one of Langley's closest councillors, and Thomas Holden was steward of Durham. Robert Strangways was chief forester of Weardale and his brother James was appointed as one of the Bishopric's Justices; he was later to become chief justice of the County of Lancaster. All came from north Manchester as did Thomas Hebden, his spiritual chancellor, and Thomas Lyes who was his vicar–general; as such, he shouldered the greatest responsibilities due to Langley's absence in London.

Without these men, the house of Lancaster would not have had the benefit of Langley's uninterrupted service. Middleton and its adjacent parishes are owed a great debt by the Lancastrian Kings. Many men owed their careers to Langley, and similarly, Langley owed *his* promotion to the abilities of his back–room staff. These servants enabled Langley to concentrate his energies to wider matters. These secretaries, chamberlains, etc, all ensured that his diocese functioned proficiently.

He appears not to have made any enemies, an achievement in itself. His humble origins, the fourth son of a small tenant–farmer, add a lustre to his career. He showed no pomp, there was no show of the gratuitous use of power or the flaunting of wealth. As a model of loyalty and dedication there are few, if any, to match his record. A workaholic certainly, ruthless in his efforts to maintain the Lancastrian dynasty, but above all this is his tirelessness. The fact that when he died he was not exceptionally wealthy is a testimony to his self–effacement. It took a man of outstanding single–mindedness to achieve what he did.

His epitaph from the House of Lancaster can be read in the tribute that was paid to him by the parliament in 1433. His franchise in Durham was the subject of attack and he had petitioned the Council against this. The guarding of his Episcopal rights over his tenants was a strongly upheld privilege. The Council found in his favour, and on the record of the decision it is stated that this was because of:

the countless magnificent and fruitful services, profitable to himself and his realm of England, diligently and faithfully shown and given by the said Bishop in the time of our lord the King, as well as in that of his noble forbears, without stint of toil, cost or expense, nor without grievous bodily hurt. **(18)**

The title of this book is Thomas Langley, *The* First Spin-Doctor: I apologise for allowing a word of the nineties, spin-doctor, to intrude into the cognomen, there are two reasons for this. Firstly, in writing this book it was my intention to appeal to a wider audience than just academics and scholars. It was my small way of endeavouring to introduce history to a wider audience. By using the modern terminology I hope that someone who is not necessarily a history-lover may be intrigued by the epithet. The phrase "Spin-Doctor" a neologism I know, yet one which in some ways seems remarkably appropriate – of course Langley was vastly more that a manipulator of propaganda – to leave him with this epithet is to belittle him by ranking him alongside the sad practitioners of hyperbole and denigration when he is abundantly qualified to take his place among the greatest of statesmen. The definition of propaganda, that which it is expedient for others to know applied as much in Langley's time as it does today.

Secondly I hope that this book has shown that the politics of the Middle Ages have modern day parallels. The entire ethos and continuation of the House of Lancaster relied on propaganda. From the justification for the usurpation, through Agincourt to the Treaty of Troyes, and throughout the minority of Henry VI, a "spin" was put on events. The public presentation of policies became of such importance that a whole new breed of civil servant became essential. The pronouncements that were given after the diplomatic embassies were carefully crafted and presented. Creating a climate in the country and amongst the mercantile classes whereby there was a ground swell of public support for the invasion of France was one of the significant factors in the 100-years-war. Langley, firstly as privy seal, and then again in the reign of Henry V when he controlled the office from the chancery, dealt exclusively with the propaganda. It was the first government to have a full-time public relations machine that manipulated events so successfully. Ergo: *The* First Spin-Doctor, Thomas Langley. Any person who is able, as he was, to partially legitimise the usurpation, at least in the minds of the general public, was certainly a spin-doctor.

Today's practitioners would be proud if they were able to include in their C. V. the fact that they created a whole new royal family, one that was to become so popular that the son of a murderer became deified both in England and Europe. Not only that, but the illegitimate relations of the murderer became the most popular and wealthy family in the country. Even the execution of the second-highest churchman in the country was presented as a legitimate act, a little local difficulty. I can only define this as Medieval Spin-Doctoring.

There is a point to this. Every nation at time of war has relied on propaganda. The neutral observer will weigh what is said and come to a balanced decision as to the rights and wrongs. The cynical amongst us would also ask the propagandists if they really believe what they were propagating? This applies particularly to Langley for a number of reasons. Did he really believe that Bolingbroke had the legitimate right to occupy the throne? The point has been made elsewhere that should the matter have been decided by an international court of law, then the Lancastrians would have lost their case. Despite this Langley not only supported the actions taken once Richard II was a prisoner but he also acted as a prime mover in the documentation that was provided to support this shaky position. Langley was no fool, this goes beyond blind loyalty, ambition had a hand here.

The initial stance that he took in respect of England's territorial claims against France is understandable and in essence was a correct position. The escalation of the claims to include the French throne again cannot be recognised as being sound in law. The only reason that I can offer is that matters had reached the point of no return. By this I mean two things. Firstly, the support of the baronage would have been withdrawn from Henry's regime. Secondly, had this support been withdrawn then the House of Lancaster would have been threatened, *realpolitik*, the barons had to be brought into line behind a political cause. I have made these points to underline the fact that Langley's commitment to the House of Lancaster contained an element of self-interest.

I have also stressed his humble upbringing – did this make him more ruthless in his pursuit and maintenance of power? Did the twin demons of poverty and obscurity have a bearing on his actions? I believe they did. As a fourth son his only chance of a career lay in the church, probably as a local rector or as a member of a monastery. The civil service offered a greater chance of better rewards. Luck played a part in his early career in that he lived in Lancashire and owing to the fact that his neighbours, the Radcliffes, who were already members of Gaunt's household, aided his early career. Their initial support was crucial. From that time onwards all the promotions that he earned were by dint of his assiduousness and his abilities. The civil service provided someone Langley's political skills with a more interesting and demanding challenge.

The men who usually occupied the position of Chancellor were drawn from the families of the higher nobility or from the upper echelons of the church. At the time that Langley was first appointed to the chancery he was not from either of these strata of society. That alone marks him out as possessing outstanding abilities, and I stress here that I do not find sufficient evidence to show that Langley's was an especially privaleged background, he was the son of a minor tenant farmer. It is also salient to remark that he was not a particularly outstanding churchman at the time of his first occupation of the office of Chancellor.

There is another pertinent point: he had not occupied the position of Chancellor to the Duchy of Lancaster, his first experience of chancery being as England's chief minister. This indicates that his appointment was internal in that he was appointed for his political abilities. Being born in Lancashire and having the Radcliffes for neighbours being the first and only piece of luck to come his way, any other fortune was self-created. Natural ability and an uncle who was prepared to educate him coupled with his service in Gaunt's chancery meant that he was given the opportunity to develop his talents. These talents, coupled with his loyalty over-rode any questions regarding "experience" as a minister of state.

The fact that he was able to rise to the prominence that he enjoyed is also a reflection on the changing times through which he lived. The importance of *"bone governance"*, as stated by Bishop Beaufort, placed the civil service in the spotlight. Bad governance would not be tolerated by the populace in the early 15th century. His motivation? the wielding of power. He enjoyed the game of statecraft, many were totally dependant on him which is why so little was written about him. This total dependence reveals the weakness in those who were the recipients of his largesse.

His early mission to Richard II on behalf of Gaunt was the beginning of his career, I feel that he made his ultimate decision to use all his considerable skills to assist the Lancastrians at Leicester when Bolingbroke was exiled.

The place in which he died was a far cry from the surroundings of his birth, and in this we can summarise his life. The palace at Bishop Auckland was set in parkland by the River Wear, designed and built by Antony Bek; the carved roof of the great hall supported by columns of purbeck marble. This hall alone was three times the entire size of the house of his birth. A large chapel with an adjoining smaller one and a *"great fair chamber with a smaller room off it"* **(19)**. A palace fit for one of the greatest statesmen of his age. A far cry from the steading adjacent to the small hamlet set in the rolling moorland at the foot of the Pennines. A fit place in which to die for the second most powerful man of his day, servant, and friend to the Papacy and three kings. A Diplomat, Chancellor, Bishop, and Councillor, a pillar of the House of Lancaster. A remarkable journey for a boy born into a world that held little prospect for a fourth son from a poor family. He had ascended the mountain-face of life from the bottom to the top. Truly the proverbial local boy made good. As they still say in the town of his birth, Owd a thawt it. I doubt that his mother and father did when the infant took his first breath when he was born into the shire of Lancaster seventy-four years before.

He was not a particularly wealthy man when he died, he tended to use the money he earned from his offices to pay for his daily expenditure. He left thirty-three books in his will, mainly concerned with theology. Robert Rolston, who was the keeper of the great wardrobe, and archdeacon of Durham from 1421, received a copy of the *Moralia* of St. Gregory. John Frank, a canon of Salisbury received the *Historia Scholastica* of Petrus Comestor, another copy of this work was bequeathed to the Chancellor John Stafford. The three volume *Dictionarium* was given to the Convent of Durham, this was valued at £60, with his copy of the Nottingham *Super Evangelia* having a value of £20. Other books of note are the *Polichronicum,* the *Corpus Juris Civilis,* and *Bestiarum Figurations.*

William Eure, the son of the Steward of Durham received £5 in his will with five marks being bequested to his yeomen and £2 to each groom, his esquires also received £5 each. In total he left monetary gifts that totalled £600, his long serving chamberlain, Thomas Holden was given Old Ford. This he sold to Ralph Legh, eventually after two other owners Thomas Bourchier, archbishop of Canterbury acquired the house. His successor Thomas Cranmer gave the house to Henry VIII when the King hinted that he found the house most attractive.

Gilt and silver crosses and plate were bequethed to various religious houses, in all 14 legatees benefited from his will; twelve more persons were given horses with two beds also listed as specific bequests.

He had funded the repairs of a number of his residences as well as rebuilding the Galilee Chapel. His lasting gifts were in his foundations at Middleton and The Collegiate of St. Mary's now Manchester Cathedral.

Thomas Langley was the unassuming, unknown power behind the strength of the Lancastrian dynasty. The controller of every facet of the medieval government that ruled England. I find it an interesting quirk that the headquarters of the modern day equivalent of the hidden face of the system of administration of the most puissant nation on earth, America, The Central Intelligence Authority, has its headquarters at *Langley*, Virginia. Would it not be interesting to know what they might make of this tenuous connection?

It is because he was so unobtrusive that his political career has not received the recognition that it should have done. As a statesman there were few to equal him in dedication and service. A school is named after him in the town of his birth but their is no lasting memorial in Middleton to their most illustrious son. Perhaps this book has helped to rectify his omission from the history of the times in which he lived, but only you the reader can be the judge of this.

Notes and References

(1) Coghill, N. (trans), "The Canterbury Tales, The Monks Tale", (London 1951).
(2) Sharman, I, C., "Thomas Langley", unpublished lecture paper, 1998.
(3) C. C. R. 1422–1429, P 46; Foedera, x, p 259.
(4) Jacob, E, F., "The Fifteenth Century, 1399–1485", (Oxford 1961) p 212.
(5) C. P. R., 1422–29, pp, 1 and 109; R. P. iv, 171.
(6) Rot. Parl. iv, 201.
(7) P. P. C. iii, 99–100 and 133; PRO, E403/658–64; E28/43/63; Foedera iv, 94, 96, 107; C. P. R. 1422–29, pp 112 and 179.
(8) Rot. Parl. iv, pp 197, 200 and 201.
(9) P. R. O., E28/44/34, 5; C. P. R. 1422–29, p 179; Rot. Parl. iv, 211–12; P. P. C. iii, 137 and 139–42.
(10) Foedra, x, pp 340–1; C. C. R. 1422–1429, p, 154.
(11) P. P. C. iii, pp, 316, 323–4.
(12) Griffiths, R, A., "The Reign of King Henry VI", (London 1981) p 77.
(13) Roskell, J, S., "The Commons in the Parliament of 1422", (Manchester 1954).
(14) Rot. Parl. iv, 175–6.
(15) C. C. R., 1429–35, p 118; P. P. C. iv, 68, 70–1; Bain, J, (ed), iv, 213–4, "Calendar of Documents relating to Scotland preserved in the Public Records Office", (Edinburgh, 1881–84), 4 vols. .
(16) "Historical Collection of a Citizen of London", (Camden Society, 1876), p 168.
(17) Reg. Langley, no. 478.
(18) Rot. Parl. iv, p 431.
(19) Itinery of John Leland.

GENEALOGICAL TABLES

The Family of Thomas Langley

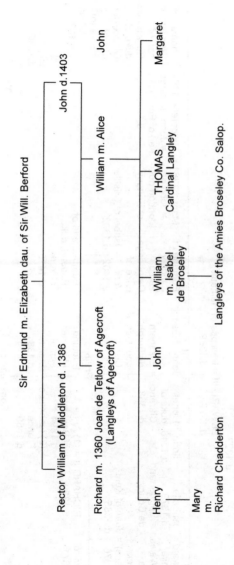

Sir Edmund m. Elizabeth dau. of Sir Will. Berford

John d. 1403

John

Margaret

Rector William of Middleton d. 1386

Richard m. 1360 Joan de Tetlow of Agecroft
(Langleys of Agecroft)

William m. Alice

THOMAS
Cardinal Langley

John

William
m. Isabel
de Broseley

Langleys of the Amies Broseley Co. Salop.

Henry

Mary
m.
Richard Chadderton

The House of Lancaster

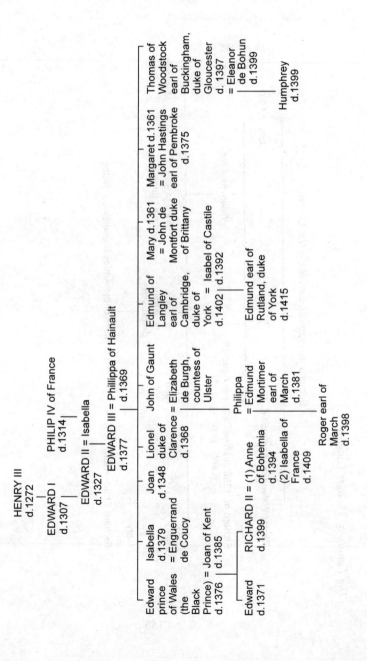

The Beauforts

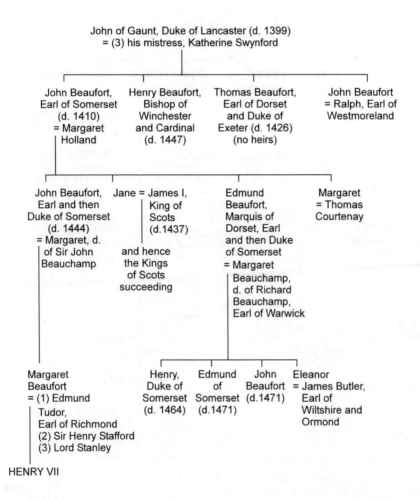

John of Gaunt, Duke of Lancaster (d. 1399)
= (3) his mistress, Katherine Swynford

| John Beaufort, Earl of Somerset (d. 1410) = Margaret Holland | Henry Beaufort, Bishop of Winchester and Cardinal (d. 1447) | Thomas Beaufort, Earl of Dorset and Duke of Exeter (d. 1426) (no heirs) | John Beaufort = Ralph, Earl of Westmoreland |

| John Beaufort, Earl and then Duke of Somerset (d. 1444) = Margaret, d. of Sir John Beauchamp | Jane = James I, King of Scots (d.1437) and hence the Kings of Scots succeeding | Edmund Beaufort, Marquis of Dorset, Earl and then Duke of Somerset = Margaret Beauchamp, d. of Richard Beauchamp, Earl of Warwick | Margaret = Thomas Courtenay |

Margaret Beaufort = (1) Edmund Tudor, Earl of Richmond (2) Sir Henry Stafford (3) Lord Stanley

| Henry, Duke of Somerset (d. 1464) | Edmund of Somerset (d.1471) | John Beaufort (d.1471) | Eleanor = James Butler, Earl of Wiltshire and Ormond |

HENRY VII

The French Succesion after 1328

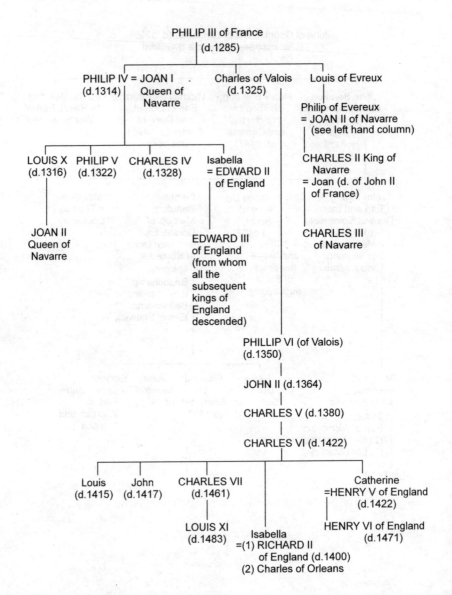

PHILIP III of France
(d.1285)

PHILIP IV = JOAN I   Charles of Valois   Louis of Evreux
(d.1314) Queen of   (d.1325)
          Navarre   Philip of Evereux
                                         = JOAN II of Navarre
                                           (see left hand column)

LOUIS X   PHILIP V   CHARLES IV   Isabella   CHARLES II King of
(d.1316) (d.1322)   (d.1328)   = EDWARD II   Navarre
                                  of England   = Joan (d. of John II
                                                    of France)

JOAN II   EDWARD III   CHARLES III
Queen of   of England   of Navarre
Navarre   (from whom
                                  all the
                                  subsequent
                                  kings of
                                  England
                                  descended)

                                  PHILLIP VI (of Valois)
                                  (d.1350)

                                  JOHN II (d.1364)

                                  CHARLES V (d.1380)

                                  CHARLES VI (d.1422)

Louis   John   CHARLES VII   Catherine
(d.1415) (d.1417) (d.1461)   =HENRY V of England
                                              (d.1422)

                   LOUIS XI   HENRY VI of England
                   (d.1483)   Isabella   (d.1471)
                              =(1) RICHARD II
                              of England (d.1400)
                              (2) Charles of Orleans

HERALDRY

The Arms of the Hopwoods, Gregges and Langleys

HOPWOOD

GREGGE

MIDDLETON

LANGLEY
OF
LANGLEY

CARDINAL
LANGLEY

MAPS

The Environs of Langley Hall

191

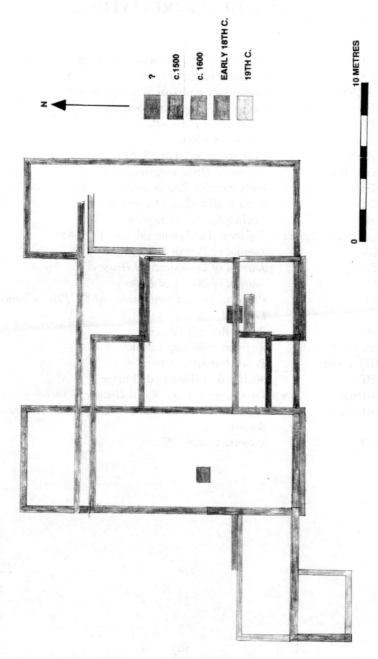

Plan of Langley Hall

N

? c.1500 c. 1600 EARLY 18TH C. 19TH C.

0 10 METRES

LIST OF ABBREVIATIONS

BJRL	*Bulletin of the John Rylands Library*
CCR	*Calendar of Close Rolls*
CARYS	*Canterbury and York Record Society*
CHJ	Cambridge Historical Journal
CPR	*Calendar of Patent Rolls*
CS	Camden Society
C&YS	Canterbury and York Society
Econ. HR	*Economic History Review*
EETS	Early English Text Society
EHD	*English Historical Documents*
EHR	*English Historical Review*
Foedera, T. Rymer	*Foedera* (The Hague Edition, 1739–45)
JBS	*Journal of British Studies*
JEH	*Journal of Ecclesiastical History*
JMH	*Journal of Medieval History*
PPC	*Proceedings and Ordinances of the Privy Council of England*
PRO	Public Records Office
Reg Langley	Register of Bishop Langley
ROT PARL	*Rotuli Parliamentorum*
SHF	Société de l'Histoire de France
TRHistS	*Transactions of the Royal Historical Society*
TRLCAS	*Transactions of the Lancs and Cheshire Antiquarian Society*
VCH	Victoria County History

SELECT BIBLIOGRAPHY

Printed Sources

Adam of Usk, *Chronica 1377–1421*, ed. Thompson, E. M., (London, 1904). *Ancient Correspondence*
"Annales Ricardi secundi et Henrici quarti", J. de Trokelowe et Henrici de Blaneforde, *Chronica et Annales*, ed H. T. Riley (RS, London, 1866).
Anonimalle Chronicle, 1333–1381, ed. V. H. Galbraith (Manchester, 1927).
Anthology of Chancery English, ed. J. H. Fisher, M. Richardson and J. L. Fisher (Knoxville, 1984).

Book of London English, 1384–1425, ed. R. W. Chambers and M. Daunt (Oxford, 1967).
Brut, or The chronicles of England, ed. F. W. D. Brie, ii (EETS, London, 1908).
Calendar of Charter Rolls, 1341–1417 (London, 1916).

Calendar of Close Rolls, 1399–1422 (London, 1927–32).
Calendar of Patent Rolls, 1399–1422 (London, 1903–11).
Calendar of signet letters of Henry IV and Henry V, ed. J. L. Kirby (London 1978).
Capgrave, J., *The Chronicle of England*, ed. F. C. Hingeston, (RS, 1958). *Chancery Warrants*.
Chronicles of England, Stow, J., (1592).
Chronicle of John Hardying, ed. H. Ellis (London, 1812).
"Chronicle of John Streeche for the Reign of Henry V (1414–1422)", ed. F. Taylor, BJRL, 16 (1932).
Chronicle of London, from 1089 to 1483, ed. N. H. Nicolas and E. Tyrell (London, 1827).
Chronicles of London, ed. C. L. Kingsford (Oxford, 1905).
Chronique du Religieux de St. Denys, (Coll. des Documents Indentis, 1829–52).
Chronicum of Adam de Usk, A. D. 1377–1421, trans. E. M. Thompson (2nd Edition, London, 1904).
Chronique d'Enguerran de Monstrelet, ed. L. Douet d'Arcq, ii, iii (SHF, Paris 1858–59).
"Chronique de Normandie de l'an 1414 a 1422", *Henrici quinti Angliae regis gesta*, ed. B. Williams (London 1850).
Collection general des documents francais qui se trouvent en Angleterre, recueillis et publies par Jules Delpit (Paris, 1847).
Common Pleas: Fleet of Fines.
Complete Peerage of England, Scotland, Ireland and the United Kingdom, ed. J. Nichols (London, 1780).
Council of Constance: the unification of the church, ed. L. R. Loomis (New York, 1961).

De Praesulisbus Angliae Commentarius, Godwin, F., ed, Richardson, W., (Cambridge, 1743).

Dugdale, William, *Monasticon Anglicanum*, vi (London, 1830).

Elham, Thomae de, Vita et Gesta Henrici Quinti Anglorum Regis, ed. T. Hearne (Oxford, 1727).

English chronicle of the reigns of Richard II, Henry IV, Henry V, and Henry VI, written before the year 1471, ed. J. S. Davies (CS London, 1856).

"Extracts from the plea rolls of the reigns of Henry V and Henry VI", ed. G. Wrottesley, *Collections for a history of Staffordshire* (William Salt Achaeological Soc., 17, 1896).

Fasti Ecclesiae Anglicanae, Neve, le, J., ed, Hardy, T. D., (Oxford, 1854).

First English Life of king Henry the Fifth, ed. and trans. F. Taylor and J. S. Roskell (Oxford 1975).

Froissart, *Chroniques*, ed. K. de Lettenhove, xvi (Brussels, 1872).

Gesta Abbatum Monasterii Sancti Abini, ed, Riley, H. T., (RS, 1867–8).

Gesta Henrici Quinti. The Deeds of Henry the fifth, ed. and trans. F. Taylor and J. S. Roskell (Oxford 1975).

Gesta Normannorum Ducam, ed, van Houts, E. M. C., (Oxford, 1992–5).

Great Chronicle of London, ed. A. H. Thompson and I. D. Thornley (London, 1938).

Harlain Manuscript, British Museum.

Hardyng Chronicle, Chronicle of John Hardyng, ed. Ellis. H., (London, 1812).

"Historical Collection of a Citizen of London", (CS, 1876).

Hoccleve, Thomas, *Works, i, The minor poems*, ed. F. J. Furnivall (EETS, London, 1892).

——, iii, *The Regement of princes*, A. D. 1411–12, ed. F. J. Furnivall (EETS, London, 1897).

Issues of the Exchequer... from Henry III to King Henry VI inclusive, ed. F. Devon (London, 1837).

Itinerary of John Leland.

John of Gaunts Register

Kirkstall Abbey Chronicles, ed, Taylor, J., (Thoresby Society, 1952).

Lichfield Act Books

Lydgate, John, *Troy Book*, A. D. 1412–20, ed. H. Bergen (EETS, London, 1906).

Memorials of Henry V, king of England, ed. C. A. Cole (RS, London 1858).

Memorial of London and London Life in the XIIIth, XIVth and XVth centuries, ed. H. T. Riley (London, 1868).

Novum Repertorium Ecclesiasticum Parochiale Londinense, Hennessy, G., (London, 1898).

Otterbourne, Thomas, *Chronica Regum Anglie, I*, ed. T. Hearne (Oxford, 1732).

Paliamentary Proxies
Procedings and ordinances of the Privy Council of England, ed. N. H. Nicolas, i, ii and iii (London, 1834).
Proceedings in Chancery, Record Commission, 1827–32.

Register of Henry Chichele, Archbishop of Canterbury, 1414–1443, ed. E. F. Jacob (C & YS, 45, 42, 46, 47, 1938–47).
Register of Robert Hallum, bishop of Salisbury, 1407–17, ed. J. M. Horn (C & YS, 72, 1982).
Register of Archbishop Scrope
Registrum Sacrum Anglicanum, Stubbs, W., (Oxford, 1897).
Rotuli parliamentorum, iii–vi (London, 1767–77).
Rymer, T., *Foedera, conventiones, literae, et cujuscunque generis acta publica, iv* (The Hague, 1740).

Sacrorum Conciliorum Collectio, ed, Mansi, J. D., (Florence and Venice, 1759–98).
St. Alban Chronicle, 1406–20, ed. V. H. Galbraith (Oxford, 1937).
Select cases in chancery, 1364–1471, ed. W. P. Baildon (Seldon Soc., 10, London, 1896).
Select cases in the court of the king's bench. Henry V, ed. G. O. Sayles (Seldon Soc., 88, London, 1971).
Select documents of English constitutional history, 1307–1485, ed. S. B. Chrimes and A. L. Brown (London, 1961).
Selections from Hoccleve, ed. M. C. Seymour (Oxford, 1937).
Storia dei Cardinali di Santa Roman Chiesa, ed, Cristofori, F., (Rome, 1888).
Stow, J., *The Chronicles of England*, (1592).

Testamenta Vetusta, ed, Nicholas, N. H.
The Great Chronicle of London, ed, Thomas, A. H., (1983).

Vetus Liber Archidiaconi Eliensis, ed, Feltoe, C. L., (Cambridge Antiquarian Society, Octavo Publications, 1919).
Vita et Res Gesta Pontificium et S. R. E. Cardinalium.

Walsingham, Thomas., ed, Riley, H. T., *Historia Anglicana, ii, 1381–1422*, ed. H. T. Riley (RS, London, 1863–4).
Warants for Issues

Secondary Authorities

Allmand, C. T. *Henry V* (London 1992).
——, *Lancastrian Normandy, 1415–1450. The History of a medieval occupation* (Oxford, 1983).
——, "Henry V the soldier, and the war in France", *Henry V. The practice of kingship*, ed. G. L. Harriss (Oxford 1985).
——, *The Hundred Years War* (London, 1988).

Armitage-Smith, S,. *John of Gaunt*, (London, 1904).
Aston, M., *Lollards and Reformers* (London, 1984).
——, *Thomas Arundal*, (Oxford, 1967).
Axon, E., "Thomas Langley, Bishop of Durham", TRLACS.

Baines, E., *History of the County Palatine and Duchy of Lancaster*, vol 1, (London, 1836).
Bain, J., ed. *Calendar of Documents relating to Scotland preserved in the Public Records Office*, 4 vols., (Edinburgh, 1881–84).
Baldwin, J. F., *The King's Council in England during the Middle Ages* (Oxford, 1913).
Barraclough, G., *Papal Provisions* (Oxford, 1935).
Barron, C., "Richard Whittington: the man behind the myth", in, *Studies in London History Presented to P. E. Jones*, (London, 1969).
Baye, de, N., *Journal of the Society de L'Histoire de France*, (Paris, 1885–88).
Bean, J. M. W., "Henry IV and the Percies", *History* vol. 44 (1959).
——, "Plague, population and economic decline in England in the later Middle Ages", (EHR, 2nd series, 15, 1962–3).
Bliss, W. H. et. al. eds, *Calendar of Entries in the Papal Registers relating to Great Britain and Ireland*,(HMSO, 1896),: *Petitions to the Pope, vol, i, 1342–1419*, (1897),: *Papal Letters, vols., 3 and 4, 1362–1404*.
Bolton, J. L. *The Medieval English Economy*, 1150–1500 (London, 1980).
Brown, A. L., *The Governance of Late Medieval England 1272–1461* (London, 1989).
——, "The commons and the council in the reign of Henry IV", EHR, vol. 79, (1964).
Bevan, B., *Henry IV* (London, 1994).
Bradbury, J. *The Medieval Siege* (Woodbridge, 1992).
Brown, A. L. "The Commons and he council in the reign of Henry IV", EHR, 79 (1964).
——, "The privy seal clerks in the early fifteenth century", *The study of medieval records. Essays in honour of Kathleen Major*, ed. S. B. Chrimes, C. D. Ross and R. A. Griffiths (Manchester, 1972).
——, "The reign of Henry IV", *Fifteenth –century England*, ed. S. B. Chrimes, C. D. Ross and R. A. Griffiths (Manchester, 1972).
Burne, A. H., *The Agincourt war* (London, 1956).

Catto, J., "The king's servants", *Henry V. The practice of kingship*, ed. G. L. Harriss (Oxford, 1985).
——, "Religious change under Henry V", *Henry V. The practice of kingship*, ed. G. L. Harriss (Oxford, 1985).
Chaucer, G., ed, Skeat, W. W., *The Complete Works*, (Oxford, 1951).
Chrimes, J. B., *English Constitutional Ideas in the 15th Century*, (Cambridge, 1936).
Church, A. J. *Henry the Fifth* (London, 1891).
Clarke, M. V., ed, Sutherland, L. S., and, McKisack, M, *Fourteenth Century Studies*, (Oxford, 1937).
Coghill, N., trans, *The Canterbury Tales*, (London, 1951).
Contamine, P. trans, Jones, M. *War in the Middle Ages* (London, 1984).

Daniel, S., *The first fowre Bookes of the ciulie wars between the two houses of Lancaster and Yorke*, (London, 1595).

Davies, J. D. Henry V (London 1935).

Davies, R. G. and Denton, J. H., eds, *The English Parliament in the Middle Ages* (Manchester, 1981).

Davies, R. R., *The Revolt of Owain Glyn Dwr* (Oxford, 1995).

Dobson, R. B., *The Peasants' Revolt of 1381*, (London, 1981).

Douet, d'Arcq, L., ed, *Chronique d'Enguerron de Monstrelete*, (Paris, 1857–62).

Douglas, D. C., ed, *EHR, vol. iv, 1327–1485*, (London, 1969).

Earle, P. *The life and times of Henry V* (London, 1972).

Earwaker, J. P. "An account of the Charters, Deeds, and Other Documents now preserved at Agecroft Hall; Co. Lancaster", TRLCAS, 1887.

Fowler, J. T. "On the St Cuthbert window in York Minster", *Yorkshire Archaeological Journal*, 4, (1875–6).

Fowler, K. A., *The king's lieutenant. Henry Grosmont, first duke of Lancaster, 1310–1361* (London, 1969).

———, ed, *"The Hundred Years War* (London, 1971).

Fryde, E. B., *Studies in Medieval Trade and Finance*, (London, 1983): also in *The Cambridge Economic History*, vol.,iii, (Cambridge, 1961).

Given-Wilson, C., *Chronicles of The Revolution 1397–1400*, (Manchester 1993).

Goodman, A. E., *John of Gaunt. The exercise of princely power in fourteenth–century Europe* (London, 1992).

———, *The Loyal Conspiracy*, (London, 1971).

———, "John of Gaunt", *England in the fourteenth–century*, ed. W. M. Ormrod (Woodbridge, 1986).

———, "John of Gaunt: paradigm of the late fourteenth–century crisis", TRHist S, 5th series, 37 (1987).

Gottfried, R. S. *The Black Death* (London, 1984).

Gower, J., ed, Macauly, G. C., *The Complete Works of John Gower*, (Oxford, 1889–1902).

Gray, H. L., "The Production and Export of English Woollens in the Fourteenth Century", (EHR, xxxix, 1924).

Griffiths, R. A., *The reign of King Henry VI. The exercise of royal authority 1422–1461* (London, 1981).

———, "Wales and the Marches", *Fifteenth–century England*, ed. S. B. Chrimes, C. D. Ross and R. A. Griffiths (Manchester, 1972).

Harriss, G. L., *Henry V. The practice of kingship* (Oxford, 1985).

———, *Cardinal Beaufort. A study of Lancastrian ascendancy and decline* (Oxford, 1988).

———, *King, Parliament and Public Finance in Medieval England* (Oxford, 1975).

———, "Fictitious loans", *Econ*, H. R. 2nd series., vol. 8 (1955).

Harvey, J. H., *Catherine Swynford's Chantry*, Lincoln Minster Pamphlets, 2nd series, no. 6.

Hatcher, J., *Plague, Population and the English Economy* (London, 1977).

Holmes, G. A., *The Later Middle Ages 1272–1485* (Edinburgh, 1962).

——, *The Good Parliament*, (Oxford, 1975).
Hibbert, C. *Agincourt*, (Gloucester, 1978).
Hicks, M., *Bastard Feudalism*, (Longman, 1995).
Highfield, J. R. L. "The Promotion of William Wykeham to the see of Winchester",
    JEH, iv, 44, (1953).
Hill, F., *Medieval Lincoln*, (Stamford, 1948).
Hilton, R. H., *The Decline of Serfdom in England* (Economic History Society, 1969).
Hutchinson, H. F., *Henry V. A biography* (London, 1967).
——, *History of Durham*

Jacob, E. F., *Henry V and the Invasion of France* (London, 1947).
——, *The fifteenth century, 1399–1485* (Oxford, 1961).
——, *Archbishop Henry Chichele* (London, 1967).
——, "The Register of Henry Chichele", (CARYS, 1937–47).

Keegan, J., *The Face of Battle*, (Harmondsworth, 1978).
Keen, M. H., *England in the later Middle Ages* (London, 1973).
——, "Diplomacy", *Henry V. The practice of kingship*, ed. G. L. Harriss (Oxford,
    1985).
Kingsford, C. L. *Henry V. The typical medieval hero* (London/New York, 2nd edn,
    1923).
Kirby, J. L., *Henry IV of England* (London, 1970).
Knowles, D., *The religious orders in England. ii: The end of the middle ages*
    (Cambridge, 1955).

Legge, M. D., ed, *Anglo–Norman Letters and Petitions*, (Anglo–Norman Text Society,
    1941).

Macdonald, C. S., *A History of Hopwood Hall, including the life of Cardinal Langley,
    Lord Chancellor (1360–1437)*, (London, 1963).
McFarlane, K. B. *John Wyclif and the beginnings of English nonconformity* (London,
    1952).
——, *Lancastrian kings and Lollard knights* (Oxford, 1972).
——, "Henry V, bishop Beaufort and the Red Hat, 1417–1421", *EHR*, 60 (1945).
——,*The Nobility of Later Medieval England*, (Oxford, 1973).
——, "England: the Lancastrian Kings", *Cambridge Medieval History*, vol. . viii,
    chap. xi (1936).
——, "Loans to the Lancastrian Kings: the problem of inducement", CHJ. vol. 9,
    (1947).
McKisack, M., *The Fourteenth Century 1307–1399*, (Oxford, 1959).
McNiven, P., "Prince Henry and the English political crisis of 1412", *History*, 65
    (1980).
Maddicott, J. R. *Thomas of Lancaster 1307–1322*, (Oxford, 1970).
——, "The problem of Henry IV's health, 1405–1413", *EHR*, 100 (1985).
Maitland, F. W., *Roman and Canon Law in the Church of England*, (Cambridge,
    1898).
Myers, A. R., *England in the later middle ages* (Harmondsworth, 1952).
——, ed, E. H. D. vol. iv, 1327–1485, (London, 1969).

Newhall, R. A. "The war finances of Henry V and the Duke of Bedford", EHR, vol., 36, (1921).
——, *The English Conquest of Normandy 1416–1485*, (New York, 1924).

Otway–Ruthen, A. J. *The King's Secretary and the Signet Office in the Fifteenth Century* (Cambridge, 1939).

Perroy, E., *The Hundred Years War* (London, 1951).
Phillpots, C. J. "John of Gaunt and English policy towards France 1389–1395", *JMH*, 16.
Pfaff, R. W. *New Liturgical Feasts in Later Medieval England*, (Oxford, 1970).
Post, J. B., "The Obsequies of John of Gaunt", (Guildhall Studies in London History, History, 5, 1981).
Post, J. B., and, Hunnisett, R. F., eds, *Medieval Legal Records Edited in Memory of C. A. F. Meekings*, (London, 1978).
Powell, E., "*The Restoration of Law and Order*", Henry V. The practice of Kingship, ed. Harriss, (Oxford, 1985).
Powicke, M, R., "Lancastrian captains", *Essays in medieval history presented to Bertie Wilkinson*, ed. T. A. Sandquist and M. R. Powicke (Toronto, 1969).
Priestly, E, J., *The battle of Shrewsbury, 1403* (Shrewsbury, 1979).

Radford, L. B., *Henry Beaufort*, (London, 1908).
Ramsey, Sir, J. H., *Lancaster and York*, (Oxford 1892).
Rosenthal, J., and, Richmond, C. eds, *People, Politics and Community in the Later Middle Ages* (Gloucester, 1987).
Roskell, J. S., *The Knights of the Shire for the County Palatine of Lancaster (1377–1460)*, Chetham Society, Manchester, 96.
——, *The Commons in the Parliament of 1422*, (Manchester, 1954).
Richardson, M., "Henry V, the English chancery, and chancery English", *Speculum*, 55 (1980).
Richmond, C. F., "The keeping of the seas during the Hundred Years War: 1422–1440", *History*, 49 (1964).
——, "English naval power in the fifteenth century", *History*, 52 (1967).
Robbins, R. H., *Historical Poems of the 14th and 15th Centuries*, (New York, 1959).
Rogers, A., "Henry IV, the commons and taxation", *Medieval studies*, 31 (1969).
Ross, C. D., ed, *Patronage, Pedigree and Power in Later Medieval England* (Gloucester, 1979).
Russell, J. C., *British Medieval Population*, (Albequerque, 1948).

Sandquist, T. A., "The holy oil of St Thomas of Canterbury", *Essays in medieval history presented to Bertie Wilkinson*, ed. T. A. Sandquist and M. R. Powicke (Toronto, 1969).
Sayles, G. O., "The Deposition of Richard II: three Narratives", from Corpus Christi College, Cambridge, (Bulletin of the Institute of Historical Research, 1981).
——, "The English Company of 1343", (Speculum, vol., vi, 1931).
Saul, N. *Richard II* (London,1997).
Seward, D., *Henry V as Warlord* (London, 1987).
Scot, T., *The Peasantries of Europe*, (London, 1998).

Thomas Langley

Shakespeare, W., *The Tradegy of Richard II.*
———, Macbeth.
———, King Henry the Fourth, Parts 1 and 2.
———, *King Henry V.*
Sharman, I. C., "Thomas Langley, a Political Bishop", unpublished lecture paper.
Somerville, R., *History of the duchy of Lancaster 1, 1265–1603* (London, 1953).
Steel, A., *The Receipt of the Exchequer*, (London, 1954).
———, *Richard II*, (Cambridge, 1941).
Storey, R L., *"Thomas Langley and the bishopric of Durham, 1406–1437* (London, 1961).
Stubbs, W., *Constitutional History of England*, (London, 1903).
———, "The wardens of the Marches of England towards Scotland 1377–1489 ", *EHR* 72.

Thompson, A. H., *The English Clergy and their Organisation in the Later Middle Ages*, (Oxford, 1947).
Tout, T. F., *Chapters in the Administrative History of Medieval England, i–vi*, (Manchester, 1928).

Unwin, G., ed, *Finance and Trade under Edward III*, (Manchester, 1918).
Ursins, J., ed, Godefroy, D., *Histoire de Charles VI*, (Paris, 1653).

Vale, M. *The Origins of the Hundred Years War. The Angevin Legacy 1250–1340* (Oxford, 1996).
Vaughan, R., *John the Fearless. The growth of Burgundian power* (London, 1966).

Walker, S. K, *The Lancastrian affinity, 1361–1399* (Oxford, 1990).
———, "Lordship and Lawlessness in the Palatinate of Lancaster", (JBS, 28, 1989).
Waugh, W. T., and, Wylie, J. H., ed, *The Reign of King Henry Fifth*, (Cambridge, 1914–29).
Webb, ed, "Metrical History", from, Buchon, J. A., ed, *Collection des Chroniques Nationals Francais*, (Paris, 1826).
Wilkinson, B., *The Later Middle Ages in England, 1216–1485*, (Longman, 1969).
Wilson, C. E. M. and Coleman, O., *Englands export Trade 1275–1547*, (Oxford, 1963).
Wolffe, B. P., *Henry VI* (London, 1981).
Wylie, J. H., *History of England under Henry the Fourth* (4 vols., London, 1884–98).

Zeigler, P. *The Black Death* (London, 1969).

APPENDIX A

THE HISTORICAL BAGGAGE

The Hundred Years War, a festering sore

To have woven into the main book a full history of the Hundred-Years-War would have detracted from Langley's biography. This lengthy appendix is included for two reasons. Firstly Langley would have studied all the available Chronicles concerning the history of the enmity between England and France before he embarked on his diplomatic initiatives that resulted in the resumption of the war. Secondly this issue dominated the greater part of Langley's political career, it being the European issue of its day.

The two Treaties so often referred to in the main body of this work are reproduced, again to better illustrate the depth of knowledge that Langley had to acquire before promulgating one and "selling" the other to a compliant Commons.

A further point is that although the excepted date for the commencement of the war is the 1330's the enmity between the two nations goes back far further than the fourteenth century hence *"the festering sore"*.

In "selling" the war to both the Commons and those, principally the merchants, as one that was just Langley would have had to study all aspects of the conflict; he needed to know what the likely cost of mobilisation would be. Do not forget that he was chancellor from the 23rd of July 1417 until the end of Henry's reign. All warfare is about profit and loss, particularly if you are chancellor of England. Langley needed to know the plus's and minus's, the fact that he managed to raise the finance to keep the war going was as vital to Henry's war effort as the actual campaign itself.

The roots of the Hundred Years War were planted by the Angevins when on the 18th of May, 1152, Henry II married Eleanor of Aquitaine **(1)**, bringing a considerable swathe of territory situated in mainland France into the hands of the crown of England. From that date all English foreign policy centred on the sustaining of, the expansion of, and the recovery of these lands. Gascony became the rock upon which foundered the ship of monarchy of successive French and English Kings. It was the one single issue that dominated above all others, affecting relations between the two nations, *a festering sore*. The sea upon which successive governments poured copious amounts of oil on the proverbial troubled waters. The major battles, Crécy,

Poitiers and Agincourt, were won by the English; the minor, but more numerous conflicts were cumulatively won by the French. The diplomatic war was won by the English, and the price this country had to pay for this was the fall of the House of Lancaster. Had England concentrated on keeping the theatre of war within the confines of Gascony, things could have turned out differently. Once Henry V began to shift the focus of the campaign to what were indisputably French sovereign lands, the war was lost. One would not have visualised this when viewing the euphoria that followed the victory of Agincourt, but by shifting the focal point and the stated aims of the campaigns as Henry did, England became embroiled in a war of attrition the outcome of which became inevitable. The thirst for uniting the thrones of the two countries provided the French with a just cause that united the French temporal Lords around the monarchy, producing a unity between king and subjects that was previously lacking. This disharmony between the Valois monarchy and the major families of the realm had previously allowed the English monarchy to fight a divided enemy. The campaign that followed Agincourt was a campaign too far. To quote and paraphrase General Browning after the fiasco of operation Market Garden "I always said that it was a bridge too far". Conversely, the warfare that followed Agincourt proved to be a campaign too far, but why then did no one make this point in the proceeding years ? We will return to this.

The accepted dates for the hundred years war are 1337–1453, but we shall begin before these dates because the conflict was brewing for a long time. The problem that the Capetian and later Valois Kings encountered, firstly with the Plantagenents and later with the Lancastrians, was one of the exercise of sovereignty. This issue was not new, the change in status that came with William's invasion of England. The change in status from vassal Duke in Normandy to a King in England meant that his followers and major landholders had two kings, and effectively, three different types of allegiance/vassalage to govern and control their lives. This was exploited by King and subject alike, the diktats of foreign policy having a bearing on events. The real beginnings of the enmity that successive generations of the English and French peoples have inherited lie in the formation of Normandy. For anyone interested in the formation of the area that became known as Normandy, I would recommend that they obtain a copy of, *"Normandy before 1066"* by David Bates, Longman, 1982.This is still the seminal work on the formation of Normandy, and provides an excellent starting point. The terms and conditions under which the area was ceded became the fulcrum upon which success Kings and Lords expended the resources at their disposal.

This joint allegiance whereby those who held lands in Normandy could be called upon to serve the Kings of France often caused friction. Initially William, as Duke of Normandy, used the vassalage to his own advantage. In 1035 William had performed homage to Henry I, King of France, in order to obtain the King's assent to his ascension as Duke. Guy of Burgundy gathered around him a powerful group of lords in an effort to seize control of the Duchy and displace William, in which he was later joined by Grimold of Plessis. The young Duke rode to Poise to appeal to the French King, asking for his support. This was on the basis that William, as a vassal of the King, claimed his right to call on his liege lord to uphold his position as *Duc de Normerrum*. In the early months of 1047, Henry I entered the Duchy joining with the levies raised by Duke William to rout the rebels at the battle of Val-es-Dunes **(2)**. This set a precedent that created enmity between the Duke and his successors and the Kings of France that was to last for four hundred years.

The stronger the grip that the Duke held his vassals in, the less easy was it for the French monarchs to exert their feudal rights. After 1066 it became harder for the Capetian kings to safeguard their rights within the Duchy. The stronger the Duke, the more difficult did it become for the Capetians to claim their rights of vassalage from the lords of the Duchy. Ordericus Vitalis tells us that Count William of Evreux declared, *"Regem et ducem diligio ... sed uni hominium faciam, eique ut domino, legaliter serviam"* **(4)**, literally meaning that he will serve only one lord, either Henry I of England or Duke Robert of Normandy, but not both. The problems that this could lead to are obvious, this exploitation being practised by all strata of society. There is a side issue that intrudes here. This joint landholding could be, and was, exploited by the English Kings.When Robert of Belleme was disinherited from his Shropshire lands by Henry I in 1102, he renounced his allegiance to Henry in the Duchy of Normandy and, until the battle of Tinchebrai (1106), created considerable problems for Henry in Normandy. As a significant landholder in Normandy he appealed to the court of the King of France for justice, a court that, by dint of the position of Henry I, could exercise judicial supremacy over Henry in the Duchy.A number of those disaffected by Henry gathered around both Robert and his brother Roger. The defeat at Tinchebrai, a much overlooked minor battle that lasted barely longer than one hour and involved less than a thousand men, broke a number of the families that were a threat to Henry's stability. There is a Lancastrian connection here-Roger of Poitou. Roger, being the younger brother of the notorious Robert, was the first lord of the vast tract of land that centred on Lancaster; he was the *de facto* first Duke of Lancaster in geographical terms.

This vassalage has been described by Professor F. L. Ganshof as representing "the personal element in feudalism ... regarded as its most essential feature" (3). The use of the word "personal "is the primary factor which governed men's actions when confronted with the choices which came with this duality of loyalties. The oath of vassalage was usually taken publicly so that the recipient was able to call on witnesses to the act if this fealty was withdrawn. This was an important point when a King had to call on his other vassals to support him against a recalcitrant lord. The act of homage, the placing of a person's hands between the hands of a lord, was a symbol of the relationship between giver and recipient. This act was given additional meaning by a declaration on holy relics, which enabled the recipient to invoke the powers of the church as support should it be needed.

The form of words of the oath varied from country to country, but the ethos of the deed remained the same and was the basic tenet upon which medieval Europe functioned. As society developed and became more complex, so this vassalage became bound by written contracts. These contracts induced political implications which could result in sanctions in the severest of cases. If the penal clause and the ensuing penalties were disputed then the inevitable outcome was that one or both parties resorted to the use of armed intervention to assert their rights. This homage was a top-to-bottom binding together of society so that those lower down the order became embroiled in the disputes of those higher up the ladder of society. This is how an entire nation could become drawn into a conflict, the spreading of the fires of insurrection. Conversely, should a major lord, or lords, decide that they could not support the monarchy in a dispute, the outcome was internal warfare. The act of homage became a double-edged sword to be exploited for personal as well as political gain. By personal gain I am alluding to the giving and extraction of favours to induce support from reluctant allies. England became the first country to allow a monetary payment so replace physical service. This in turn allowed the King to hire mercenary forces to supplement his feudal host and became known as scrutage. This method became more favoured by the Plantagenets in that it allowed them to hire men whose loyalty could be bought, making them more pliable and flexible when following royal policy. This system of payments, known as *droit de franc-fief* in France, was not utilised by the Capetian monarchs until the later period of the thirteenth century. The implications behind this vassalage meant that the King had to prove.

The Beginnings of the Conflict, 1066–1340

Henry II of England had proved a constant thorn in the side of the Capetian Kings of France. The inheritance that Eleanor of Aquitaine brought with her roughly equalled half of the entire lands of France south of the Loire. The increasingly monastic Louis VII's powers were impotent when he tried to exercise them outside of the *Ile de France*. Henry was all-powerful in his family's French dominions centred on Anjou, he also controlled Maine and the lordship of Touraine. His autocratic father Geoffrey had also taken over control of Normandy which had come to him through his wife Matilda, daughter of Henry I of England, the conquest being completed in 1141–4. Henry II's expansion came to embrace an area which also included the *de facto* overlordship of Brittany and Toulouse as well as the Auvergne.

"*Un empire en latitude, en aucun point il ne mord profondement sur le continent*". **(5)**

The inheritance that passed to Richard, the eldest surviving son, was vast. His pre-occupation with the Crusading movement meant that conditions for the re- assertion of the Capetian rights over their feudal territories could be exploited should the House of Capet find a ruler who was equal to the task. With the ascension in 1280 of Philip Augustus, Philip II, France was to find a monarch equal to the enterprise **(6)**

As a prelude to open warfare being declared against King John Philip contrived to dispossess the English King of his French lands through the process of law. A court was contrived in1202, judging "that the King of England should be deprived of all the land which up to then he and all his ancestors had held of the kings of France, because for a long time they had refused to furnish nearly all the service due for the lands and they were not willing to obey their lord in anything" **(7)**.

This judicial ruling enabled Philip to call on his vassals to uphold his rights against a recalcitrant lord. The denouement came at Bouvines in 1214 which followed the reconquest of Caen, Falaise, Poitiers and Chinon. This defeat on the borders of Flanders curtailed England's influence in the low countries. The surrender of La Rochelle after a siege of three weeks in 1224 compounded the obedience that the Capetians re-exerted. This defeat has been described as "the end of the Angevin Empire" **(8)**. These losses had a profound effect on the trading position of England with its continental neighbours. The revenues of the crown and principal lords suffering greatly as a consequence. It is salient to underlined that the Constable of Bordeaux was financially responsible to the exchequer at Westminster.

This policy of reconquest continued during the reigns of Philip's heirs, Louis VIII (1223–6), and Louis IX (1226–70). In particular, the capture of Caen and Rouen in the Duchy provided access via the Seine to the French merchants whilst at the same time removing a rich outlet for the English traders. The loss of the other main sea ports, Bordeaux and Bayonne, will be dealt with later. As a result of these losses, English foreign policy underwent a rapprochement. The power vacuum created by the collapse of the Hohenstaufen dynasty allowed Henry III to elicit the election of his brother, Richard, Duke of Cornwall, to the position of King of the Romans **(9)**. He was married to Beatrix, daughter of Dirk II, in 1257, but these plans ultimately collapsed. It was not until the second decade of the fifteenth century that imperial help, in the form of Emperor Sigismund, proved beneficial to England Henry III endeavoured to save what he could by diplomatic means. His agreement to the Treaty of Paris (1259) was resented by many of his barons. They felt, with some justification, that Henry was devoting too much of his time to his overseas territories. Henry had performed the act of homage for the Duchy of Aquitaine; thus, the feudal ties were re-established. The fact that the inhabitants of the Duchy preferred to be under the control of the monarchs of England played a significant part in Henry's decision to preserve England's interest in its last continental holding. The loss of La Rochelle meant that the preservation of the sea port of Bayonne became of prime importance. Bayonne's importance was twofold: the obvious one was as the gateway from the sea into the Duchy, and secondly, geographically it was a convenient staging post for ships on their way to the Mediterranean **(10)**. This connection which flourished over the centuries did much to assist in the establishment of the merchant guilds in both London and the Cinque ports. The treaty contained clauses that were flawed, terms that, as Edward I emphasised, were based on certain premise that were not in existence, and yet refereed to as being fact. Principally that in order for the giver to be able to perform the act of homage he must firstly be in possession of the lands upon which the treaty was based **(11)**. The most serious clause, from the English point of view, concerned Normandy; Henry renounced all rights to not only Normandy but also Anjou, Touraine, Maine and Poitou. In this Treaty and its terms lies the foundations of the Hundred Years War

As England's export and import trade increased, and together with this the revenues accruing to the crown, so to did the influence of the mercantile classes. Their power was to be of the greatest assistance to the Lancastrian Kings, and also to Bedford during his regency in France. This economic importance was a two-way thing thus ensuring the support of the people of the region for the continuation of English rule. This co-operation of the populace became of prime importance to England's foreign policy aims over the coming centuries, economic dependency over ruling the ties of nationhood and feudalism. The Lancastrian connection with the Duchy can be traced from the investment of Edmund of Lancaster with large portions of

Ponthieu, through the investiture of Edward the Black Prince to John of Gaunt. Many retainers of the Dukes of Lancaster were to make their fortunes in Gascony over the next centuries.

It is pertinent to note that the blood ties between France, England and the French dominions were to dominate the foreign policy that Bedford endeavoured to uphold from 1422 until his death. His grandfather Gaunt occupied the position of Duke of Aquitaine between the years 1390–4. This had caused problems in that only the eldest son of the King could hold the position (12). Richard II was to remain childless.

The problems previously referred to in regard to homage, and the Duke of Normandy also being a King, equally applied in Aquitaine. Guillame de Nogaret commented that "the King of France is subject to no-one" (13). When the councillors of Louis IX questioned the wisdom of his entering into the Treaty of Paris, Joinville reports that he replied "it seems to me that what I give him (Henry III) I am employing well, because he was not my man, and now he enters into homage" (14). This standpoint was not unique, and the Kings of England would have been justified if they had uttered these words apropos their connection with the English baronage. Had the situation have been reversed then Henry would have expected the same response from Louis.

There follows an interesting first hand account of the response of Edward II to a request by one of Philip V's advisers that Edward should swear an oath of fealty as well as homage. This reply was made by Edward at Amiens around the 2nd of July 1320, it being reproduced to exemplify the English view of their position in Aquitaine

We well remember that the homage which we performed at Boulogne (1308) was done according to the form of the peace treaties made by our ancestors, fate the manner in which they did it. Your father agreed to it, for we have letters confirming this, and we have performed it already in the same fashion; no one can reasonably ask us to do otherwise; and we certainly do not intend to do so. As to the fealty we are certain that we should not swear it; nor was it ever asked of us at the time. (15)

This is consistent with the views of his father who 1273 said, when paying homage to Phillip III, "Lord King I do you homage for all the lands which I *ought* to hold from you" (16). This was restated in 1286 when Edward said "I become your man for the lands which I hold from you on this side of the sea according to the peace made between our ancestors". Legally a defensible tenet. This was the view which remained constant through to

Langley's lifetime, that of the English territories being the monarchy's by right, not held by the largesse of the French Kings, the French position being the antithesis. This was an insoluble situation with each of the protagonists being entrenched in intractability. Here lies the genesis of an enmity that lasts, in a lesser measure, to this day, the pride of two nations being locked by xenophobia in a whirlpool of discord and enmity, the causation of a ruinous conflict, the treadmill of Medieval politics and policy, a constant channel of hatred fed from the well of nationalism that was topped up by zealots promulgating covert self-interest. A harsh analysis maybe, but I believe an accurate one. Certainly in Normandy, prior to its reconquest, self-interest was encouraged when it could provide discomfort for the other side, policies of cynicism practised under the cloak of national interest, the real interest being self.

Unquestionably, under Henry V the national interest was the mantle under which the Lancastrians masked their hidden agenda, namely, the perceived need to "legitimise" Henry's Kingship by leading his country to victory in a "just" war. This perception, unspoken except by those of the inner circle, principally Langley, had its roots in the demons that pricked Henry's private conscience. These ghosts from the past had their roots in the illnesses and premature death of Henry IV, visited on Henry's father, some privately said, as a punishment for the deposition and murder of Richard II and the murder of the archbishop Scrope of York. The triumph would provide a balm for the King, God's support for the victor pushing the demons into the farthest corners of his inner thoughts. His premature death reawakening the "curse of the House of Lancaster", the premature death of Clarence and Bedford adding credence to the legend. History and superstition were the heavenly twins that governed Langley's life.

Edward I installed a defined hierarchy of governance in Aquitaine which was ultimately controlled by England,. This gave the Duchy a semblance of autonomy which became the focus for the defence of the Duchy and its rights in the disputes with the French crown. In 1294 the Duchy was viewed by Edward as an area where he held complete powers of judicial control, the French view being that the supreme court of appeal lay in Paris. At the beginning of the fourteenth century Edward was arguing that the terms of the Treaty of 1259 had been breached, making the Treaty invalid.The main points were that Louis IX had failed to surrender the territories as defined in the Treaty of 1259, and that the Duchy had not been properly invested on Henry III. Of equal importance to this was the inheritance in the form of the lordship of Ponthieu which Eleanor of Castile brought to her husband through the death of her mother on the 16th of March 1279 **(17)**. The lands of

Ponthieu were centred on the estuary of the Somme, with Abbeville, Le Crotoy and Montreuil being the main towns. This area was to provide a valuable foothold in northern France for future English Kings.

The ties between the Duchy and England were strengthened when Edward I and his son employed Gascon nobles in their campaigns against the Welsh and Scots. There was a rich pool of armed retainers to be drawn from, particularly after the collapse of the internal and external Crusading movement in Europe. This service was strictly for payment and was not performed as a commutation for feudal dues. Whilst the two Edwards were engaged in warfare this had the additional benefit of removing from the Duchy large groups of armed retainers and their lords who, from boredom, would indulge in border raids. The Gascon nobles viewed the right to indulge in private warfare as an historic privilege, their *droit de guerre,* something that the French Kings did very little to check. Not unsurprisingly the distant Capetian monarchy periodically encouraged the Gascon nobles to indulge in this fratricide if by doing so they would cause problems for the Duke and his Duchy officials. a mirror of the policies adopted by their forebears in Normandy some two hundred before.

This led to a proliferation of castle building that had, by 1337, seen in excess of 1,000 castles and fortified manors, *maison-fortes,* dotted about the Duchy, principally along the river valleys.

The preferred settlement of disputes by the English crown was by judicial means, but generally appeals to the court of the King in Paris were for obvious reasons discouraged. English pride did not need to be reminded of its feudal ties which bound it to the Capetian monarchy. The political manoeuvrings that the Gascon nobles indulged in can be compared to the conduct of the Norman barons who held manors in or adjacent to the Vexin. For the family of Montgomery read the house of Foix who were engaged in a protracted feud with the Armagnacs. An inevitable consequence that follows conflict between major landholders is that in turn the feuding percolates down to their vassals, thus broadening the conflict both geographically and in terms of the numbers of armed men involved. Further, should the gains from any dispute be of a high enough value in terms of finance or additional territories, then mercenaries would be hired. In this, the Great Schism, with the Papacy based in Avignon, added a religious/political dimension to issues of contention. This is mentioned as a factor.

The approximate number of people living in the Duchy in 1316 was 625,000, equivalent to one-seventh of the population of England **(18)**. Bordeaux, the largest City, had a population of 30,000, 14.4% of the population of the Duchy. A further 16% of the population resided in the

City's suburbs. The economic yield to be derived from the region was considerable. The average number of tuns that were exported was 83,000 between the years of 1305 to 1336 (19). The income to the exchequer exceeded the yield from the English Shires (6 to 10% of the price of the wine was paid as duty). The exporters of this highly lucrative trade, the vintners, formed their own guild in Vintry ward in the City of London. They were granted significant privileges and built large warehouses adjacent to the Thames. This strengthened the ties with England, the influence being a two-way thing, ebbing and flowing with the diktats of international policy. The rich grain and soft fruit produce from the region also became fundamental to both exchequers.

Malcolm Vale has described Bayonne as in effect the sixth cinque port (20). Maritime unions were formed by a number of the Duchy ports with their counterparts in England. 464 ships are recorded as loading supplies at Bordeaux as well as 119 Breton ships and 59 Norman vessels at the turn of the 14th century. The importance of these maritime links can be seen in the outbreak of hostilities between England and France. On the 15th of May 1293, a fleet from the Cinque ports defeated a Norman fleet off the coast of Brittany at Cap Sainte-Mathieu and they then went on to sack La Rochelle. This was the precursor to Philip the Fair confiscating Aquitaine. How much encouragement Edward 1 had given to the Bayonnese is a matter for debate. Philip demanded 20 hostages to be selected from officers of the Duchy. He also demanded that all the lands held in fief were to be taken back into French control. This demand merely provoked further defiant attacks on French officials. I would make a point here that those indulging in the plainly unlawful attacks must have been given at least tacit support from Edward to risk escalating the situation. The Capetians had begun to reinforce their garrisons and Edward's officials sent men and supplies by sea to the strategic ports.

In general, the people of Gascony retained their loyalty to England and refused to recognise the citations sent by Philip in regard to the proclamation of his rights. In an effort to defuse the situation, Edward sent his brother Edmund of Lancaster to Paris in February 1294. The outcome was the partitioning of the Duchy as Edward agreed to the surrender of Aquitaine to the French but significantly, the Treaty was never sealed. This was chiefly due to the request by the English that in future the Duchy should be held by any children that were born to Edward and Margaret, Philip's sister. The effect of this would have been that Edward's heirs would perform homage firstly to him for the Duchy thereby any attempt by the Capetians to exert their rights would firstly have to be put to Edward and his successors, effectively annexing the Duchy from Capetian control. The views of the chroniclers on these events differ, being dependent upon the nationality of the author, just as today various newspapers adopt various stances dependent upon their political ideology and so too it was in the Middle Ages.

As a side issue, French ambitions in Aragon had foundered through, amongst other reasons, a lack of good communications and supply lines. Gascony was strategically well placed to be utilised should an expedition be mounted. On the 20th of June, 1294 Edward renounced his homage to Philip IV. From that moment each side placed its vassals on a war footing. Edward had to resort to pardoning criminals and outlaws to increase his forces (21). In 1295, 40,000 men were raised through the shire levy. The war in the Duchy was one of siege, counter-siege and relief. The towns of Rions (1295), St. Sever (1295), Dax (1296) and St.

Macaire were all besieged. It has been estimated the Philip spent 61.5% of the Duchy's gross domestic product on financing the war between the years 1294–97 (22). As long as the sea-lanes remained open, England could relieve and re-take the towns of the Duchy. Thus the war stagnated.

The cost of the war has been calculated at £100,000 during the reign of Edward I (23), and this high figure represents virtually the entire revenue of Edward I. This clearly indicates the fundamental importance to England that the crown attached to the preservation of the Duchy. Compare this with the expenditure incurred by the French crown, £432,500, this between the years 1294–99 this being indicative of the nature of the war. In reality, it was more costly to besiege a town than adopt a posture of defence.

A truce was finally agreed on the 9th of October 1297 at Vye-St-Bavon in Flanders, a truce that was to last until the 6th of January 1298. The cost of French occupation to the English crown was heavy as Edward had to compensate over 450 Gascon nobles who had been dispossessed of their lands. This dispossession caused deep and lasting enmity towards the French nobles from the people of Gascony. Edward's feelings towards his Gascon subjects are exemplified in a letter written under his instruction from Ghent dated the 16th of October 1297:

we wish that you should always have such concern for the needs of Gascony that our men who are there shall be relieved and aided as far as possible in the best manner. . . For our honour or dishonour lies in this business, and that of all those who love us, and especially those responsible for our affairs in the places where you are at present. (24)

This letter was addressed to the men of Bayonne and shows the honourable intentions which Edward attached to his obligations. Further, had Edward not adopted this tone he could have alienated his supporters in the Duchy thereby making the recovery of the crown territories virtually impossible.

French occupation came to an end when Philip began to voice his resentment concerning Boniface VIII's interference in the internal affairs of France. The Pope was becoming increasingly concerned that the privileges of the church, particularly in Aquitaine, were being encroached upon. The majority of the French clergy supported Papal interference, and this was not to be the last time. During the diplomatic exchanges that preceded the resumption of the Hundred Years War in 1413–15, Thomas Langley openly voiced England's support for the French clergy when they threatened to withdraw their obedience from the Avignonese Pope, a threat they were to carry out. Combined with this, the citizens of Aquitaine were becoming more vociferous in their complaints against the French officials who were endeavouring to supplant the Duchy officials. The defeat of Robert of Artois by a force of Flemings at Courtrai in the July of 1302 merely compounded matters.

In 1303 the citizens of Bordeaux rose in revolt against Philip's men and it seems likely that they had been aided and abetted by the Bayonnese exiles in England. These events brought about the restoration of the Duchy to the Plantagenets in June 1303 in a ceremony held in St. Emilion. The French rancour that had accompanied the occupation could not be expunged by any single act. The debts that Edward had run up supporting the war were still outstanding in the reign of his grandson Edward III; the same applied to the French crown. The dispossession of the Templars and the confiscation's from the Jews and Lombard bankers were a consequence of the debts run up by the Capetians. Thus the seeds of prejudice are planted. England's preoccupation with the Scottish wars and French involvement with the subjugation of Flanders meant that matters in Gascony quietened down until 1322.

Charles of Valois, uncle to Charles IV (1322–28), had faired badly from the war in Aquitaine. Disturbances in the Duchy began to increase, bribery by Charles and others exacerbating matters. In April 1323 outright attacks were launched on Marsan. Matters escalated quickly and Edward II diverted money from the Scottish war to Gascony as the French attacks increased. A truce was agreed in June 1323, but the "Marsan War "was a harbinger of the real conflict that was to burst across Gascony. Edward II postponed performing the act of homage for the Duchy, pleading that the war against the Scots prevented him from leaving England, partially true. In frustration the French invaded, capturing the Isle of Oleron in October.

The priory of St. Sardos in the Agenais, a dependency of the Benedictine house of Sarlat claimed that it held a privilege from the King of France binding the abbey to the crown of France. They further claimed that the privileges could not be transferred without the consent of the brethren of the abbey, and they also claimed that the dependencies of the abbey were similarly bound. On this basis Charles IV authorised the building of a new fortified town-a *bastide*. Matters came to a head when the people of Agen wrote to Edward II that:

> *the people of the king of France insist upon founding a new settlement at the place of St. Sardos, lying in the middle of the land of Agenais ... which is under the ... jurisdiction of the seneschal of the Agenais ... Hence, if this (new) population is established in the said place, the land of the Agenais will be lost, because almost all the people of this land will flock there on account of the privileges which have been granted to the inhabitants by the King of France (25).*

Not for the first time, nor the last, were the privileges of the church to become the subject of dispute between the two nations. The church was not entirely blameless in that it used the conflict to its own advantage in certain instances.

Do not forget that the higher civil servants were drawn from the upper echelons of the clergy. In England's case Langley was Bishop of Durham, Henry Beaufort was Bishop of Winchester and Richard Courtenay was Bishop of Norwich these being the most noteworthy from the English side.

The French Parlement duly passed an arret authorising that a settlement should be established. On the night of the 15th of October a group of men set fire to the priory at St. Sardos and killed a number of French soldiers. In retaliation the Capetians ordered the confiscation of the castle of Montpezat but its garrison refused to hand over the castle. Diplomacy at Paris ended in stalemate and Charles IV personally led an army to the Toulouse. Despite the intervention of the Pope both sides remained intractable, Edward hired mercenaries and criminals to fight in Gascony. Agen surrendered early in the war after a long siege. The significant majority of the people of Aquitaine steadfastly supported Edward, particularly the citizens of Bordeaux. Again the war petered out and on the 25th of September 1325, Edward, earl of Chester, the future Edward III, performed homage for Aquitaine in Paris.

One thing is clear, despite the various truces and underlying tension never leaving the Duchy, that outright war was inevitable. Further spasmodic outbreaks of conflict broke out, gradually increasing in intensity and frequency. On the 6th of June 1329, Edward III performed homage to Philip VI for Aquitaine at Amiens. Matters rumbled on until the summer of 1336 when, after failing to win the support of Pope Benedict XII for his crusading intentions, Philip moved the fleet that he had assembled from Marseilles to the Norman ports. Edward placed the coastal ports on a war footing and war was now unavoidable. Philip demanded that all the Gascon officials should be ordered to allow his French officers entry to all the towns of Gascony.

Aquitaine was formerly confiscated on the 24th of May 1337. Sir Oliver Ingham, Edward's lieutenant in the Duchy, refused to surrender and again the French began to appropriate the Duchy town by town. Edward opened another front from Flanders, a sensible tactic in that the Flemish coast was closer to England and easier to reinforce. In June 1340, Edward formerly assumed the title King of France, claiming that his title was superior through his mother's line, and he had a point. He was, through his mother, the nephew to Charles IV, Philip VI being Charles's cousin , his father being merely a Comte. This pedigree would be recited, when it suited, by successive English Kings and not least by Henry V, although Henry IV's usurpation did weaken the claim. By aligning himself with the Flemings he, in effect, encircled France. His allies in Aquitiane and Gascony took heart from this latest twist. All this took place only fifty years before Bedford was born, and it should also be born in mind that Edward III was Bedford's great-grandfather.

One thing above all that is clear is that the Truces which permeated this period of Anglo-French relations were merely a veneer masking a deep-seated animosity. These Truces were merely sticking plaster and beneath the surface the wound still bled. The festering sore required cauterising, but only total warfare would do this.

The events that preceded the resumption of the war in 1413–15 mirrored the events of the first two decades of the fourteenth century. For Aquitaine read Normandy, the principal difference being that Henry V and the Lancastrians were in a hurry, his demons needing the act of exorcism; only a victory over the French could provide this.

Victory and the Uneasy Peace, 1340–1389.

The Gordian knot that was the problem of Gascony was woven by strands of discord strengthened by a series of judicial disputes that served to further entangle matters. The rights of the vassals in Aquitaine were subordinated to the issue of homage between the Kings of England and the French crown. For every positive reaction there is a negative reaction; the conduct of the two nations more than underlines the truth of this rule.

Edward III shifted the focus of the war from the south to France's northern borders; this was a sensible move. Flanders's dependence on the import and export of English wool provided England with an economic lever that the French could not match. The economy of Aquitaine and the southern regions was interwoven with its exports to England; Edward could now open a war on two fronts. The armed dependants in the south could be relied upon to halt any French attempts at insurgence . Flanders and Normandy were considerably nearer to England and through Normandy, principally via the mouth of the Seine, the way to Paris could be opened. Also, historically, the links between Normandy and England were old and strong dating back to before 1066.

It was at Ghent in January 1340 that Edward formerly assumed the title of King of France. He quartered the arms of France having the fleur-de-lis engraved on his seal. The symbolism was continued by weaving leopards and lilies into a surcoat. In April his wife Philippa of Hainault, who due to her heavy pregnancy had remained in Flanders, gave birth to a son at the abbey of St.Bavo **(26)**. This child was the fourth from the marriage, being preceded by three brothers and a sister; he was christened John born in Ghent, the English spelling of which was Gaunt. He was the son of a king and the great-nephew of Philip VI, king of France. The birth of a son of the royal blood always carries political significance. His godfather was John, Duke of Brabant **(27)**, and he was carried to the christening font by Jacques van Artevelde, Edward's principal ally in Flanders. This son was Bedford's grandfather, the inherent ties to mainland Europe being made forty-nine years before the grandson's birth. The spiritual roots that were to dictate Bedford's career being planted half a century before his arrival in the world; English, French and Flemish blood flowed in his veins.

A desultory raid into the Cambresis on the borders of Flanders and France petered out. England needed to establish a bridgehead, a port was needed in Normandy. Edward lifted the embargo on wool exports and moved the staple from Antwerp to Bruges with the addition of a payment of £140,000 towards the defence of the low countries. Between the years 1338–1340, seventy-six days were spent in actual conflict, involving a total of 12,002 troops **(28)**. Raid and counter-raid across the channel had been undertaken during the years 1338–9. This came to a head in the summer of 1340 when a French fleet anchored in the mouth of the River Zwin opposite the town of Sluys. The cities of Ghent and Bruges provided 2,202 troops, the conflict beginning on the 9th of June. Froissart puts the number of French ships at 120 from Normandy, Genoa and Picardy, under the command of admirals, Hugh Quieret, Peter Behuchet and the Genoese Barbanera. Even allowing for

Froissart's tendency to exaggerate the numbers it was still a substantial threat to England's coastal ports.

Edward, in his cog the "Thomas ", attacked on Midsummer Day, the French ships being moored closely together thus restricting their ability to manoeuvre. The 12,000 English archers wreaked havoc, the battle lasted from the early morning until noon, and the French were routed with their three admirals dead. A year's truce known as the truce of Esplechin followed. During this time the internal bickering of the Flemings continued, and their help would always be subject to their internal squabbles.

The death of Duke John III of Brittany, in the April of 1341, shifted the focus of royal policy. Not surprisingly Edward supported one candidate, Philip supported another. Edward's choice was the younger brother of the Duke, John de Montfort, Charles of Blois, whose claim came through his marriage to the daughter of the elder brother. Edward conferred the earldom of Richmond on de Montfort who promised to recognise his claim to the French crown. Because of this, Philip, understandably, accepted the claim of Charles sending his eldest son, John, Duke of Normandy to Brittany where he captured de Montfort. This side-show tied up a good many of Edward's men which necessitated his invasion of Brittany in the autumn of 1342. He met little resistance and overran the area without meeting any substantial resistance. Added to the defeat at Sluys this gave England uninterrupted passage for its ships in the channel. There is a point missed by many historians who have bemoaned this campaign as tying up too many resources for too little gain, a view I cannot agree with. A considerable number of privateers acted with impunity, and even encouragement, from Brittany. A further truce was agreed at Malestroit in the January of 1343.

Edward redirected his commanders to Gascony where Henry, Earl of Derby and Sir Walter Manny achieved some notable successes at Bererac, La Reole, Aigillion and Montsegur (29). John of Normandy countered the following year by taking a large force into Gascony, recovering Angouleme and laying siege to Aiguillon. Edward had been busy in Flanders endeavouring to bring the various factions together. This was partially successful although van Arteveldt was murdered shortly after he left. The Flemish reliance on English wool ensured that the alliance held, Hugh Hastings being appointed to command the Anglo-Flemish troops. Edward was busy assembling an army, estimated at 15,000 strong. This was made up of 2,400 cavalry and 12,000 foot-soldiers half of which were archers. To put the war effort in perspective, it is worth noting that the estimates of the number of arrows that were supplied are put at 133,200 for 2,380 bows. The views of historians as to

Edward's intentions is mixed, but given that Derby was holding out in Gascony I believe that it was always his intention to invade Normandy. The point should be made that the victories at Sluys and in Brittany had afforded unrestricted passage to Edward in the channel. Once in Normandy he could rely on his Flemish allies, and also, by opening up such a front, he could exert pressure of Philip to redirect his son's forces to the north, whilst at the same time preventing Philip from leading reinforcements from France.

Medieval generals were keen students of tactics and battle plans and they were often preoccupied with all aspects of warfare. Henry V remarked that "warfare without battles is like sausages without mustard ", Froissart also made the point that "the English will never love or honour their King unless he be victorious and a lover of arms "this being an indication of the expectations of the people that Henry carried into France, Froissart was only recording the general popular conceptions and opinions.

To this end what follows is salient in that the tactics that were employed at Crécy and Poitiers were replicated at Agincourt and in later encounters when Bedford was in command. Fortunately all three battles have been the subject of numerous studies, and in Langley's lifetime the information available was readily accessible. Bedford was engaged in the French wars some sixty-five years after Crécy and Poitiers, and the art of war had changed little. Therefore what follows is highly relevant to our understanding of the thinking of England's position it's inherited traditions.

A large amount of this tradition was of an oral nature, the recollections of those who actually fought at these battles being passed down by word of mouth through families. A lot of this is, sadly, unrecorded. However the tactics employed throughout the 120 year period of the war prove that the oral tradition was strong, because these tactics hardly varied during the period, which is somewhat surprising when one considers that the French, who suffered so badly at Crécy and Poitiers, appear not to have learnt from the previous follies by the time of Agincourt.

When Shakespeare wrote his histories towards the end of the sixteenth century, he drew heavily on the chronicles, particularly upon the work of Ralph Hollinshead's written in 1587, and when Titus Livius's *Vita Henrici Quinti*. These authors were drawing on earlier works whose roots lay in oral accounts. Froissart had presented a copy of his *Chronicle* to Richard II, and Henry V and Bedford would be familiar with the work. There is another point for us to consider. During Bedford's regency the role of England was primarily defensive as opposed to offensive, the lessons of siege warfare having to be reversed; the aggressors became the defenders, a largely new

218   *Thomas Langley*

role for the English. During the era that preceded Bedford's regency the French had developed an aptitude for withstanding long bombardments. When the roles were reversed, the adroitness they had developed stood them in good stead.

Crécy

Edward landed at St. Vaast-de-la-Hogue, 18 miles south-east of Cherbourg, on the 12th of July, and launched a *Chevaunchee* across Normandy, sacking Caen. The purpose of the *Chavaunchee* was to spread panic across the countryside and to coerce the people into supporting the invaders by reminding them that their King was powerless to halt these raids. The French had taken the precaution of breaking all the bridges that crossed the Seine as Philip moved to defend the Norman capital of Rouen; they were to adopt similar tactics thirty-one years later with the bridges over the Rivers Bethune, Bresle, and Somme. The armies tracked each other on opposite sides of the Seine as Edward marched towards Paris, this causing Philip to re-enter the capital. His thinking on this was that Edward might by-pass the city and sweep towards Gascony trapping John of Normandy between the English forces in Gascony and Edward's army. In reality the English carpenters had been repairing the bridge at Poissy which Edward crossed, after which he moved eastward fording the Somme at Blanchetaque; Philip VI, chasing behind, was unable to traverse the ford due to the high tide. The comparisons with his great-grandson's army in 1415 are remarkable. The English troops were tired and short of supplies and confronted by superior numbers. They were to benefit from luck and an overconfident undisciplined French force. A further blow to Edward was that his Flemish allies had been driven back in a skirmish at Bethune.

  The English army, numbering around 12,000 men, occupied a good position on a plateau above the river Maie, with the woods of Crécy-en Ponthieu, four to five miles deep and eight miles wide, to the fore. On the 26th of August the French forces, approximately 38,000 strong, inexplicably commenced their attack in the late afternoon within a few hours of their having reached the field of battle. Philip appeared to be overruled by his commanders, prudence dictating that they should have waited until the morning. Chaos ensued as the front line of Genoese crossbowmen ran out of arrows and were trampled in their retreat by the advancing heavy cavalry. The heavy rain that had fallen in the afternoon meant that the cavalry were slowed to virtually walking pace. The late autumnal sun made an appearance shining directly into the eyes of the French army. Edward's troops were far better organised and they held their positions using their Welsh longbows to good effect, a legend being born. Their herce formations suited the conditions perfectly. The word herce means a harrow, the medieval harrow being triangular or oblong in shape.

There has been a good deal of debate as to exactly what Froissart, the main source for the word herce, meant. When one considers the carnage which the archers were able to inflict, an oblong or triangular formation would be the best shape to allow the maximum damage to be wrought. These archers could fire between ten and fifteen arrows a minute, with a maximum range of three hundred yards. Edward had ordered the archers to dig pits in front of their positions, the positioning of the archers on the flanks meaning that the French were caught in a crossfire. The French cavalry had to withstand between five and seven-and-a-half thousand arrows a minute. Each man carried approximately 100 arrows, and therefore there were around half a million arrows available for use at each of the main battles (**30**). It is little wonder that all but a small party of French nobles escaped to Amiens, a blanket of fog that descended aiding their escape.

The 16–year-old Edward the Black Prince commanded the right wing; Henry V was the same age when he fought at the battle of Shrewsbury (1403), both establishing their reputations early in their short lives. The aura of invincibility that both carried meant that their deaths, in the prime of their lives, were the harder to understand by their subjects. The mantle of responsibility that was handed to Bedford was one that was inappropriate, *a poisoned chalice*, one that had profound effects on the internal politics of England. The creators of sepia-tinted legends bequeath to those who follow an inheritance that it is unfeasible to emulate. Today we would say that the ruling clique, the Lancastrians, were guilty of believing their own publicity. There is a further link between the battle and Henry V: the nearly blind John, King of Bohemia, fighting on the French side. He was roped to his household knights in the forefront of the French advance, and needless to say he was killed. The courage he showed in fighting whilst blind is the stuff of chivalry, his motto being "Ich Dien", his emblem being white feathers. When Henry V became Prince of Wales he adopted both the motto and the symbol, the imagery linking him by inference to this brave man. The dead king's body was removed from the battle field on Edward's orders and was treated reverentially by his men who washed and cleaned the body before wrapping it in a shroud of linen.

Boosted by their success, the English army moved to Calais which was well fortified. Edward invested the town, a siege being the only option. Almost unbelievably the army was joined by the Queen and her ladies-in-waiting, treating war as a spectator sport; markets were held on Wednesdays and Saturdays. Despite Papal interference Edward refused to lift the blockade. The siege lasted a year, Philip taking this long to gather a relieving army. After marching to Calais, he viewed the English positions and withdrew, the town surrendering on the 4th of August 1347. England's near two-hundred-year occupation of the town had begun. Coupled with the defeat of the Scots at Neville's Cross and the withdrawal from Gascony of John of Normandy and his army, it had been a good year for England.

The most important gain for Edward was the capture of Calais which gave him a secure port thereby removing his reliance on the Flemish points of embarkation. The views of the English chroniclers give hints as to the general perception of the war. The prevalent opinion was that Philip was a usurper (31) who headed an undisciplined army that was riven by rivalry and jealousy. Added to this was the praise to God for supporting the English in a just cause.

So what had Edward gained? What was the return on the country's investment in the expedition? From the battle itself the answer is "not very much", those in the front ranks of the cavalry being all killed, and these were the ransoms that would have produced the best returns. The chaos of a medieval battle meant that it was virtually impossible for a commander to control his troops, the chain of command could never be held steady. The fluidity of the protagonists in a set-piece battle along with blood-lust overtaking rationale, meant that any financial gains could be negated by one moment of uncontrolled aggression. Even with the commander in the front line, as with both the Black prince at Crécy and Henry V at Agincourt, the melee of conflict could not be controlled. The noise alone would prevent this, also a good many of the combatants, particularly the rank and file, were intoxicated. What we today call "Dutch Courage", whilst this induced the rank and file to fight, it also had negative effects in terms of the taking of ransoms. Ransoms were the medieval equivalent of today's mortgages, the family of those captured frequently bankrupting themselves in order to meet the cost of the ransoms demanded. The film Braveheart it certainly was not.Unless the person captured was "well-connected ", i.e. was a highly-placed retainer in a rich lord's household or from the upper nobility, they could languish in captivity for years. The only substantial gain was the capture of Calais, a bridgehead into Normandy, and also a port from which England could effectively put a strangle-hold on traffic entering or leaving the Seine. The axiom that one battle settled a war was false. As will be seen after Agincourt, the main objective , namely the subjugation of France, lay beyond the grasp of Edward's army.

The general perception that one gleans from the chronicles is that they were written with the purpose of reassuring the English populace that the campaign had merit and was worth pursuing. This perception, strengthened by the further victories at Poitiers and Agincourt, did much to place Bedford in an impossible position. The sensible position would have been for English to accept the loss of their French territories. Pragmatism was a lesson that the English were slow in learning. Had they concentrated on the part that luck undoubtedly played, more caution may have been exercised.

The first visitation of the black death which began later in the decade of Crécy, forced a halt to be called to the continuation of the war. The plague spread from France to England via Bordeaux, and ships carrying wine brought the disease first to Melcombe Regis. The plague was to spread across England from the ports of Bristol, London, Southampton and Plymouth (**32**). Henry Knighton has left us the best description of the way that the plague affected England:

*Then the dreadful pestilence made its way along the coast by Southampton and reached Bristol, where almost the whole strength of the town perished, as it was surprised by sudden death; for few kept their beds more than two or three days, or even half a day. Then this cruel death spread on all sides, following the course of the sun. And there died at Leicester, in the small parish of Holy Cross, 400; in the parish of St. Margaret's, Leicester, 700; and so in every parish, in a great multitude. Then the bishop of Lincoln sent notice throughout his whole diocese, giving general power to all priests, both regulars and seculars, to hear confessions and give absolution with full episcopal authority to all persons, except only in the case of debt. In such a case, the debtor was to pay the debt, if he were able, while he lived, or others were to be appointed to do so from his goods after his death. In the same way, the Pope gave plenary remission of all sins to all receiving absolution at the point of death, and granted that this power should last until Easter next following, and that everyone might chose his own confessor at will (**33**).*

Knighton's comments regarding the two parishes in Leicester were replicated across the entire country, as they were in France. The effects of the plague on both countries were diverse, and England's export trade suffered, not only with Gascony, but also with Flanders. The shortage of labour across Europe affected all countries and the inter-action of trade between importers and exporters. The immediate effect at this time was that the hostilities were put in abeyance, enforcing a breathing space for both sides. Certainly a number of skirmishes at sea continued, but not of the previous scale.

Philip VI had died in 1350 to be succeeded by John II, a man whose abilities and judgement did not match his ambitions. Edward III flirted with an alliance with the King of Navarre, the aptly named Charles the Bad. Charles was treating with both sides at once, something that the Duc de Burgundy was to do in Bedford's lifetime, but the negotiations came to nothing.

Pope Innocent VI's mediator, the Cardinal of Boulogne, brokered a treaty at Guines in 1354. In return for Edward renouncing his claim to the throne of France, he would receive Aquitaine, Poitou, Anjou, Maine, Touraine and the march of Calais in full sovereignty. In essence this was almost all the lands that England had been demanding as theirs by historic right, the significant omission being the greater part of Normandy. Mutual mistrust meant that the treaty was never ratified, and, given the mistrust, even had the treaty been ratified, enforcing it would have eventually induced further conflict. Both countries were now so steeped in retrograde policies that any solution was always going to be unworkable. Each of the three major set-piece battles of the discord that was the Hundred Years War was preceded by desultory negotiations.

Poitiers

Edward's eldest son, Edward, Prince of Wales, known as the Black prince, took a small army to Gascony in 1355. A *Chevaunchee* into enemy territory was undertaken against the Comte d'Armagnac whose lands bordered Gascony. The expedition penetrated to within four miles of Toulouse before wheeling across country to Carcassonne and Narbonne. The French prudently refused to offer battle, the memory of Crécy being still fresh in the more sagacious commanders. The plunder gathered on this raid justified a further campaign the next year, the object of which was to join with Henry of Lancaster's army in Brittany; the two forces could then sweep into central France. By the September of 1356 the Prince's army had reached the Loire, meeting little opposition on the way. The English force decided to march to Bordeaux, the rumours of a large force that had been mobilised by King John dictating that caution should be exercised. The two armies stumbled upon each other when on Saturday the 17th of September the Black Prince's force of 5,000–6,000 found its route to Poitiers blocked at near Maupertuis by a French force numbering 16,000; a force of Scots under the command of Douglas were with the French. Douglas had previously benefited from French aid in Scotland, something that became a feature of the next sixty years or so, the French endeavouring to keep the English busy in their backyard, much the same as England was doing in Gascony. The point that I have been making in regard to Langley is that like the royal Princes before him, being well versed with the history of this and other conflicts in the Hundred Years War. This is exemplified by the address that the Black Prince gave to his men before the battle. Geoffrey le Baker (**34**) records that the Prince said:-

"Your courage and faith are well known to me, for in many great dangers you have shown yourselves as not unworthy sons and kinsmen of those who, under the lead of my father and forefathers, the Kings of England, found no labour to impossible, no place to difficult to take, no mountain to hard to climb, no tower too strong to win, no army unbeatable, no armed host to great. Their efforts tamed the French, the Cypriots, the Syracusans, the Calbrians and the Palestinians, and overcame the Scots, the Irish, and the persistent Welsh. Occasion, time and danger is wont to make bold men out of timid, quick-witted men out of dull. Honour and patriotism, and the hope of the rich spoils from the French, call you as much as my words, to follow in the footsteps of your fathers. Follow the standards, obey without question, in action and thought, the commands of your leaders, so that if we live to see victory, we shall continue as comrades together, always of one heart and one mind ... Again, if envious fortune decrees, which God forbid, that in this present labour we should go the way of all flesh, your names will not be soiled with infamy, but I and my companions will drink of the same cup with you. To conquer the French will be glorious, to be defeated, which God forbid, misfortune and disaster, but not disgrace.".

The tone and tenor of this speech was replicated by the Prince's great-nephew, Henry V, at Agincourt. My point in respect of the history of battle that Princes of the royal house like Bedford studied, is underlined by the words spoken before Poitiers. It is easy to see where Shakespeare found his inspiration from. The bulk of Edward's army occupied a hill, the archers being again placed in fierce formations on the flanks. A hedge, with areas of marshy ground behind it, dissected the battlefield. The French sent the cream of their army, the cavalry forward to break a hole in the hedge, but the English archers sheltering behind it annihilated them.The French dismounted, partly on the advice of Douglas, and they appear to have learnt at least one lesson from the defeat ten years before. As the dismounted French forces advanced they suffered extremely high losses as the English archers again showered them from the flanks. Le Baker remarks that the archers ran out of arrows and that they had to run forward to retrieve arrows from the dead bodies of the French vanguard. At a crucial moment in the battle Edward's Gascon ally, Captal de Buch, led a charge against the French rear causing panic to spread to the front ranks. Combined with this Edward led the bulk of his forces down the hill towards the front line of the beleaguered French forces. The French broke and fled, leaving behind them the bulk of their commanders, including their nineteen-year-old King, John II, who had broken one of the first rules of warfare and had charged into the battle when he should have retreated, above all, when a monarch's duty was to avoid capture.

It should be noted that the number of men involved in this battle were approximately half the number that fought at Crécy. The principal consequence of this was that the Black Prince was able to exert a control over his men and their conduct on the field of battle that was not available to his father. Also, Agincourt was a combination of the two previous major battles. Henry was able to exert some measure of control over his men, greater than Edward III but not as much as the Black Prince. Some ransoms were taken, but not as many as there should have been. Remarkably, the tactics employed by the English were virtually the same in all three battles. Post-Agincourt, the French had finally learnt the painful lesson that in open conflict, the English, with their superior archers, could withstand the larger numbers of the French cavalry. Had Bedford been able to engage the French in a major set-piece battle, his task in conquering the areas of France that were outside English control would have been made easier. John II was carried to London after a two-year truce had been agreed at Bordeaux. On the expiration of the truce Edward III engaged in yearly campaigns against a demoralised and divided France. In Paris a struggle had begun between various factions for control of the Dauphin. The first terms of a proposed settlement collapsed due to the French being unable to raise even the deposit for their King's ransom. The second set of proposals were so outrageous that the French rejected them almost immediately.

The Treaty of Brétigny

By the late summer of 1359, Edward III had landed at Calais with an army of 12,000 men, and it was time to capitalise on the gains. He presumptuously carried a gold crown with him to be used to crown himself king of France when Rheims had been taken. He failed to take Rheims and was forced by the sickness that depleted his forces to retreat to Calais. The French proposed a treaty which was negotiated at the town of Brétigny near Chartres. This treaty which bore the name of the town in which its terms were agreed was to be become the single most important document in Langley's life. The attempts to implement the terms of the treaty were the foundations upon which firstly Henry V and later Bedford, conducted the war in France. Langley, more than any other politician strove to compel the French to adhere to the terms of this treaty and the treaty of Troyes. This endeavour was his life's work, and it was to cause his premature death. The majority of the terms of the treaty are reproduced at *appendix a*. I would ask the reader to study the terms in the appendix as well as the summary that follows. This document, and the Treaty of Troyes, were the single most important to be enrolled in the history of the Hundred Years War. The events that ensued as a result of the endeavours of Bedford to implement the terms contained in the treaties had the profoundest effects on the history of not only France but of England also. These documents, together with Magna Carta, are the greatest constitutional changes of the medieval period. But for Salic law, which debarred Edward from pressing his claim by descent to the French throne, the treaty of Brétigny would not have had the importance that it came to have. The terms of the treaty in many ways were shaped as much by Salic law as they were by the two crushing defeats suffered by the French. The treaty of Troyes, which will be discussed later, negated a good deal of the problems caused by Salic law.

The treaty was sealed by Edward III and King John II in the October of 1360 at Calais after various amendments to the original terms that had been agreed on the 8th of May at Brétigny. The basic terms were which in return for the payment, in instalments of 3,000,000 crowns, and for the recognition of English rights to the territories of Gascony, Ponthieu, Calais, Marck, Montreuil and La Rochelle, Edward would renounce his claims to the throne of France.

Any interpretation of the treaty has to take cognisance of the events that had occurred in the previous two decades in Gascony. Whilst there can be no doubt that the English were negotiating from a position of strength, the terms of the treaty would appear on first reading that England did not press the advantage that they had. This has perplexed historians, with many varied theories being advanced, but I believe that the key to understanding the thinking of Edward III and his advisors lies in their belief that in the future the terms of the treaty would be breached and the war would be resumed. Edward would need the agreement of parliament to commence hostilities, and also the war, to date, had been costly, and the treasury needed replenishing. The plague had placed an additional strain on the country's finances, and so the priority had to be to gain, through the terms of the treaty, as much financial benefit as could be immediately realised. To this end the sovereignty of Gascony had to be the first priority, the duchy at this time being the provider of the greatest source of revenue.

Likewise, the retention of Calais and the counties of Montrieul and Ponthieu would ensure that the trade with Flemish weavers could continue. Had Edward pressed his claim to Normandy, and here let us hypothesise that the French would have conceded this, in financial terms England would not have benefited.However true that it is, Edward was making a great sacrifice by not insisting on the ceding of Normandy. May I make the point that, in England the failure to insist on Normandy as being part of the package did not raise a great deal of consternation. In any event England had established a bridgehead with the capture of Calais.

It should also be remembered that the plague had decimated the numbers of men available to serve in the English army. Edward also had to provide troops in the border regions, and quite simply he would not have the manpower needed to garrison all the conquered territories. The Black Prince had an army of circa 5,000–6,000 men, his father had approximately double this available, and with the minimum number of troops needed in the borders being in the region of 5,000, England's entire manpower of 23,000 men was stretched to breaking-point. Also, financially the country could not afford to maintain a standing force of the size permanently in the field. Normandy would have needed a high proportion of the available manpower without being able to afford the income to warrant such a high concentration of resources. The resources needed to protect the duchy's borders were extremely high, and territorially Edward had as large an area as he was able to protect. I feel that Edward took the pragmatic view that he should settle for what he knew the French would be able to agree to.

This then leads to the next question: why did he renounce all claims to the French throne? The point has already been made that, given the previous ways that past treaties had been broken, did the English really expect the French to adhere to what was agreed? From the French point of view, they needed to gain a respite to recover, not least because their King was a captive and Paris was deeply divided due to the vortex that the removal of the head of government caused. Also the ransom of 3,000,000 crowns had to be found. Should Edward have pressed his claim, then the French parties which were diametrically opposed would have found common cause in resisting an unwanted "foreigner" as King. Also, had he insisted on being recognised as King then he would have not have been able to pursue his ransom demands. You cannot demand a ransom for a King when you are claiming to be the King of the country whose royal personage you firstly expected to be ransomed and then deposed. A juxta-position, the only alternative for Edward, was to forego the ransom and allow John II to remain on the throne with the agreement that on his death Edward's heir, Edward the Black Prince, would be recognised as heir to the throne of France.

This would have had the consequence of having to forego the huge ransom money whilst at the same time committing England to defending English interests by aiding John against his sons and others who would undoubtedly rebel. Henry V and Bedford were to find that to sustain a King on the throne of France when in actuality he was King of only a third of the country, was an impossible position to sustain. In this context, Edward actually engaged in *real politic* when he agreed the Treaty of Brétigny.

The final point concerns the renunciation clause, this being added as a separate document in the October at Calais. In essence the clauses stated that Edward would only renounce his claim to the French throne if the process for the ceding of the lands had been completed by the 1st of November 1361. This was an impossible deadline to meet. By linking the two issues together Edward was being prudent, his thinking being that once the claim to the throne was made the French would not deliver the lands as listed in the Treaty. The detail needed to transfer the lands was complex and could not be completed in slightly over a year, and it therefore follows that, after the 1st of November 1361, the main treaty would be nullified by non-compliance. In plain English, the English had inserted a "get-out clause", a loophole. This also left Edward with the option of still maintaining his title as King of France, something which acted as a unifying cause around which he could garner the support of the people of England, a cause that Henry V, and later by Bedford as regent for Henry VI, used to good effect when gathering support for firstly the resumption, and later the continuation, of the war with France. Edward accepted a payment of 400,000 crowns as the deposit on the ransom releasing King John in return for hostages. Within a year the hostages had been moved to Calais to await the further payment of another 200,000 crowns which they had confirmed would be paid. King John stated that he was unwilling to meet the arrangements that the hostages had claimed he was in agreement with. On receiving this news, one of the hostages, his second son, the duke of Anjou, broke his parole. King John honourably returned to London as a prisoner, and he was to die in the capital in April 1364, being succeeded by Charles V.

When Henry V determined to re-open the war with France, the basis of the propositions put forward by the English diplomats, Langley and Courtnay, was that the terms of the treaty of Brétigny had not been met. Therefore, at least initially, England required that the ceded lands be handed over and that the balance of the ransom for King John be paid. As matters escalated Henry renewed his claim to the French throne, this leading to the resumption of the war. The treaty of Troyes finally solved, on paper only, the problems whose roots had been planted in the treaty of Brétigny. However, any agreement on paper had to be ratified by action, and the dauphinist party refused to recognise what had been agreed at Troyes. The attempt to win through conquest what had been agreed by diplomacy was to lead to the deaths of both Henry V and his brother Bedford. This in turn was to begin the stirrings of discontent in England that led to the deposition of Henry VI. Here lies the genesis of the Wars of the Roses, the Lancastrians actually propagated their removal from power by pursuing matters in France. Anyone wishing to consider the points of view put forward by others should consult the works cited at (35).

The war was resumed in 1369, but during the interim a number of "freebooters", discharged from the army, had indulged in privateering by plundering the French countryside. During this period John de Montfort defeated Charles of Blois at Auray, and Charles V accepted the homage of de Montfort for the duchy of Brittany. This allowed him to turn his attentions to the internal stabilisation of France. During this period the Black Prince had entered into a treaty of alliance with King Pedro of Castile, and not unsurprisingly the French backed the claim of Henry of Trastamara. This was a sensible move, that by advancing large sums of money to Henry the French were able to rid themselves of the mercenary forces who were terrorising their countryside. These forces now found employment in the France-Navarrese war. The battle of Najera again resulted in an English victory, the Anglo-French forces being routed with the capture of the French captains, Du Guesclin and Marshal d'Audreham. Pedro was restored to the throne but it became clear that he was unable to pay the sums agreed to the English forces for the payment of their troops. Without the support of the English, Pedro could not maintain his hold on the throne, and he was defeated by a French force at Montiel in 1369. John of Gaunt, the Prince's younger brother now became involved in matters and this ensured that England remained involved in the politics of Castile for the next two decades. Gaunt took Constanza as his second wife. The consequences of this contributed to the animosity that gathered pace against Gaunt at the English court. The actions of Bedford's grandfather were partly responsible for the usurpation of the throne by Bedford's father and this will be discussed in the next section. The Black Prince had to look to Aquitiane to pay his troops and additional taxation measures were put in place. The Aquitainians balked at this and appealed to Charles V as their overlord to intercede.

The overall positions of the two protagonists had altered as England now had to defend the conquered territories. England did attempt to mount *Chevaunchees*, notably in 1373 when John of Gaunt lost a number of men in a sweep across the *massif* of central France. Also a Castillian fleet under the command of the earl of Pembroke was carrying goods to Aquitaine when it was destroyed off the coast of La Rochelle, and in Brittany, de Montfort rebelled against Charles, this being settled by a truce agreed by Gaunt at Bruges. By 1372 the French had regained all of Poitou as well as pushing the English back to the area around Bordeaux. In 1373 the Constable of France, Du Guesclin, together with the Duke of Bourbon, had recaptured Brittany. They accomplished this by copying the English tactics of the *Chavaunchee* whilst at the same time prudently avoiding an outright battle.

The death in 1376 of Edward the Black Prince was a major blow to England, not only in terms of the pursuit of the war but also in regards to the succession to the throne, his father was to die within a year, leaving the infant Richard as King of England. This was against a background of discussions between French and English envoys, the aim of which was to agree a permanent peace. The main sticking-point was sovereignty, the insoluble problem that had started in 910 when Normandy was ceded to Rolf the Red.

With the death of Edward III in 1376, the French mounted a two-pronged attack against Bordeaux and Calais whilst at the same time sending a fleet to raid the English coast. John Neville's appointment as lieutenant in Gascony partially stemmed the tide. Progress and set-back in equal measure accompanied the progress of the war, the outbreak of the Great Schism in 1378 adding a new dimension to the war. Urban VI who had been elected in the spring of 1378 was deserted by a number of his cardinals who, in the September, elected Robert of Geneva who took the title Clement VII, and he made Avignon his seat. England and Germany supported Urban France, Scotland and the Flemings supported Clement. Charles V died in 1386 leaving England with a small coastal strip stretching from Bordeaux to Bayonne and Calais as all they had to show for 46 years of warfare, a negligible political gain when set against the efforts that had been expended during the previous half-century. The question of homage still lay unresolved, the victories of Crécy and Poitiers having merely papered over the crack of disunity which were deepening in England, their apogee being reached in the Poll Tax riots and the aftermath which resulted in the seizure of the throne by the Lancastrians led by, Henry Bolingbroke, Earl of Derby.

No study of Langley's political life could effectively be undertaken without cognisance being taken of the inherited historical baggage which permeated the thinking of the hierarchy of society in the early fifteenth century. Whilst the rank and file of English society were bound by feudal obligations to their lords, the upper echelons of society viewed France from an entirely different perspective. Certainly the monarchy perceived the reconquest of France as an assertion of rights and privileges which they had been unlawfully deprived of. When Henry V began to contemplate mounting an invasion of Normandy the historic precedents were pored over by the civil service. The advent of a more pluralistic governance meant that the need to seek the approval of the Commons in terms of the raising of finance to meet the cost of mobilisation was a prerequisite, and so all facets appertaining to a conflict were employed to unite the various strata of society. It became a common enterprise, the monarch and his people in unison in pursuit of a mutually agreed objective.

The protection of the hereditary rights of monarchy occupied the minds of successive rulers across Europe from the Holy Roman Empire through France and Spain to England. The prime aim of all monarchs was the protection of, and where necessary the re-establishment of, their hereditary rights and principles. This to a lesser degree applied to the immediate family of a monarch. This is particularly true in the case of Bedford. For a brief period, from the death of Clarence in March 1421 at Bauge to the birth of Henry VI on the 6th of December 1421, Bedford was a heartbeat away from the throne of England. Again, from the ascension of Henry VI to the Duke's death he was heir to the throne. The assertion of these hereditary rights had a particular significance for Bedford. Not only would the regaining of these rights benefit him as one of the senior lords of the realm, but should the throne become vacant then it would fall on him to continue the policies of his brother. The principal political aim was the regaining of the lands which by historic right formed part of the patrimony of the House of Lancaster, held in the personage of the monarch as titular head of the realm. Langley was particularly close to Bedford, they had worked together since the prince's early days as Warden of the Eastern Marches.

In order to create this climate of acquiescence it was necessary to promulgate the proposition that England as a *nation* had been deprived of its legitimate rights in territories which were traditionally the property of the realm, and by extension, belonged to the collective wealth of the nation. It was seen as a "just" war, a crusade, in truth a contradiction in terms, but one that in the mind of Medieval man struck a chord of resonance. This cause had to be presented as being based on sound precedents, and to this end the history of the causation of the enmity between the two countries had to be placed before both the Commons and the citizens of the realm. This last was done by way of the production of pamphlets.

Langley, as a member of the ruling clique, was well tutored in the history of the former Kings, his ancestors, and their dealings with France. This would have seeped into his consciousness and would have had a profound bearing on his thoughts and the actions that ensued. Specifically, when he was regent of France, his knowledge of the past history of the dispute became as important as his military capabilities, the more so when Joan of Arc and the propaganda that she invoked did so much to sow the seeds of doubt in the minds of some of the English protagonists.

A further factor was the resurgence in the power of the Papacy after the resolution of the Schism. Any Papal interference in the quarrel was based, in the main, on the legality of each nation's stated position. In the briefing of, and the hearing of, the reports of the diplomatic embassies, Langley had to know his precedents when countering the arguments which were put forward. Once the overall strategy had been determined, principally by the King and his council, Langley became bound by all the aspects of the dispute which included the legal and diplomatic sides of the conflict.

The other salient issue for us concerns the unwritten desire, virtually a necessity, for the son of Henry IV, an usurper in many peoples eyes, to legitimise his kingship. Henry V's demons, solely discussed with those closest to him, could only be vanquished by triumphing in what was perceived as a just war, victory being a sign of his divine right to occupy the throne and God's blessing, being an extension of the divinity that had been invoked through the use of the Holy Oil of Canterbury as the unction at his coronation. Victory in a conflict, especially if this victory is won against overwhelming odds, as Agincourt was, acts as a unifying catalyst. The same rule applied to Poitiers and Crécy, set-piece battles being remembered long after sometimes more important minor skirmishes; such is the psyche of a race in wartime, the English nation more so than most. The spirit of nationhood is embodied in the celebration of victory, a lustre being added when the triumph is on foreign soil and against the traditional enemy. Today, war is almost a spectator sport with instant pictures relayed to our living rooms via television. In the Middle Ages it took many weeks for news of a triumph to spread across the kingdom, magnified in its magnificence with the retelling, and thus legends have their genesis.

Langley, like those before him, will have studied the histories of earlier campaigns in order to learn from the past mistakes. Unfortunately, politics got in the way of some of these lessons.

This can be dangerous for the ruling clique in that the euphoria of victory can propel a country's leaders causing them to endeavour to emulate previous spectacular victories. Rather than be in control of events the reverse becomes the case, events controlling the conduct of the war, and the drivers become the driven. This, I believe, became the case with Bedford. In today's language, the people of the kingdom began to believe the P.R. that Langley promulgated. To an extent, Bedford and his lieutenants in France had to continue pursuing a course of action which they knew would not lead to England winning the war. To withdraw from some of the conquered territories would have been perceived as failure and this in turn could have sown the seeds of unrest at home. Bedford became the victim of his brother's success, the holder of a *poisoned chalice*, the defender of an untenable position. Langley's semi-retirement, through old age, meant that there was no-one in the government who had the willpower, or the skills, to coerce parliament. By the time that the Commons began to voice concerns over the way that the war was going, the tide had turned against England and the trickle of reversals had become a flood of defeats.

It is also salient to point out that many of the senior barons in England used events in France to their own advantage as profiteers motivated by self-interest, the pursuit of power for self-aggrandisement, Medieval carpet-baggers.

In many ways the Hundred Years War was the last of the truly Medieval wars. The advent of more powerful and reliable cannon began to make the mounted knight, swathed in armour, an anachronism. As man devised newer ways to inflict damage on the enemy, no matter how thick the plate armour, so the practice and tactics of conflict altered. Bedford was one of the last English commanders who fought a campaign on foreign soil under the rules that governed the conduct of a Medieval army. Certainly the Wars of the Roses that followed the end of the Hundred Years War was still waged using Medieval tactics, but the dawning of the age of the gunner and his tools of war was imminent. The experimentation that Henry V and Bedford undertook in France was the prelude to this. The stronger fortifications of the towns played a large part in bringing this about. Also, with Agincourt, the French finally learnt the painful lessons begun with the battles of Poitiers and Crécy, namely, that in set-piece conflicts the longbow negated the heavy cavalry charge.

Notes and References

(1)   Warren, W. L., *Henry II,* (London, 1973).
(2)   Douglas, D. C., *William the Conqueror,* (London, 1964).

(3)   Ganshof, G. L., *Feudalism,* (London, 1952).

(4)   Chibnall, M., (ed), *The Ecclesiastical History of Orderic Vitalis, book x,* (Oxford,1969); also reproduced in, Ganshof, F. L., *Feudalism,* p 93, (London, 1952).

(5)   Renouard, Y., *Etudes d'histoire medievale,* 2 vols., (Paris, 1903).

(6)   Bradbury, J., *Philip Augustus, King of France 1180–1223,* (London, 1998). An excellent new study into this most interesting of all the Capetian Kings.

(7)   Ganshof, G. L., *Feudalism,* (London, 1952).

(8)   Gillingham, J., *The Angevin Empire,* (London, 1984).

(9)   Denholm-Young, N., *Richard of Cornwall,* (Oxford, 1947).

(10) *Foedra, 1, ii.*

(11) Vale, M., *The Origins of the Hundred Years War, The Angevin Legacy 1250–1340,* (Oxford, 1996). pp 52–5 for an analysis of the flaws in the Treaty.

(12) Vale, M., *The Origins of the Hundred Years War,The Angevin Legacy 1250–1340,* (Oxford, 1996). One of the best recent works on the subject.

(13) Strayer, J. R., *The Reign of Philip the Fair,* (Princeton, 1980).

(14) Joinville, J., (ed), Wailly, N, de, *Histoire de St. Louis,* Paris, 1868).

(15) Pole-Stuart, E., "The interview between Philip V and Edward II at Amiens in 1320 ", EHR, xli (1926).

(16) Luard, H. R., (ed), *Flores Historierum,* (R.S., London, 1890).

(17) Johnstone, H., "The county of Ponthieu, 1279–1307 ", *EHR, xxiv,* (1914).

(18) Renouard, Y., "Conjectures sur la population du duche d'Aquitaine en 1316 ", *Etudes d'histoire medievale, i,* (Paris, 1968).

(19) Carus-Wilson and Coleman, O., *England's Export Trade, 1275–1547,* (Oxford, 1963).

(20) Vale, M., *The Origins of the Hundred Years War, The Angevin Legacy 1250–1340,* (Oxford, 1996), p 149.

(21) Prestwich, M., *Edward 1,* (London, 1988).

(22) & (23)   Vale, M., *The Origins of the Hundred Years War, The Angevin Legacy 1250–1340,* (Oxford, 1996), p 203, and appendix ii: Strayer, J. R., "The cost and profits of war: the Anglo-French conflict of 1294–1303 ", in *The Medieval City,* ed. H. A. Miskimin, D. Herlihy and A. L. Udovitch, (Yale, 1977).

(24) Prestwich, M., (ed), *Documents Illustrating the crisis of 1297–98 in England,* (Camden Society, 4th set., London, 1980). p. 163.

(25) SC 8/287, no. 13303.

(26) Armitage-Smith, S., *John of Gaunt,* pp 1–3, (London, 1940).

(27) Lucas, H. S., *The Low Countries and the Hundred Years War, 1326–1347,* (Michigan, 1929).

(28) Contamine, P., (trans, Jones, M.) *War in the Middle Ages, p 240,* (London, 1984).

(29) McKisack, M., *The Fourteenth Century 1307–1399, p 132,* (Oxford, 1959).

(30) Hardy, R., *Longbow, A social and military history,* pp 68–9, (London, 1976). An excellent history of the longbow, particularly useful for the technicalities of the weapon.

(31) Thompson, E. M., (ed), *Chronicle G. Le Baker,* (Oxford, 1889).

(32) Gottfried, R. S., *The Black Death,* p 58, (London, 1983).

(33) Lumby, J., (ed), *Henry Knighton, Chronicon,* p. 61. (RS, 92, London)

(34) Thompson, E. M., (ed), *Chronicle G. Le Baker,* (Oxford, 1889).

(35)   Le, Patourel, *Review historique de droit francais et derenger, 4e Series., t. xxx* (1953), pp 317–8: Cosneau, *Les Grands Treales de la Guerre de Cent Ans,* pp 39–68, 173–4, (1899): Petit-Dutaillis, M. M., and Collier, "La Diplomatie francais et le traite de Brétigny ", *Moyen Age, 2e Series. i.* (1897), 1–35: Chaplais, P., "Some documents regarding the Fulfilment and Interpretation of the treaty of Brétigny ", *Camden Miscellaney, xix,* (1952).

APPENDIX B

THE TREATY OF BRÉTIGNY, 1360

This was the document that formed the basis for the discussions in Paris between the French and the two embassies led by Langley.

1. First, that the King of England, in addition to what he holds in Guinne and Gascony, shall have perpetually, for himself and his heirs, all the things which follow, to be held in the same manner as the king of France and his son or any of his ancestors, Kings of France, held them; that is to say, what was held in demesne, in demesne, and what in fee, in fee, for the time and in the manner specified below:

The city, castle, and county of Poitiers, and all the land and county of Poitou, with the fief of Thouars and the land of Belleville.
The city and castle of Saintes, and all the land and country of Saintonge, on both sides of the river Charente.
The city and castle of Agen, and the land and country of Agenais.
The city and castle and the whole country of Perigord, and the land and country of Perigueux.
The city and castle of Limoges and the land and country of the Limousin.
The city and castle of Cahors, with the land and country of Caoursin.
The city and castle and county of Tarbe, and the land, district and county of Bigorre.
The city, land and county of Gorre.
The city and castle of Angouleme, and the county, land, and country of Angoumois.
The city and castle of Rodez, and the land and county of Rouergue.

And if there be any lords, like the Count of Foix, the Count of Armagnac, the Count of L'Isle, the Count of Perigord, the Viscount of Limoges, or others who hold any lands or places within the bounds of the said regions, they shall do homage to the King of England, and render all other services and payments, due on account of their lands and holdings, in the same manner as they have done in times past.

2. Also the King of England shall have that all the King of England or any of his predecessors formerly held in the town of Montreuil-sur-Mer and its appurtenances.

3. Also the King of England shall have the whole County of Ponthieu; save that if any of the County and its appurtenances have been alienated by former kings of England to any other person than the King of France, the latter shall not be bound to restore them to the King of England. And if such alienation's have been made to former kings of France, and the King of France holds them at present in his hand, he shall release them wholly to the King of England; except that if the Kings of France have had them in exchange for other lands, the King of England shall either restore what was had in exchange or leave in his hands the land thus alienated. But if the former kings of England had alienated anything to other persons than the King of France and these be since come into the hands of the latter, the King of France shall not be bound to restore them. Also if such lands owe homage, the King shall deliver them to others, who shall do homage for them to the King of England; and if not, the King of France shall present them to a tenant who shall do homage for them within a year of his leaving Calais.

4. Also the King of England shall have the castle and town of Calais; the castle, town and lordship of Marck; the towns, castles, and lordships of Sangatte, Coulogne, Ham, Le Wal, and Oye; with land, woods, marshes, rivers, rents, lordships, advowsons of churches, and all other appurtenances and places lying within the following limits and bounds (specified in detail).

5. Also the King of England shall have the castle, town, and the whole county of Guisnes (Guines), with all the lands, towns, castles, fortresses, places, men, homages, seigneuries, woods, forests, and the rights within them, as wholly as the recently deceased Count of Guisnes held them at the time of his death. And the churches and the good people within the limits of the said County of Guisnes, of Calais, of Marck, and the other places, shall be subject to the King of England as they were to the King of France and the former Count of Guisnes. And all these possessions, of Marck and of Calais, contained in this article and that immediately preceding, the King of England shall hold in demesne, excepting the inheritance of churches, which shall remain wholly to them wherever they are situated; excepting also the

inheritance of other persons of the districts of Marck and Calais, situated outside the town of Calais, to the annual value of £100 of land and below, in current coin of the countryside, which shall remain to them. . . . .

7. Also, it is agreed that the King of France and his eldest son, the Regent, shall as soon as possible, and at latest before the Feast of St. Michael next year, restore, transfer, and deliver to the King of England and his heirs and successors without fraud or cunning, all the honours, obediences, homages, allegiances, vassals, feofs, services, recognizances, and rights, etc. . . . . . by any cause, title, or colour of right, to the king or crown of France, on account of the cities, counties, castles, etc.., and all their appurtenances and appanages, wherever they may be, and each one of them. And the king and his eldest son shall command, by their letters patent, all archbishops, bishops, and other prelates of the Holy Church, and also the counts, viscounts, barons, nobles, citizens, and all others whatsoever of the cities, counties, lands, countrysides, isles, and places, that they shall obey the King of England and his heirs, and be at their command, as they have obeyed the kings and crown of France. And by the same letters they shall acquit and absolve them, as well as they can, from all homage, faith, oaths, obligations, subjections, and promises made by any of them to the kings and to the crown of France in any manner whatsoever.

8. Also it is agreed that the King of England shall have the counties, cities, castles, lands, countrysides, isles, and places, with all their appurtenances and appanages, wherever they may be, to hold himself, and to be held in heredity and perpetuity by all his heirs and successors, in demesne in so far as the King of France held it in demesne, and also in fee and service, as the Kings of France did; excepting all that is said above in the article touching Calais and Marck . . .

13. Also it is agreed that the King of France will pay to the King of England three million gold crowns, of which two are worth the noble of English money. And of this sum 600,000 crowns shall be paid to the King of England or his deputies at Calais within four months from the time of the King of France's arrival there. And within the following year 400,000 crowns shall be paid to the city of London in England until the 3,000,000 crowns shall be paid.

14. Also it is agreed that in return for the payment of the 600,000 crowns at Calais and for the delivery of the hostages named below, and for the surrender of the town, castle, and fortresses of Guisnes, and the towns of its county, the king's person shall be released from prison, and he shall be permitted to depart from Calais, and return to his own realm without hindrance; but he shall not be able to arm himself or his people against the

King of England until he shall have performed what he is bound to by this present treaty ... (Here follows the names of 41 hostages and prisoners of war who are to be held by the English as pledges of good faith.)

(17. Within three months of the King of France leaving Calais, four hostages from Paris and two from each of 18 other towns are to present themselves at Calais. . .)

19. Also it is agreed that as soon as possible within a year from the King of France's departure from Calais John, Count of Montfort, shall have the county of Montfort, with all the appurtenances, doing liege homage to the King of France and promising duty and service in all cases, as a good and loyal liege vassal should do to his liege lord, in respect of the county; and also there shall be delivered to him his other inheritances, which were never part of the duchy of Brittany, doing homage or any other duty which if fitting.

20. Also, on the question of the demesne of the duchy of Brittany, which is disputed between John of Monfort on the one hand and Charles of Blois on the other, it is agreed that the two Kings should call before them or their deputies the principal parties of Blois and Montfort, either in person or by deputies, and should inform themselves of the rights of the two parties; and should try to bring the parties into accord on all matters in dispute between them or on as many as possible of these matters ...

21. And it should happen that one of the parties should not wish to appear in satisfactory manner before the kings, or their deputies, when they shall meet; and also if the kings or their deputies shall have ordained or declared that the parties ought to be in agreement, or should have given their judgement in favour of one party, and one of the parties is unwilling to agree to this or to obey the declaration; then the said kings shall proceed against him with all their might and help the one who is willing to agree and obey; but in any event the two kings shall not, either in their own persons, or through others, make or undertake war against the others, make or undertake war against each other, for the cause above said; and the sovereignty and homage over the duchy shall always remain with King of France.

(**22**. The lands of Philip of Navarre and his adherents to be restored with full pardon. . . .)

(**25**. All persons banished or deprived during the war as adherents of either party are to be restored entirely to their rights and possessions.)

26. Also it is agreed that the King of France must deliver to the King of England all the cities, towns, countrysides, and all other places named above, which must be handed over to the King of England by this present treaty, as soon as he can, and at the latest within a year of his departure from Calais.

27. Also ... the King of England, at his own cost and expense, shall deliver all the fortresses taken and occupied by him by his subjects, adherents, and allies, in France, Touraine, Anjou, Maine, Berri, Auverge, Burgundy, Champagne, Picardy, and Normandy, and in all the other parts and places of the kingdom of France, except those of the duchy of Brittany, and of the districts and lands which by this present treaty ought to belong and remain to the King of England.

28. Also, it is agreed that the King of France shall cause to be offered and delivered to the King of England, or to his heirs or deputies, all the towns, castles, or fortresses and other lands, districts, and places above named, with all their appurtenances at his own cost.And if there shall be any persons so rebellious that they should refuse to restore to the King of England any cities, towns, castles, districts, places, or fortresses, which by this present treaty ought to belong to him, the King of France shall be bound to deliver them to the King of England at his own expense. And in the same way the King of England shall deliver at his own expense the fortresses which by this present treaty ought to belong to the King of France. And the kings and their people shall be bound to help each other, if necessary, at the cost of whichever party shall make the request ...

29. Also, it is agreed that the archbishops, bishops, and other prelates and people of Holy Church, by reason of their temporalities, shall be subject to that one of the two kings under whom they hold their temporalities; and if they hold under both kings, they shall be subject to each of them for the temporalities which they hold of each. . . (A firm alliance and friendship is to be established between the two kings and realms; and this shall involve the abrogation of alliances directed by either side against the other, including especially the French alliance with Scotland and the English alliance with Flanders. All the foregoing clauses of the treaty shall be confirmed by the pope.)

34. Also, all the subjects of the kingdoms who wish to study in schools and universities of the kingdoms of France and England shall enjoy all privileges and liberties of such schools and universities as fully as they could before the war, and as they do at present ...

38. Also it is agreed that neither of the kings aforesaid shall procure or cause to be procured any innovations or hindrances to be made by the court of Rome or by others of the Holy Church, whoever they may be, against this present treaty, and against the said kings, their helpers, adherents, and allies ... And if our Holy Father or any other wishes to do it, the two kings shall stop him to the best of their ability, without any deceit ... Given at Calais, 24 October, the year of grace, 1360. (The following important stipulations, included in Articles 11 and 12 of the treaty of Brétigny, were omitted from the final treaty of Calais.)

11. (The King of France and his eldest son promise that within a year from the next Michaelmas they will transfer to the King of England all their rights within the ceded territories) without retaining or reserving for themselves or their heirs in these territories anything whereby they or their heirs and successors ... might be able to challenge or demand in time to come anything of the King of England, his heirs and successor, or any of his vassals and subjects, by reason of the districts and places ... And that the King of England, his heirs and successors, shall have and hold in perpetuity all the above named districts, with their appurtenances and appanages, and shall retain them fully in their lordship, sovereignty, and obedience, allegiance, and subjection, as the kings of France had held them at any time past; and that the King of England, his heirs and successors, shall have and hold in perpetuity all the districts above-named. . ... in full franchise and perpetual liberty, as sovereign and liege lord, and as neighbours to the king and realm of France, without recognising any sovereignty in them, or doing any obedience, homage, resort, or subjection, and without doing, at any time to come, any service or recognition to the kings or crown or France for any of the cities, counties, castles, lands, districts, islands, places and persons.

12. Also it is agreed that the King of France and his eldest son shall expressly renounce the jurisdictions and sovereignties, and all rights which they have or could have, in all things which by this present treaty ought to belong to the King of England. And similarly the King of England and his eldest son shall expressly renounce all the things which by this present treaty ought not to be offered to or remain with the King of England, and all the demands which he has made to the King of France, to the homage, sovereignty and demesne of the duchy of Normandy, Touraine, the Counties of Anjou and Maine, and the sovereignty and homage of the duchy of Brittany and of the county and districts of Flanders.

APPENDIX C

THE TREATY OF TROYES, 1420

When Langley read this document out to the Commons it was ratified without dissent, he had prepared the ground well. Also the fact that Henry V was · seated beside him cowed any dissenters into acquiesce.

Henry, by the grace of God, King of England, Heir and Regent of France, and Lord of Ireland, for perpetual remembrance, to all Christian people ... we notify and declare that ... we have taken a treaty with our father-in-law (Charles of France); in which treaty between our father and us, it is concluded and agreed, in the form according to the following manner:

First, it is agreed between our said father of France and us, that for as much as by the bond of matrimony made for the good of peace between us and our most dear and most beloved Katherine, the daughter of our said father and of our most dear mother, Isabel his wife, those same Charles and Isabel are made our father and mother, therefore we shall regard them as our father and mother, and honour them as such, and it is fitteth such and so worthy a prince and princess, to be honoured especially before all other temporal princes of this world.

Also, that we will not disturb, distress, nor harass, our said father; but he shall hold and possess, as long as he lives, as he holds and possess at this time, the crown and the royal dignity of France, and the rents, fruits, and profits of the same, to the sustenance of his estate and the charges of the realm; and our foresaid mother shall also hold, as long as she lives, the estate and dignity of queen, according to the manner of the said realm, with a suitable and convenient part of the said rents and profits.

Also that the foresaid Katherine shall take and have dower in our realm of England as queens of England hitherto were wont to take and have, that is to say, to the sum of 40,000 crowns a year; of which two shall always be worth an English noble ... Also, that after the death of our said father, and from thence forward, the crown and realm of France, with all their rights and appurtenances, shall remain and abide and belong to us and our heirs for evermore.

Also for as much as our said father is afflicted with various infirmities in such manner that he may not attend in his own person to arrange for the needs of the realm of France, therefore during the life of our said father the faculty and exercise of governance and disposition of the public good and common profit of the realm of France, with the counsel of nobles and wise men of the realm, ... shall remain and abide with us, so that henceforward we may govern the same realm, both by ourself and also by others whom, with the counsel of the said nobles, we may be pleased to depute ... Also that we will do our utmost to see that the court of the parlement of France be kept and observed in its authority and superiority, and in all that is due to it, in all manner of places that now, or in time to come, are, or shall be, subject to our said father.

Also that we diligently and truly to the utmost of our power, shall work and act so that justice may be administered and enforced in the realm of France, according to the laws, customs, and rights of the same realm without exception of persons ... Also that we to the utmost or our strength and as soon as it may conveniently be done, shall labour to put into obedience to our father all manner of cities, towns, castles, places, countries, and persons, within the realm of France disobedient and rebellious to our said father, holding or belonging to the party commonly called Dauphin of Armagnac. Also that all manner of conquests that shall be made by us in the realm of France over the said rebels, outside the duchy of Normandy, shall be done to the profit of the said father ... Also by God's help when it shall happen to us to come to the crown of France, the duchy of Normandy and all other places conquered by us in the realm of France shall be under the commandment, obedience and monarchy of the crown of France.

Also that we will not impose any impositions or exactions, or cause them to be imposed, on the subjects of our said father without reasonable and necessary cause, nor otherwise than for the common good of the said realm of France, and according to the rules and demands of the reasonable and approved laws and customs of the realm.

Also that neither our father nor we nor our brother the Duke of Burgundy shall begin nor make with Charles, styling himself the Dauphin of Viennes, any treaty of peace or accord, except by the counsel and assent of all and each of us three and of the three estates of both of the aforesaid realms.

(*ii*)   *The commons fear for the independence of England when Henry becomes king of France, 1420.*
Also pray the commons that as the Lord Edward, formerly king of England, great- grandfather to our present king, at his parliament held at Westminster ... in the 18th year of his reign in England and the first year of his reign in France. . . the said late king, having regard to the estate of his said kingdom of England, and especially to the fact that it had never been, nor ought to be, in subjection nor obedience to the kings of France. . .. willed, granted, and established for himself, his heirs, and successors, in his said realm of England in his said parliament, that. . ..his said realm of England and the people of it. . ..should never in any time to come be put into subjection nor obedience to him, his heirs, and successors as kings of France.

That it may please the very noble and very powerful prince the Duke of Gloucester, Guardian of England, to ordain and establish by authority of this present be affirmed and kept in all points. And moreover, to ordain by the aforesaid authority that because our said lord the king is heir and regent of the realm of France, and King of France ... the said kingdom of England and the people of it ... shall never be put in subjections or obedience to him, his heirs, and successors, as heir, regent, or king of France ... Reply: Let the statute then made be held and kept.

(iii) Approval of the treaty by parliament, 1421.
Our most serene lord, for his part, wishing to have the said peace and all and each of its articles, in the like manner sworn, confirmed, and ratified by himself and the three estates of his realm, as he is obliged to do by the terms of the said treaty, swore and promised to observe the said peace well and faithfully in all things, on the word of a king, and by the holy Gospels of God corporally touched by him, and caused to be summoned the said three estates, that is to say, the prelates and clergy, nobles and magnates, and the commons of the said realm, on the second day of May in the ninth year of his reign, for the greater confirmation and strengthening of the aforesaid peace, and for other reasons touching his estate, his kingdom and his realm ... in the presence of these three estates the same most serene lord our king expound and declare in detail by the venerable father in God, Thomas (Langley) by grace of God, Bishop of Durham, his chancellor. . ..The three estates, considering, concluding, and deciding that the said treaty was praiseworthy, necessary, and useful to both realms and their subjects, and indeed to all Christendom, approved, praised, authorised, and accepted the treaty of all and each of the articles in it, by the command of our lord the king, as it appears, as the three estates of the aforesaid kingdom approved, praised, authorised, and accepted, and promised on behalf of themselves and their heirs and successors to observe and fulfil these articles and each of them well and faithfully in all time to come, as far as it lay in their power.

APPENDIX D

THE MANIFESTO OF THE DAUPHIN AGAINST THE TREATY OF TROYES, 1421

Refutation of the Treaty of Troyes and an appeal to the French in favour of the Dauphin against the King of England, 31st January, 1421. (After 24 points against the treaty the document proceeds:) For the honour of the fleurs de lys there follow some conditions founded in right to rebut the damnable treaty which Henry of England has asked for and wishes to have.

1. The honour of the fleurs de lys and the right of the crown of France neither can nor ought to be conveyed to strangers, especially those who are ancient enemies, against the king's consent and the consent of those who can reasonably claim right and interest in the said crown and its preservation.

2. The honour of the fleur de lys and the right of the crown of France belongs clearly ... to the very noble prince Charles, only son and heir of the said crown, so that neither the king nor any other person whatsoever can reasonably dispose of it against his will under pretext of peace by marriage or any other excuse.

3. The honour of the fleur de lys and of the crown of France extends not only to the king and queen and their children but to all those of the royal house of France present and future, such as nephews, cousins, nieces, and more generally to all the three estates of France according to various grades and obligations.

4. The honour of the fleur de lys and of the crown ought to be upheld and guarded by all the faithful and loyal subjects of the crown without giving any consent to the contrary which might be to the prejudice of another right of interest of lordship, for to do otherwise would be against the law of God, natural, civil, and canonical, and against good judgement of reason.

5. The honour of the fleurs de lys and of the crown ought not to be damaged by those who owe fealty and loyalty to the crown, on pain of treason, crime of lese-majeste, and rebellion, and concessions made to the contrary and confirmed by oaths would be felonious and iniquitous and tending to everlasting damnation.

6. The honour of the fleur de lys and the right of the said crown ought to be guarded by those who are sworn and bound to it, so that they ought to bear all corporal pain that a loyal person ought to suffer before forsaking their faith and loyalty ...

7. The damnable treaty that Henry of England has asked for under pretext of marriage with the daughter of the King of France and of total peace between the said kingdoms of France and England is full of malignity and fraud and deception, for under pretext of peace and marriage it tends to innumerable and perpetual divisions ...

11. The treaty tends to promote and nourish all treasons, perjuries, disloyalties, and rebellions, and tends to the shameful servitude of all those members of the noble kingdom of France-clerks, nobles, and laymen-and to very unworthy subjection.

12. The treaty must be resisted and prevented by every good Christian having ecclesiastical or temporal power, each one according to his right, and as they wish to expel from Christendom the evils named above, especially by the peers, notables, and citizens of France and all those who hate tyranny, and uphold virtue and freedom.

INDEX

Index